Where
The
Truth
Lies

WRITER AS CRITIC SERIES XIV

WHERE THE TRUTH LIES

selected essays

RUDY WIEBE

NeWest Press

LIBRARY AND ARCHIVES CANADA CATALOGUING IN PUBLICATION
Wiebe, Rudy, 1934–
[Essays. Selections]
Where the truth lies : selected essays / Rudy Wiebe.

(Writer as critic ; 14)
Issued in print and electronic formats.
ISBN 978-1-926455-75-4 (paperback).
ISBN 978-1-926455-76-1 (epub).
ISBN 978-1-926455-77-8 (mobi)

I. Title.   II. Title: Essays. Selections.   III. Series: Writer as critic ; 14

PS8545.I38A6 2016   C814'.54   C2016-901691-9   C2016-901692-7

EDITOR: Smaro Kamboureli
BOOK DESIGN: Natalie Olsen, Kisscut Design
COVER IMAGE: "Lethbridge High Level Bridge" by dave_7 on flickr
(www.flickr.com/photos/21612624@N00/2335895061) is licensed
under CC BY-SA 2.0. Image has been modified.
AUTHOR PHOTO: Joseph Gascho

NeWest Press acknowledges the support of the Canada Council for the Arts the Alberta Foundation for the Arts, and the Edmonton Arts Council for support of our publishing program. This project is funded in part by the Government of Canada.

201, 8540 – 109 Street
Edmonton, AB T6G 1E6
780.432.9427
www.newestpress.com

No bison were harmed in the making of this book.
Printed and bound in Canada   1 2 3 4 5   18 17 16

To the memory of

H.F. Klassen

(1900 – 1969)

WINNIPEG

Carl Kreider

(1914 – 2002)

GOSHEN, USA

Henry Kreisel

(1922 – 1991)

EDMONTON

who gave me jobs

When you write, you lay out a line of words.

ANNIE DILLARD
The Writing Life

To touch this land with words...you must lay great black steel lines of fiction...build giant artifact over and into space.

RUDY WIEBE
Passage by Land

I became a writer many times.

ROBERT KROETSCH
A Likely Story

Acknowledgements

These pieces are a selection of essays and presentations I have made in sixty years of writing. Others are available in *A Voice in the Land* (1981), *Playing Dead* (1989, 2003) and *River of Stone* (1995), but no comprehensive bibliography has been made and so I do not know how many I have written. The twenty-one selections included here often reflect the particular times when they were composed. They have been slightly edited to fit the requirements of this book; also, deletions have been made in some to avoid redundancies. I gratefully acknowledge the following first appearances:

"Terminal Disease": *Writers Guild of Alberta Newsletter* (1991).

"A Frontier Visit": University of Alberta's 75th Anniversary Celebrations; published in University of Alberta's *Folio* (23 December 1982).

"With the Flow": *Rhubarb* (Spring 2009).

"Documenting a Writer's Life": *Prairie Fire* (Spring 2002).

"Hold Your Peace": BC Mennonite Historical Society, Abbotsford, 2012.

"On the Trail of Big Bear": Western Canadian Studies Conference, University of Calgary, March 1974; published in *Journal of Canadian Fiction*, 3. 2 (1974).

"Where the Truth Lies": Various versions presented at several Canadian and American universities, 2007.

"In the West": *Globe and Mail,* March 25, 1978.

"On the Civil Right to Destroy Canada": *Edmonton Journal,* November 8, 1995.

"Land, Language and Law": The Shumiatcher Lecture, University of Saskatchewan, February 1999; published in *Saskatchewan Law Review,* 63, 1 (2000).

"The Elusive Meaning of 'North'": *Canadian Geographic* (January–February 1996).

"The Wind and the Caribou": *Edmonton Journal,* September 24, 1995.

"On Being on the Top of the World": *Brick,* 64 (Spring 2000).

"Acceptance Speech, Governor General's Award": Award Ceremonies, Montreal, November 15, 1994.

"Where the Black Rocks Lie in the Old Man's River": *Place: Lethbridge, A City on the Prairie,* Rudy Wiebe (author) and Geoffrey James (photographer). Vancouver: Douglas & McIntyre, 2002.

"The Sweet Fiction of Owning Land": *Collection Canada 2004.* Ottawa: Canada Post, 2004.

"On Death and Writing": American Association of Canadian Studies, Bangor, Maine, September 1983; published in *Canadian Literature,* 100 (Spring 1984).

"Killing our Way to Peace": The Thomas Merton Celebration, Vancouver, February 2003.

"The Body Knows as Much as the Soul": Samuel Yoder Lecture, Goshen College, Indiana, March 1995; published in *Mennonite Quarterly Review* (April 1997).

"Flowers for Approaching the Fire": Edmonton Mennonite Centre for Newcomers Benefit, March 1998; published in *Conrad Grebel Review* (Spring 1998).

"Look to the Rock": Thanksgiving Worship Service, 200th Anniversary of the founding of the Molotschna Mennonite Colony, Tokmak, Ukraine, October 2004.

Permissions

©1987 Di Brandt, reprinted by permission from *questions i asked my mother,* Turnstone Press (Winnipeg, MB).

"The Body Remembers" from *Sleeping Preacher,* by Julia Kasdorf, © 1992. Reprinted by permission of the University of Pittsburgh Press.

WRITING
A
LIFETIME

TERMINAL DISEASE

Several years ago, after long and serious introspection, I finally admitted to myself what my life problem has been; and is. I suffer from a terminal mental disease called writing.

I panicked for a moment, and talked to numerous people in whom I had recognized similar symptoms; they laughed at my apprehensions. They told me there were no known practitioners who specialized in treating such cases, no medicines, and there certainly were no institutions, anywhere where one could go for a cure. Besides, I had been infected for so long — who knows when chromosomes and cells first run amuck, but in my case it was at least forty years — there was really no question about it, they told me. In fact, it had been clear to some of them for a long time: I would die of it. The deadly Writeritis.

Where did it come from? I have no idea. I was a perfectly normal Canadian kid, last child of refugee immigrants who had found in Canada all they ever dreamed of in a country, and as a child I was taught all the sensible, practical things: to hold a good job and be a decent, contributing member of society — pay my fines and taxes, give donations to worthy causes, be polite, help those less privileged than I, behave decently in public — all that salt-of-the-earth citizen stuff. So I went to school to become a medical doctor, but after the first year of university I didn't want to do that. First class marks in science, second class in literature — and I changed my major and shifted to Arts and English. What was the matter with me? Was it a symptom that, even then, I did not recognize? My parents were the first not to understand what I was doing; I was the second.

It was almost as if I had been struck by polio, which was what happened to several of my friends then in the early fifties. They were ordinary kids, not a thing visibly wrong with them until suddenly they were sick. And even if they survived the initial attacks, their lives were forever marked.

Well, what does all that matter now, after so many years? No one should have to be bored with a stranger's biography. The point is, infected as I am, I engage with the world through writing: by putting words together into sentences, paragraphs, stories, essays, novels, scripts, diatribes, whatever — by typing them on paper and getting (if possible) editors and publishers to print and publish them — that is, *make them public*. For a lifetime, the only lifetime I presently know I have. I could be growing food (like my brother) or building houses or cutting out cancers or singing operas or running governments (Brian Mulroney is younger than I) or playing golf or preaching some kind of gospel, anywhere, or shopping at West Edmonton Mall for the good of the economy, but what am I doing? Sitting in a small room, trying to find words on a computer screen.

You have been warned: writeritis is terminal. There are no known cures, but there are people about who can make your disease worse. Teachers and editors aid and abet it when they tell you: "This manuscript is good; please show me more." Even more dangerous are those who insist on giving you a grant of money "so you will have more time to write more." Worst of all are publishers who offer you advances, who insist on giving you contracts and dragging you before the attention of readers, who in turn can become enthusiastic about what you have written. At that point you may as well recognize that you are irretrievably diseased; fit only for a writer's disability pension.

Such being the case, some of us have come to a sad and most sobering conclusion. Writing, as all forms of art, is more a calling than a job. As Flannery O'Connor, a writer of ineffable grace, imagination, and beauty once wrote: "There is no excuse for anyone to write fiction for public consumption unless he has been called to do so by the presence of a gift. It is the nature of fiction not to be good for much unless it is good in itself" (O'Connor 81).

I can only say, "Amen."

1991

A FRONTIER VISIT

My English Department office at the University of Alberta over-
looks the North Saskatchewan River bending through Edmonton.
That is where I was on the evening of Sunday, 22 August 1982.

It had been a vivid summer day, and now the level sunlight
suddenly struck every downtown window ablaze, every tower
across the river exploded upward like a flame. For an instant one
could only see the city as beautiful. I needed that; five days of the
past week I had had to spend in Ottawa trying to be wise about a
national cultural policy many cynics believed would never get past
the politicians. (They were right; the five-hundred-page Federal
Cultural Policy Review Committee Report, better known as
the Appelbaum-Hébert Report, didn't survive the 1984 change
of government). I am no cynic, but I now longed for nothing so
much as a few quiet days with the novel that had been gradually
shaping itself — much, much too gradually, would it ever truly
metamorphose and live? — a few days with the novel before university registration and classes moved in like glacial inevitability.
And now there came a knock at my door.

Not hesitant, or timid, not clamouring, demanding prerogatives — students so often betray themselves facing a closed door. This knock was exactly loud enough to fill a professor's small office. At 9:33 on Sunday night, dear god I can't be this wicked.

But after fifteen years at this university I am programmed; without conscious refusal I am on my feet and opening the door. To a medium-sized man with great bushy eyebrows, large sharp eyes, a salt and pepper moustache. And a small mole under his left eye. Fortunately I am holding onto the door very firmly.

His left eyebrow cocks at me. "Good evening, Mr. Wiebe," he says. I am simply standing there. "You used to be more polite."

"I'm sorry, I…" already I'm apologizing and I remember like a stroke the first time I saw Professor F.M. Salter: September, 1954, student registration day and an inner office in the Old Arts Building, its door wide open and I poked my head in seven times or walked up to it eight and kept on going; there was always someone in there with him I thought and so I had an excuse to delay what would inevitably happen anyway, he never would let me into English 65, his renowned creative writing course. "I hardly…expected you, so good…come in, astonishing…to see…"

He enters and I close the door quickly. He considers the long panorama of Edmonton, the High Level Bridge still lined across the river, then the sprawl of my papers and books about desk, typewriter, floor. "I hardly expected…" but I get myself stopped. Unless I repeat something banal, I am speechless.

He turns to me, easily, "Shakespeare had his regal ghosts, Dickens his Spirit of Christmas. Surely after twenty years you can be permitted one irascible old professor."

Of course. August 22, 1962.

We both sit down together abruptly, laughing. He is in my swivel chair, I in the visitor's and that is perfectly proper; while he was alive, I never had a university office to welcome him into with his round face and unbluffable, implacable eyes glittering like the memory of both pleasure and terror and flaring anger and a ripping, overwhelming happiness. He continues now:

"You always were such a dour young man, like some heavy-laden Scot. But when you smiled, and then finally laughed, ahhh, that was different."

I remember where he was sitting when he first said that to me; I went back to St. Steve's residence and tried faces in the mirror, not daring to believe him. Life at twenty still too serious to be smiled away.

"I couldn't smile that first year," I tell him, "because I was working so hard in your Shakespeare class and you didn't give me the prize in it anyway."

"I know, I know," he says. "Spring 1955, it was Mr. Baker, he wanted to be a lawyer, he needed the prize more than you. Besides, anyone who tries like you did to prove that *Romeo and Juliet* is a shallow play doesn't deserve any…"

"I still think a blood-feud is a stupid hill-billyish basis for a play!"

"Hasn't life taught you anything yet?"

"Not about serial revenge killing, that's just…"

"*Romeo and Juliet*," he interrupts, but patiently, "is a tragedy of fate, the beauty of love between star-crossed lovers."

"Dr. Salter, let me assure you, if I had known that as a young Dean of Men here you used to pace your rooms in Athabasca Hall intoning aloud the love sonnets Juliet and Romeo whisper to each other, to the giggling delight of eavesdropping freshmen, I certainly would never have tried to prove it a poor play."

"You would then, as it were, have kissed by the book, eh?"

"I would have been collared into it," I answered as grimly, and then we are laughing again, aloud together. I was in his Shakespeare class twice, once for credit and four years later for instruction and delight. So I heard him discourse on twenty-seven of the thirty-seven plays, and even in the time of his growing illness the classes were kaleidoscopic with play-acting, critical and character analyses, minute differentiations of plot (there are thirty-nine possible plots and Hamlet is a perfect multi-layered example of "the biter bit" plot), of rhetoric explained and presented and above all marvelous words, words singing, exhorting, pleading, crying, thundering words that clove through or stuck in the mind, sliced you finer than the swords of any Elizabethan bloody dandy.

"What work are you doing now?" he asks gesturing, abruptly as always.

"I'm writing another novel." And somehow, his steady eye again makes me want to confess. "Trying...it's...a kind of love story."

He considers me; his eyebrow arches slightly. "Do you think," he says, "you are old enough already to write a love story?"

I certainly never tried one in his writing class...well, that's not quite true. I did several times with an amazing lack of success. The enormous exception of Shakespeare proved his rule: you had to be old, through and preferably beyond the singing riot of the blood before you could write of love, capably. Tragedy, irony, the black holes of inexplicable or malignant fate, these were my small beginning successes, but joy, love, whistling happiness... he makes me furious all over again, just studying me, daring me.

"You got me into this!" I have every right to be loud in my own office. "I was perfectly resigned to that summer job as an insurance investigator and then you got me listed as top alternate for a Queen Elizabeth Graduate Scholarship and sure enough one of the top ten didn't accept and I got one and needed to do nothing but start on a thesis and I told you I wanted to do an MA in Shakespeare of course — a perfectly acceptable subject, to investigate, reveal, analyse, maybe destroy Shakespeare's attitude on war, whatever it was I said — and you just sat there, 'Yes, yes,' with all those stacks of thick books piled around you in your summer porch and letters from scholars and thinkers all over the world lying everywhere like gold, 'yes, Mr. Wiebe, a good many people can write perfectly acceptable, or dreadful, theses on Shakespeare — but perhaps only you can write a fine novel about Canadian Mennonites.' Leaking that into me like . . . poison."

He says now, very quietly, "You never did trust any of those incredible stories you already had."

"How could I? I'd just heard or lived them, I'd never, ever, read a word of them. Low German doesn't happen on the playing fields of England or the sidewalk cafes of Paris. They were just about running from Stalin and starving and gratefully shovelling cowshit in peace."

He shakes his head. "You would out-peasant us all, wouldn't you," he says, and suddenly leans forward his eyes pinning me. "Did you honestly think the coal mines of Cape Breton, the trenches of the bloody Western Front were any better?"

"They at least had the dignity of written story, and all the manly adventure, and the killing."

"It's not that way much," he says, "when you're the one that's getting killed in the mud. But you were typical enough, all those young people coming here from prairie bush farms, grabbing for everything, their minds soaking up ideas faster than you could tell them, look there, there! I remember one very learned English scholar, if I told you his name you'd recognize it, who once ventured this far onto the frontier to lecture and I made a point of introducing him to every one of my students, individually, and he said to me in private, later, 'They all have such…' and then he caught himself but he couldn't quite get out of it, 'such… difficult…names.'" He chuckles, his face soft with memory. "That was long before the jet plane; Oxford was two weeks away, and even Toronto four days. You remember why I accepted you into the writing course?"

"I would forget? You gave me 40% on the *Romeo and Juliet* midterm and the same day you handed back our first essays, and I'd written on *The Tempest* and that mark was 90."

"Of course," he laughs. The subject was 'off-stage and interscene dramatic action' and you wrote about Ariel, we hadn't discussed the play yet, you brilliantly explained how Ariel doesn't sweep fire over the ship, but how he sets it all aflame *with himself!*"

"And you wrote in the margin," I say, "in that inimitable spidery red fountain pen — sometimes the page was redder than black and white with three arguments you offered and then destroyed to show why they would have been wrong if I had used them, which I hadn't — you concluded, 'I don't know you from Adam — well, I didn't make the world — but if you want to take a writing course, I'll give you one, wherever, whenever you want it. Come to see me.' That's what you wrote, on a handwritten Shakespeare essay."

He leans back; I see the words form on his tongue; his face, his entire body changing:

Prospero: Hast thou, spirit,
Perform'd to point the tempest that I bade thee?
Ariel: To every article.
I boarded the king's ship; now on the beak,
Now in the waist, the deck, in every cabin,
I flam'd amazement. Sometime I'd divide,
And burn in many places. On the topmast,
The yards and bowsprit, would I flame distinctly,
Then meet and join. Jove's lightnings, the precursor's
O' th' dreadful thunderclaps, more momentary
And sight-outrunning were not; the fire and cracks
Of sulphurous roaring the most mighty Neptune
Seem to besiege, and make his bold waves tremble,
Yea, his dread trident shake.
Prospero: My brave spirit!
(*The Tempest*, I, ii, 193–206)

I am in the bare lecture room that is Arts 135, one of forty or fifty students, some sitting on the floor because there are never enough desks in Professor Frederick Millet Salter's classes. Outside, November snow drives chips of ice against the windows, grey Alberta winter closing in. But really I am on an uninhibited tropical island, the Bermudas perhaps, and I am looking up at the most superb teacher I ever knew; the immensely learned man who would not let me dare less than the farthest edges of my wildest, most improbable, dream.

1982

WITH THE FLOW

The magazine Rhubarb asks me: what are "the TOP 10 influences that shaped" me in my seven and a half decades of life? To quote a book of mine, "Childhood [or one's entire life] can only remain what you have not forgotten" (*Earth* 7).

When, in a previous millennium, I retired from teaching writing at the University of Alberta, I gave three hour-long talks entitled "An Invention of Influences." They were:

    1. The Discovery of Deserts, Giants and Sewers

    2. The Artifice of an Iron Hand

    3. Articulating the Skull in the Swamp

The talks were never published, and *Rhubarb* has no space for these hours of wandering in the boreal bush of my scribbling past but, to go anywhere, even briefly, I do need some definitions. Influence: a lovely noun, formed by the preposition "in" plus the Latin *fluere*, "to flow." The noun "influent" is even clearer: "that which flows in." Is *Rhubarb* asking: what, in a lifetime, has flowed *in* you, Rudy Wiebe? Or is it "flowed into," or "flowed through… within… past… under… over… beside… out of… against…"

— all those powerful, essential prepositions which in English shape-shift and control our meanings? Or is the question really: what, with all this flowing somewhere *in* you, what has remained behind to make you the writer you continue trying to become? Tell us, make it up (down... out?) as necessary.

Okay. I will not comment on my immediate family, without which my actual life is unimaginable; that story is for another place, not here. So, whatever or wherever the flow, what remains behind in me:

— **The place where I was born:** the vanished homestead-farm community of some thirty-five families (perhaps 250 people) at Speedwell in the boreal forest east of Turtle Lake, north of North Battleford, Saskatchewan. No human being now lives on the Speedwell land, which is Township 53, Range 17, west of the 3rd Meridian. In 1971 the hills and sloughs and creek-beds and all the log buildings on all the homestead quarters, except for several small woodlots reserved for wild animal shelter, were bulldozed, burned and seeded to grass to make a summer cattle pasture. However, the pine log walls of Speedwell School still stand stacked in a small patch of brush, and two miles south there is the tiny clearing of the Speedwell Mennonite Brethren Church Cemetery, circled by aspen and beautifully cared for beside the cattle corrals. Thirty-two persons are buried there, one row of children, one row of men, and one row of women, 1932 to 1948, including my teenage sister in 1945.

— **Jesus Christ:** his life and his stories. It sometimes seems to me his spirit already moved in me while I grew into being in my mother's womb and, in various and inexplicable ways, has never left me. I hope.

— *My mother:* she lived her 84 years in Low German, *"Awbeid enn Hohp"* (Work and Hope, both as nouns and verbs), and in High German, *"Dem Mutigen gehoert die Welt"* (To the daring/the courageous belongs the world).

— *Reading:* numberless books that, to quote a novel of mine, "allow [you] to hear human voices speaking from everywhere and every age, saying things both sweet and horrible, and everything else that might be imagined between them" (*Sweeter* 7). Tena, my wife, tells me the foundation corner of our Edmonton home is cracked from the weight of my library; true, there is a large crack, but I'm convinced her office of books and records is making its own contribution.

— *Forms of writing:* beginning with driblets of songs and rhymes spinning in my head that I eventually thought could be poems, struggling to write short stories, essays, dramas, sermons, novels, creative non-fiction, postmodern historiographic metafictions (I never said that: blame the critics), readings, editing a news magazine and collections of short stories, illustrated children's stories, film scripts (original and adapted, with some even produced), illustrated historical books filled with participants' first-hand accounts, living and dead biography and autobiography, etc., etc. And even within such specific forms as the short story or novel, which have constituted most of my writing, the shape of any one can become so complicated that writing the next one becomes a continuation of finding the impossible possible.

— *Anabaptist-Mennonite heritage:* none of us choose our ancestors, and I have at times found my ancestral lineage, often obscure, stimulating beyond measure. Exploring over five centuries (from

Wybe Adams von Harlingen, 1584–1652) of my world-wandering Canadian, Paraguayan/German, Russian/Ukrainian, Polish/Prussian, Frisian/Flemish family offered more than enough stories for seven lifetimes.

— *Big Bear:* the wise and brilliant Plains Cree chief who in 1876 refused to "touch the pen" to Treaty 6 because he recognized it gave the Canadian government control ("it was not given to us to have the rope about our necks") over everything Native (Morris 192). His complex life, and that of his many descendants to this day: the story of the continuing creation of our shared homeland Canada, and of justice for all, especially the Aboriginal People, from sea to sea to sea.

Oh, Big Bear; a power in my life. As if I continuously dreamed him — though I have never been conscious of that dreaming in my sleep; only when awake. As though, once I had climbed Bull's Forehead Hill above the confluence of the Red Deer and the South Saskatchewan Rivers — the place where in 1838–39 he was given his bear vision — and Elder John Tootoosis of the Poundmaker First Nation had shown me the place where his body was buried in 1888 on the bank of the Battle River, and in New York's American Museum of Natural History had held in my hands the core of his scared bundle — the great bear paw complete with claws he had, as instructed in the vision, sewn onto a bib of red stroud — and I had been forgiven for opening the bundle cloths without knowing the proper songs to sing, nor prayers to pray, and alone, without a circle of believers to assist me: after that, his spirit began to live in my imagination beyond my knowing; and would remain.

— *West Germany in 1957 – 58:* no one knows his own place until he has traveled to others and learned to recognize difference. The gift of a Rotary Fellowship gave me two semesters at the University of Tübingen (founded in 1479) and, with Tena joining me in delightful marriage, travels throughout Wuertemberg, Bavaria, Austria, Switzerland, Italy, Belgium, the Netherlands, and Great Britain. Also two train trips, Lethbridge to Montreal and back, and the indescribable beauty of a sunlit day sailing down the St. Lawrence River until sunset carried us below the red-blazing fortress of Quebec City. Plus ten days on the North Atlantic, going and coming, with enough heaving ocean for bountiful seasickness.

— *Frederick M. Salter:* professor of English at the University of Alberta who taught me my first writing course and, in 1959, told me that there were no doubt numberless students capable of writing an acceptable MA thesis on Shakespeare but, perhaps, only I could write a good novel about Canadian Mennonites. He dared me; and I dared.

— *Students in creative writing workshops:* in Canada, the United States and Germany. I will not name any, some now brilliant, widely published writers, but the hundreds of imaginations I have encountered, and the places they have taken me, remain subliminally everywhere.

Ten influences: an arbitrary number and, including perhaps the first four, in no necessary sequence. An essay is possible on any one, and in a lengthening lifetime I've written a number. The problem with writer longevity can be a complicating, even contradictory, oeuvre. Hopefully.

2009

DOCUMENTING A WRITER'S LIFE: AN AGGRAVATION OF QUOTES

The Bible says that God is omnipotent, except in one respect. He has willingly given up his omnipotence over man's mind.... Why did God give man free will, which is clearly the source of all the evil in the world?

Who can answer for God's motives? If God is omnipotent, he must have known it would cost him the murder of his only Son if he created a world — and yet he made the world and he made us, as we are. Why?

We cannot comprehend because we are very little, and we can only see as a firefly with its tiny prick of light flying in the great darkness of the world's night. All we know now is that we have the right, nay, it is the freely offered gift that we are "the captains of our souls." And once we have, out of ourselves, accepted this great offering, we can only be thankful in our little way.

Recently I found the document containing these faintly August-
inian words — and others — in a file folder; I have no memory
of writing them on high school scribbler paper. They seem to be
an essay written for a class on Christian Doctrine (*Glaubenslehre,*
taught at the Alberta Mennonite High School in German, though
we could write our assignments in English) that I took when I was
seventeen, but they are obviously not what I handed in because
in the file is also the completed assignment with the instructor's
mark on it: a totally different three-page, six-point attempt at a
biblically proof-texted argument entitled "God's Rule of the Earth
in Relation to the Free Will of Man and the Laws of Nature." No
comment, just a date, "May 22," and a mark, "H-"; an "H" being
then in Alberta the highest grade.

When you read these words I wrote with an ink pen in 1952,
you are not only doing the most uniquely human thing on earth
— hearing language. You are doing so by taking the further step
into human brilliance of seeing language made visible. Using
the optical conventions we all agree upon as English spelling,
I can create precise (unbelievable?) ideas in your mind quite
different from whatever you were thinking an instant before;
ideas based on — no, I should rather say "created by" — the very
(pun intended) complex sounds we make with our mouths, a
noise-making ability which as children we prattled ourselves into
understanding as unconsciously as our bodies growing larger.
Every normal human child uses sound in ever-new combinations
to create the infinitely varied meanings of language; no other animal uses sound in that way. As Hugh Brody explains it:

> In the absence of language, inheritance is limited to the
> gene pool. Parents pass on to their offspring a bundle of

genes and very little else. But with language, they can pass on vast bodies of knowledge, moral codes, forms of social arrangements. And with language, it is possible to think.... The capacity to be human is inseparable from the capacity to think, be articulate and change life through words. (Brody 292-3)

All my life I have worked with words, trying to be a writer. Writing better is a never-ending possibility. To make a visible and oral thing with words.

Beyond any teen-philosophy scribblings acceptable in a Christian school — my mind as yet uncomplicated by a knowledge of Voltaire or Hume or Kant — I tried to write stories. Inexplicable to me now, the earliest of these were filled with cemeteries, cold moonlight, wind, mostly leafless trees; even a few written while I was at university had much the same characteristics. My first published story (1956) had a clumsy title, "Eight and the Present," that *Liberty Magazine* arbitrarily changed into the even worse "The Midnight Ride of an Alberta Boy"; it was reprinted in my initial short-story collection, *Where is the Voice Coming From?* (1974) as "Scrapbook."

My second published story, "The Power," was selected for *New Voices: Canadian University Writing of 1956*. This is the opening paragraph:

The gaunt trees crowding the road were shivering spectres, staring through him in the passing wagon. The spring, the summer, even the autumn had gone now, and the winter had not yet come. The stillness of no season at all filtered through the thin November wind as it slid, moaning, between the creaking branches of the poplars. It was no season at all, only a kind of suspension that was waiting for him to get on and do something. Yet he could do nothing, for he seemed to be, like the season, suspended by an everlasting thread in a void, and he was twisting slowly, futilely, like a strangled rabbit in a snare. He opened his eyes wide once more and stared about him, pupils fixedly dilated. The trees seemed to look, the road and wagon and horses, the huddled log church they were passing, the two men in front of him, even the woman leaning against his shoulder seemed to look and be there, yet somehow they were not there because they were flat like shadows, and, like shadows, though he could reach out and touch them, he could not *feel* them. His big hand closed upon the hard muscles of his thigh. For a moment it was absurd that he should think of himself as one of the silly rabbits he snared in winter, but it passed in an instant. He could not feel the presence of anyone, stare as he would, and he could hardly feel his empty self. (Wiebe, "The Power" 128)

And so on. Trying to wrestle into words what a person feels or, more difficult, does not feel. Since then I have myself experienced the death of children (sudden as an axe splitting my skull) and know more certainly that the "no feeling" is right — the blank yet overwhelming *feelinglessness* of a person whose children have been destroyed so completely by fire that you cannot distinguish the ashes of their hair and flesh and bones from those of the house logs within which they burned. You try, as Annie Dillard says, "When you write, you lay out a line of words" (3).

My next published attempts at writing were newspaper stuff. While attending Tübingen University in Germany, I sent the *Lethbridge Herald* several items that it published as "Rudy Wiebe Writes from Overseas." The first appeared December 5, 1957:

Spending Sunday in London

The booming bells that once awakened Dickens a hundred years ago swung in a brilliant Sunday for all Londoners. This might be the last sunny day all fall [i.e., Oct. 20] and, since every rainless day in London must be considered as probably the last for months, people strolled everywhere; with their homburgs, their umbrellas (pessimism is usually a virtue), their purple poodles (I saw one — and had to stare to convince myself)....

Now, the afternoon. Let's see the colours of St. James Park. But you get waylaid in Trafalgar Square by several polite pigeons. They are great ladies and gentlemen, as all established Londoners should be, and they never crowd when sitting on your head, shoulders and arms — only 23 per person. The others wait their turn. The Square is full of people, but there are enough pigeons to accommodate everyone — if not, a courier is sent for more to Leicester Square. The fountains spray up, the enormous wreaths hanging from the lions' paws at the foot of Nelson's Column glitter in the Thanksgiving sunlight, and the crowds of Londoners, buried behind stone canyons of their own making, have their weekly contact with domestic animal life.

But now, on through Admiralty Arch and down The Mall, where the Queen rode to her coronation. Four cavernous palaces on one side and St. James Park, where Henry VIII once had his private hunting and now scattered with colour, on the other. With all the English, you sit under a beech and eat an apple. Perhaps Henry pierced a hart with an arrow right where you are now sitting, or decided on an execution. Present or past, England is colourful.

At the end of The Mall, solemn, stony, tremendously aloof among all the searching eyes, stands Buckingham Palace. Persons with all types of noses and accents wander about, stare up under the bearskins into the unflinching faces of the Palace guards, stare through the bars [of the fence] at the empty windows, stare at each other stare — and some wonder what a fortune it must cost to heat in winter, and others marvel that a very small family should need so much living space.

You are disappointed. It is all so cold and looks just like the black and white pictures in the Grade III book at home. Well, how else can it look? And all is not cold — the monumental statue of the mother Victoria — queens still live and breathe and love their children. And all is not solemn — the bronze gargoyles about the base grin at you with their water-spouting mouths.

On to Hyde Park — just past the Palace grounds. It is quite an ordinary park — tall trimmed oaks and huge commons where small boys practice soccer with their fathers. But the real attraction is at Marble Arch Corner — the Orators Heaven.

What's on today? Since it is the first time for you, all is novel, but the various types of cranks are easily identified. Thousands crowd about in various-sized groups, and the orators, who stand on chairs, trash-cans, or even regular stands — showing thereby that they are the pros — rave, rant, laugh, sob, holler as they see fit. First, of course, you see the street-corner religious fanatic who uses his "religion" to damn everyone and shout "I told you so!" when some new disaster arises in the world. This one is interpreting the Bible by means of Russia's Sputnik, but only two old ladies are listening to him — more attracted by his grizzly beard than his tirade.

The crowd, like a bloated monster, bulges and heaves and pours about, searching for diversion. Here is the hoarse voice and the green flag of the Irish Nationalist, a queer [i.e., odd] scholar with a queerer theory; here the humourist whose face makes it impossible for him to live and be anything else, a wit snipping at world affairs (and what could be juicier for an English crowd than a salty comment on America's Sputnik reaction). And, an island among the turmoil, a Salvation Army meeting whose gospel songs attract many a person far from home. But the Communist and the coloured people's stands have the real crowds.

By beginning this essay as I have, I have entangled myself in documentary. Document: "written evidence...which furnishes information upon any subject, as a manuscript, title-deed, tombstone, coin, picture, etc" (*OED*). Laying out a line of words is a writer's coin, his picture, his tombstone of evidence; Anne Carson explains, superbly, what I am trying to do here by gathering together bits of original texts out of my personal half century:

What you enjoy in a documentary technique is the feeling that you are crossing back and forth on the frame of facts, skating from document to document, while retaining your own point of view — which is called "objective" because you make facts into objects by viewing them this way. You are not so swept along by the facts as to forget your own viewing, as you would in the midst of a poem or dramatic film. Instead you insist on seeing the edge of the frame wherever you look. In a good documentary the facts spill over the frame; then spill again. (Carson 143–144)

That fall encounter with Hyde Park and its people lived on in my memory of a memory; alone in my solitary student room that December, medieval Tübingen all around me, I tried to find an image in lines of fewer words that would reveal more of what I remembered feeling:

Fall Sunday in Hyde Park
A squall of rain in a puff of wind...
The thousand and one dreams screamed to the world
Unmarked.
Save by the swish of leaves and litter
On crumpled pavement
And a mongrel miserably nosing
A trash can.   (Wiebe, "Fall Sunday" 5)

In the Edmonton summer of 1959 I was trying to write a novel. Eventually, after some years and two excellent editors, it would struggle out of an inchoate boil of characters, places, times, prejudices, opinions, myths, ignorance, memories, life and lives I had or had never lived that roiled and continually re-shaped themselves in my head as I scrawled or typed words onto paper. But for that to happen, much would have to be left behind.

Here are twelve hundred words from a draft chapter of *Peace Shall Destroy Many*. In spring during the 1890s a large group of Mennonite settlers are moving by freight train from their home colony in the Ukraine to build a new colony in eastern Russia, and I am digging to find one of the novel's main characters, that of Deacon Peter Block — here "the boy in the red scarf":

> The adventure of travel was quickly experienced, and then came the monotony of days and nights cramped together with three or four other families in the dirty boxcars.... After nine days the train arrived at the Volga River. Everyone in car number eight crowded to the door and the small windows to gaze in dumb wonder at the skeleton of steel that leaped the mud-swollen river which they had to cross. After a pause, as of hesitation, the train crawled onto the bridge, and then slowly the shadows of the girders passed over their faces as they looked down and down in the bright sunshine at the grim, rolling river and the ice-blocks pushed up high on the banks.... Only three more days left.
>
> The boy in the red scarf was gone again before anyone could notice him. The just married young couple returned to their corner through the tight corridor of

piled boxes and pulled the sacking shut behind them. As he did so, John pulled at the tautness of the ropes that held the supplies in place. Each layer of boxes had its rope, and when they lay still they could hear the ropes creak to the swaying of the train. The tiny floor space was covered with blankets. As usual, John pulled off his boots sitting on the bed, for there was no place to stand. Greta had already lain down, her arm over her eyes pulling her long, full dress up tight around her breast. John looked at her, just beside him but not quite touching, anywhere.

"Tired?" As the last boot pulled free.

"Uh-huh." It was muffled by her wide sleeves.

The rhythmical throb of the wheels ground up through his head as he eased down beside her. After a moment he touched her dress. A bit of light filtered palely through the oiled paper over what was supposed to be the window. They lay listening to the crying of the other families' children, which echoed from the ceiling of the car.

"John" — with an odd accent.

"Yes." There was a long pause.

"No?"

"Sure, my lovely. You're tired."

In the nine days of travel he had learned more than all the previous days of his life. Neither he nor Greta had been told anything of what was involved in being married... So they had begun to discover for themselves what it was to be man and woman in their cubicle behind the supplies. John felt the trip composed his whole life. He could barely remember his home village, or what his father looked like… Greta was breathing deeply beside him, and he moved against her on the blankets.

"John — you're not supposed to — you'll drive me crazy —"

For Greta had learned from her mother that she would have to endure. "That is all. You must give him his due." Which statement had explained exactly nothing to the poor girl, who now felt that she must have fallen prey to the most devilish of devils, for she had no way to explain her body's quick, flaring desire for him. But she could not fight it; all she could do was pull down John's head against her breast so that he should not see her nakedness, and even the rip of some cloth, long carefully treasured, did not matter. Then, as she leaned back with staring, unseeing eyes, suddenly they focused on movement and a scream tore from her, past the dark boy who was leaning far out from the top of the baggage, straining to see what, though he had seen its motions day after day, the fading light or a sheltering blanket had always hidden. His face terribly concentrated in his look, his red scarf a livid scar in the gloom. In his compulsion to see he had pushed away the small, iron-bound box which had hidden his cranny and, as John jerked back at Greta's scream and followed her horrified gaze upwards, the boy realized himself, pulled back, and in so doing tipped the box forward; it's iron corner clipped him as it fell. A short cry was all they heard as the boy disappeared.

John was just able to deflect the box, which landed with a thud on a corner of their bed. He did not dare look at his wife as he pulled his clothing into place, the sound of voices rising beyond the barrier. He pulled back the curtain; the other travellers crowded there, swaying slightly with the train, their gaze questioning.

"Mr. Block," John said, "your boy —"

"If that hoodlum has bothered you, I'll —" The gruff man glared as he took two steps towards John. "Pete!" he bellowed. "Here this instant!"

"Pa," Mrs. Block murmured, "I'm sure the boy —"

"Pete!"

At that moment the boy slipped from behind a packing case through an opening no one knew was there, and collapsed at his father's feet. In the gloomy car it looked for a moment as if his scarf were wrapped about his face, and the mother with a scream of "Blood!" lurched down beside him. His face was awash with blood that pulsed freely from a long gash across the right temple and down to his eyebrow. He had fainted without a word....

It was two weeks later that a lone wagon appeared out of a draw in the hills east of the Russian town of Orenburg. The driver, a huge man who was walking beside his wagon, allowed his heaving team to stop at the crest as he looked across the level land that fell away gradually to the north. They were on the first rise of the foothills of the Ural Mountains; it was land such as he had known by the Black Sea, but infinitely more barren. It seemed to reach to the end of the world, with not a human in sight.

He turned to the woman, who was riding in the heavily loaded wagon. "They build their villages in the coulees, that's why we can't see anything." With a growl: "If it wasn't for his stupidity, we could have moved on sleighs like the others, and we wouldn't have to kill our horses."

The boy for whom this was intended was propped up beside the baggage, and did not flicker even his eyelash to show he had heard his father. He was looking north also, not concerned with the muddy trail they were following. He was not thinking about his fever that had held them at the railroad station while the other settlers used the last vanishing snow to advantage in getting their supplies to the new colonies. He was not thinking of how the fever of the infection had finally broken, and the Russian doctor had explained, "He will always have the red scar." With his unbandaged eye he was looking at the land, and he was thinking about that.

Peter Block had arrived on the Orenburg steppe. It would be years before he knew of the existence of the plains of Canada. (Personal files)

Clumsy stuff, explanatory prose too obviously constructed, even more than this in a very long chapter. Totally discarded in the final version of the novel and never published. But necessary to make for what will become a life-long apprenticeship in fiction: to discover over and over how little is essential, how much must always be shoved aside and left.

By 1967 I had returned to the University of Alberta to teach Creative Writing in the English Department, and it seemed important that a young professor should write scholarly research articles. In a paper given at the Western American Literature Association, I expatiate on the "abnormally high number of expatriate professional debunkers" of Canadian writing that seem to be in the United States, explain why I think "Canadian western fiction is particularly suited to use Canada's two [as yet] unrealized myths: our classless non-ethnicity and our widely-proclaimed non-racism, to explore where we are going in a huge world squeezed small by the media" (29), and declare with a novelist's (not a scholar's) confidence that the most interesting frontier for Canadian fiction is not in its cities:

> [The frontier of Canadian writing] is in the north. Two-thirds of Canada remains empty; one of the last great empty spaces on earth. Oh, airplanes and helicopters and hovercraft and skidoos roar over it in all directions all the time, but in two million square miles you can still get away from diesel noise and fumes; you can still, if you walk in the wrong direction, have half the circumference of the moon to go before you'll likely meet another human. There you can be alone, not "alone" as in the city. There you can still battle elements on a basic level, study your own thoughts undisturbed on the picture tube of your mind, always a private and individual production unmuddled by deodorant reminders. In a natural world man has not looted or polluted, yet, you can still look about, see what has never been seen before and in the absolute silence of never-before-breathed air, hear your own heart beat. I know there's good fiction there!
> ("Western Canada" 30)

Later in the '70s I became friends with Paul Thompson, who had created Theatre Passe Muraille in Toronto. We worked together to stage several shows out of my fiction, and in 1977 we talked Theatre 3 of Edmonton into staging a play, not yet written, about an Alberta conflict between farmers and a power company which wanted to build an enormous thermal power plant using coal dug up out of their farmland. *Far As The Eye Can See* acted out that conflict; it grew as a "collective creation" between actors, director, and writer. Throughout the final hectic days of practice Paul kept pushing that the play needed an *in vino veritas* scene; the two most powerful antagonists, brilliant mining engineer John and dedicated, stubborn farmer Joe needed an "in wine is truth" encounter. Finally I agreed; together with actors Eric Peterson (John) and Dennis Robinson (Joe) we "jammed" the scene, as they say, for some hours and then I wrote it out clean:

Joe Nussbaumer in the town bar; John Siemens enters, already drunk.

JOE: Well, what do you know, the Bigshot! I never thought I'd see you here.

JOHN (very depressed): I never thought so either.

JOE: Where's your smile? Where's your notebook, Bigshot?

John sits down at the table; Joe is about to get up and move away, but abruptly he changes his mind and leans forward.

JOE: You sit here, you put your money on the table.

JOHN (taking out money): You think it's easy being a Bigshot? You ever tried it?

JOE: Me, I'm just a dirt farmer, shovel shit.

JOHN: Okay, here (stands up) you be the Bigshot, com'mon.

JOE: Me?

JOHN: Yeah, you, I'm a flunky and you're the Bigshot.

JOE: Wha — what does a Bigshot do?

JOHN: He asks for things — and they happen, just like that — okay Joe, you're the Bigshot, ask for things, com'mon.

JOE: Okay — give me the keys to your car.

JOHN: Yes, sir! (hands over keys)

JOE: Not those, the Porsche!

JOHN: Of course — good Joe, good! — anything else, sir?

JOE: And I want a raise, fifty thousand a year.

JOHN: After taxes, sir? With bonuses?

JOE: (getting confused) Yeah — yeah —

JOHN: Look Joe, put your back into it, you're a *Bigshot!*

JOE: I — I don't know how — what do I want?

JOHN: You want *everything*, you're big, get big (Joe tries to get big) — Bigger, bigger! — (Joe tries harder)

okay — now I'm a little guy, I'm a farmer and I live on
my farm and raising my kids and I'm farming farming
farming and I see you, Bigshot, coming over the hill
and you see my farm and —

JOE: I want it!

JOHN: Yeah, you want it because I've got it and
you're the Bigshot and I get all the little people
together (he is piling bar chairs on top of each other)
and we try to be as big as you and work and work
and you...

JOE: I go BOOM!

The chairs crash to the floor.

(The scene continues until Joe achieves the "bigness"
to heave John bodily off the stage; abruptly the
fundamental "truth in the wine" overtakes them.)

JOE: I wanna thank you for buying me all these
drinks — and for showing me how to be a Bigshot.
(He stands up) But I don't want to play your game
any more. (He goes)

JOHN: (Alone at the table) I don't either.
(Personal files)

That scene was great fun, both to create and to watch. It was
never performed nor is it in the published text, yet to hone the
best out of that story it was necessary to try to make it.

The dominant entertainment of the past forty years is the moving picture, in all its variant forms, and at some point most contemporary fiction writers are tempted, or been asked, to write a script. Beginning in the '70s, I have worked on several, and one project that seemed to have a strong possibility for actual production (in contrast to the dreary numbers of scripts forever "in development" and then dropped) was a story I called "Breaking Stony Mountain." Stony Mountain is the oldest federal prison in western Canada, built north of Winnipeg in 1874, and Cree Chief Big Bear was imprisoned inside its stone from 1885 to 1887. One of the three dominant characters in this script is an imagined clone — an avatar if you wish — of Big Bear's life and personality, as throughout my writing life so many of my characters and stories have been, unpublished or published. Here is the scene in which he first appears:

INTERIOR.GERIATRIC HOSPITAL ROOM, DAY

CLOSE-UP of unbelievably ancient JOE BEAR curled almost foetal-like on the bed. He is asleep, but two female hands shift his head up gently, and another hand presents a spoon with something peach in it. The spoon is inserted into his pliant mouth; after a moment, he swallows.

WIDENING SHOT to include two elderly female nurses. One is feeding Joe while the other (a Native woman) holds his head in position. We have already been hearing their conversation with a clearly dissatisfied young doctor.

> FEEDING NURSE
> (very motherly)
> ... he's never a bit of bother, he just tucks in, full bowl
> of baby food, just so easy...

DOCTOR

Any normal functions — speech, elimination, bowel
movement?

HOLDING NURSE

Well, he never talks, and bm's no more than two little
turds a year, but I sometimes think maybe he's a —

DOCTOR

Two little…a year?

FEEDING NURSE

Well he only eats once a week, you don't expect —

DOCTOR

Once a week!

An accountant with an ancient ledger has appeared.

ACCOUNTANT

Sorry to be so long, he wasn't on the computer. There
isn't much
(he points, and the doctor studies the book as well)
just Arrived January 17 1958, Age 83, from Saskatchewan, no next of kin or address…

DOCTOR

Why would he be brought to Manitoba from Saskatchewan? Who visits him?

HOLDING NURSE

Nobody I've ever seen, but I've only been here
fourteen years and I sometimes think he —

ACCOUNTANT

(a flat-footed fact man)
83 in '58, so he's 113 years old right now.

The doctor is staring from one to the other in amazement.

DOCTOR
That's impossible, 113…

FEEDING NURSE
Never a bit of bother, the old dear.

She inserts the last spoonful; Joe swallows. The doctor leans over, pulls an eyelid up. Joe's black eye stares into his with absolute intensity; the doctor shuts it quickly.

DOCTOR
(to accountant)
Hasn't anyone ever done anything about him?

ACCOUNTANT
What's to do? He's cost the taxpayer, in thirty years, exactly $1,007,263.00.

HOLDING NURSE
(she'll have her say)
I sometimes think he's just a nice hibernating old bear and one day he'll just —

DOCTOR
From now on, no more food.

The two nurses look at him in consternation; their mouths fall open.

FEEDING NURSE
He don't cost nothing. I buy the jar of baby food myself once a —

DOCTOR
I need the bed. He's beyond recovery.

(Personal files)

To inherit in the very marrow of your birth bones, as it were, more than one language is an immeasurable gift for a writer, even (especially) when they are as linguistically related as mine: oral Russian-Mennonite Low German, the only language I spoke with my parents as long as they lived; literary High German; the English I do not remember learning when I started school. To discuss the quality of what happens when a writer can, as by instinct, without conscious word translation, see the world simultaneously in several languages is beyond what I am trying to do here; leave it for another time.

But there remains the unquenchable fascination of fiction, reading and laying the line of words on the page and reading again and laying words down again, to find that extraordinary state when you are not yourself any longer and yet you are more yourself than you ever are; being that on a perfectly ordinary weekday morning. Face the blank wall and, as Henry David Thoreau put it, "Know your own bone: gnaw at it, bury it, unearth it, and gnaw it still" (Dillard 68). Fiction: a word derived from "fict," that structure you form, that you make with words out of facts. The long months of a novel that shifts and changes through the years as you change while living through it, or the day, perhaps the hours and then the days and weeks of polish of a short story, a very, very short story — here's a concluding one I contrived to keep under five hundred words; four hundred and ninety-three to be exact, including the title:

Life Story

It began when John was born, when his mother was almost fifty. His father, sixty-seven, said it was an accident, that for years now he had thought his hose, as he called it, was set on play only. John did not speak English or French until he began school, where he learned to sing a song, two lines of which he could never forget:

But it stopped, short, never to go again
When the old man died.

He understood after reading a Bible-story book that Jesus had never laughed nor made love, though he had wept out loud and beaten several salespeople and money changers, nor had he ever touched a woman — except perhaps his mother — unless she first touched him. In high school John played hockey, and once almost scored a goal in an important game. He did not, knowingly, ejaculate while awake until he tried to kiss the woman he was convinced he could marry. She was not so convinced, and that was it. After seven years he stopped trying to teach school when he noticed a girl staring at him in horror just as he was prepared to murder, at last, by manual strangulation, his worst goof-off pupil. For two years he collected and arranged stamps. A choral society he sang in sang a song, several lines of which continued to pass through his mind:

Nothing is here for tears, nothing to wail,
Nothing but well and fair.
And what may quiet us...

Later he could not recall the ending of the third line, nor did he ever try to discover it. He began to sell real estate, there were vacant houses and shopping malls everywhere, it was obvious the world was being re-designed to be sold. He touched a woman's anus once, and circled it softly with his fingertip. "Please," she said in her Canadian way, and that was it. There were times when John suspected he might be happy, though he could never fathom a reason why. He suffered a heart attack while speaking into his cellphone; fortunately his car was halted at a four-way stop, in neutral, and no one was hurt. His will consisted of one sentence stating that his remains, such as they were, were to be cremated. Despite his enormous gifts to foundations for afflicted and famine-ravaged children, his estate was so large that his nine siblings and their spouses, their children, grandchildren and great-grandchildren, seventy-one persons in all, were momentarily at a loss as to what to do with it. Momentarily.

All final arrangements were handled by the Hurlbut and Zoom Funeral Home. The crematorium was outside the city, hidden behind aspen so that no passing motorist on the nearby highway was likely to notice the dense, oily smoke billow from the silver chimney, churn, and fray into elements that vanished in the sheer, sunlit air. Or, if anyone did notice, they would not recognize it for what it might be. (*Collected Stories* 310)

Write then, until you end where you begin, with a single word. You stare at it, look, listen, until it begins to shape-shift. Becomes transformed, achieves metamorphosis.

The word is *prairie*.

"Pr - air - ie" — air, suspended in a high and difficult, one might say an impossible linguistic balance between paired voiceless bilabial and central approximant consonants, and two gentle frontal vowels.

Or, fondled and heard in another way, "prairie" becomes two words, "pra[ye]r" and "air[y]" (*Place* 105), their knotted tail and bumpy head strung inextricably together — to create what strange, amalgam creature, what improbable verbal lion and snake and goat and eagle chimera?

2002

HOLD YOUR PEACE

The publication of my first novel *Peace Shall Destroy Many* in October 1962, was a life-changing experience for Tena and me.

We were living in Winnipeg with our two children, Adrienne three years old and Michael one. In the spring of 1961 I had graduated from Mennonite Brethren Bible College with a Bachelor of Theology degree. In fact, after high school I had been studying every winter of my adult life, and had Bachelor and Master of Arts degrees in English from the University of Alberta, and now also three more years of theology and literature study, which included ten incredible months at the 500-year-old university in the medieval castle town of Tübingen. After graduation from MBBC we thought there might be a pastorate open for us in our Mennonite Brethren Church Conference, but there seemed to be no risk-takers that spring. So, while alternating child care, Tena did night nursing at Concordia Hospital and I took a three-month teacher training course at the University of Manitoba; in August I was hired to teach English at Selkirk High School, a thirty-minute commute north of Winnipeg.

However, the day before school began, September 1, 1961, the MB Conference Publications Committee wrote me a letter inviting me to become the founding editor of a weekly English Canada-wide church paper, yet unnamed. It was an opportunity I instantly loved. By Christmas I got myself extricated from Selkirk High and in mid-December I was extremely busy with the long range planning and the first issues of the *Mennonite Brethren Herald*. I was the sole staff: not even a secretary (I did have an electric typewriter) but I was also part of the Christian Press with all the resources of an excellent printing business. Henry F. Klassen was both the manager of the Press and editor of the *Mennonitische Rundschau*, a German weekly founded in 1880. He taught me a great deal about publishing a church paper, not only the wide cooperation needed in producing such a periodical, but also the political skills required to deal with a denomination scattered across Canada with its largely venerable, German speaking leadership. At times HF and I had hefty disagreements — both of us were always highly "principled"! — but on the whole we worked very well together.

So, beginning with the first issue of the *Herald* on January 19, 1962, as editor I became a "presence" in every Mennonite Brethren household in Canada — 16 to 20 pages every week. No wonder neophyte me made errors in judgment; and every one of them in public!

Nine months later *Peace Shall Destroy Many* was published. In the fifty years since, I have been asked a great deal about that event, and have given talks and published essays about it. Most readily available are "The Skull in the Swamp" (*River of Stone* 1995) and the "Afterword" to the Vintage edition of the novel (2001). Enough said here is that on March 21, 1963 I sent a curt letter to

A.W. Schellenberg, chairman of the MB Publications Committee:

> Since I understand that I no longer have the confidence of the Publications Committee, I would herewith tender my resignation as editor of the *Mennonite Brethren Herald*. ...

And then I added, with an intent that is no longer quite clear to me, though it could possibly be ironic: "I should like to thank the Committee for the original trust that was shown me when I was appointed to this position. May God guide you in your further work." It was Schellenberg who, when they forced my hand, had smilingly assured me, "At least we don't have to worry about you getting another job!" And sure enough, they didn't. Within a month of my resignation, the Dean and President of Goshen College had invited me to come to teach Creative Writing in Indiana, USA. What some Mennonite leaders found offensive, others found creative; ejected from the "paradise" of Winnipeg, Tena and I and our sweet children found ourselves wandering "east of Eden" in the foreign land of Goshen. A superb "desert" land indeed, with barely twelve MBs in sight: we invited them all over for our first Canadian-American thanksgiving, October 1963.

The wide-spread Canadian Mennonite reaction to *Peace* was partly because I was already well known as an editor who did not hesitate to let readers voice church and theological disagreements in the *Herald*. But the book itself — the factual object — became the core of the controversy. No need to discuss here the power of language, of words — that incredible Genesis creation image: God *spoke*, and the universe sprang into existence. I will briefly comment on the controversy from four perspectives:

FIRST: A realistic novel about Russian Mennonites, published by a large secular publisher, in English.

Not the first novel about Russian Mennonites in English: that honour belongs to the American Gordon Friesen for *Flamethrowers*, published in 1936. Friesen was born in 1909; his parents were members of the Corn, Oklahoma M B Church; he was never baptized, and by 1939 was in New York as a Communist Party organizer. He died there in 1997 and his novel was never widely known. It was clearly autobiographical — about a young man who leaves his rigid family and their narrow Mennonite church — written in a style more fantastical than realistic.

But my novel was, if anything, overloaded with the day-to-day realism of facts and people. About a homestead Mennonite community in the northern Saskatchewan bush — almost every 1920s Mennonite immigrant knew of those — about a young man awakening to adulthood within such a community and struggling with whether to enlist in the Canadian military during World War II. And published in Toronto by McClelland and Stewart Ltd., "The Canadian Publishers." Just picking it up, looking at the dust-jacket cover, you saw not a picture but huge words, in Black on White and Blazing Red capitals:

IN HIS FIRST NOVEL
RUDY WIEBE
A YOUNG THEOLOGIAN
WRITES OF PREJUDICE
AND BIGOTRY ERUPTING
TO DESTROY THE PEOPLE
OF A SMALL CANADIAN
COMMUNITY
PEACE SHALL DESTROY MANY

The same statement is repeated on the back cover, the white and red reversed on black, and inside the dust jacket a long descriptive text states categorically:

> Through a careful weaving of events, Mr. Wiebe reveals the violence that lurks just beneath the surface in the lives of the Mennonites.... A Mennonite and a graduate of the Brethern [*sic*] Bible College in Winnipeg, Mr. Wiebe writes with insight and understanding of his own people.... It is a book that will appeal to all and upset many.

And under the dust jacket, the hardcover book itself: 1/3 white, 2/3s black, with W I E B E in huge black.

Well, I had been shown the dust jacket before the book was published, and I had objected to the design; not the least about calling me "a young theologian." But a first-time novelist has no power over cover copy, inside or out — that belongs to the promotion department's idea of what will sell books. It was truly a graphic, explosive cover; but not much happened in the first months — not that I heard then — but later it was said that *Peace Shall Destroy Many* was the major discussion subject at 1962 family Christmas dinners all over Manitoba. If that's true, it should have sold better!

Though it did sell well, at first. Peter Klassen did an early review in the *Herald*; The Christian Press Bookstore itself ran three ads for it in the *Herald* and by December 7 the ad announced the "paper edition is out of print" (the 700 copies of a sales promo idea). But I never mentioned a word about the novel in the paper after the review. My friend Frank Epp, editor of *The Canadian*

Mennonite (his brilliant 1920s history *Mennonite Exodus* was published a month later, November 1962), ran three long articles, and developed news items about *Peace,* and by early 1963 secular media attention mounted, both newspapers and radio, until, when I resigned, I received a phone call from CBC-TV's flagship public affairs program Close-Up hosted by Pierre Berton. At the time CBC-TV was a "really big deal"; Canada only had two national TV networks and Close-Up wanted to interview me about the controversy. I had already done several shows for CBC radio on other matters; I still have my notes on that Berton phone call:

> — would I be willing to appear live on the show,
> or be filmed — i.e., the show be more carefully edited?
>
> — what kind of questions would I be willing to answer?
>
> — would I agree to debate the book on TV with
> Frank Epp and/or Rev. F.C. Peters (the Canadian
> MB Conference moderator)?

At that time, the MB Conference still forbade its members having a television in their home, and so a national TV interview would have been especially anti-church and confrontational. Besides, after months of mounting controversy, I was feeling the need to become a "quiet in the land" Anabaptist. I refused Pierre Berton.

I did not refuse the *Free Press Weekly Prairie Farmer* when they asked to condense and serialize the novel, which would send it into nearly 200,000 Canadian homes. More on that later.

SECOND PERSPECTIVE: *a realistic novel about Mennonites and sex.*
There is no description of sex in *Peace*; only the devastating results of it. Late in the novel the daughter of the dominating

church deacon, Elizabeth Block, unmarried, age 33 and worn down by farm labour, suddenly gives premature birth to a dead boy. No one, not even her parents, knew she was pregnant. An hour later she too is dead, not having spoken a single word to anyone of how, or why, this could happen to her. Her sad life a final secret that dies with her. At that time, as a man in my mid twenties, I think I was unable to write her story.

But there was other human pain I could try to write. Her devastated father Deacon Peter Block seeks out the only man in the community he believes could have impregnated his daughter: his one-time hired hand, the local Métis Louis Moosomin. On his way to confront Louis, Block prays that he will be able to force him to confess that he raped Elizabeth. But the confession Block forces out of Louis reveals no rape: it reveals that Elizabeth came to Louis of her own free will; once; to his isolated room in the Block barn.

For a Mennonite woman to commit such a sexual transgression in a novel was, of course, the most direct, obvious reason to censure the book. Stated so baldly, as I have here, and ignoring all the complex and varied human interaction in the story — just one example: later in the novel we discover that the reason why Elizabeth is an "old maid of 33" is because, years earlier, her father would not allow her to marry Herman Paetkau because Paetkau was an illegitimate Mennonite child born in Russia. (I later wrote a short story about Herman, "All on their Knees," first published in *The Mennonite*, Newton, Kansas, 1968). I say, stating the issue of an unmarried pregnancy so baldly, it is plain to see why some Mennnonite ministers felt they had to condemn what I had written. Rev. David Pankratz, the leader of the Alberta church where I was baptized (and where my parents were faithful members) was one of several ministers who wrote me letters regarding *Peace*:

For some time I have been urged by members of our church to read the book. Younger and older members had read the book and classified it as "filth."… I have read the book from cover to cover…our Mennonite people, the M.B. church and authoritative men have been degraded, and sorry to say, our young people plastered with shame.… (Personal letter, 1963)

I could go on, but there is no need here to expand on this "absolutely obvious sin" problem. Better to consider what I think was a more basic issue raised in the novel.

THIRD PERSPECTIVE: a realistic novel about Mennonites and the inherent racism of "Christian" isolation.

Here's a quick, lop-sided view of Mennonite history. The Dutch and German Anabaptists who followed the teachings of Menno Simons survived in Europe as a religious group for four centuries because both the King of Poland in the sixteenth century and the Czarina of Russia in the eighteenth century allowed huge settlements of Mennonites into their respective lands on the condition that they would settle only in their own separate and restricted communities, develop prosperous agricultural and commercial businesses, and not proselytize their faith in any way. In particular, they would *not* promote their refusal to bear arms. In four centuries Mennonites worked hard in eastern Europe, grew in numbers and, on the whole, prospered mightily. Their social restrictions became, for some in a very clear sense, evidence of their "superiority" to the surrounding national populations. Clearly, Mennonites gained materially because of their centuries-old, and separated, commitment to "doing God's will." One might call it a form of "prosperity Gospel."

I could argue that, over centuries, this obvious material "prosperity" became self-evident proof for many Mennonites of their God-given social and spiritual "superiority." Now, a novel is *not* a history: *Peace Shall Destroy Many* never pretended to be Frank Epp's *Mennonite Exodus*. A novelist does not pretend to be recounting the facts of what literally happened in an actual place (the way historians say they do — often by quoting other historians). Rather, a novelist dramatizes a plausible human situation, creates an action taking place between believable — not necessarily statistically average, but between plausible and believable human beings — creates characters and conflicts to arouse our emotions and carry us into a world perhaps quite different from our own but which, when we are immersed in it, we feel as if we were living it far more vividly than we feel ourselves to be physically alive and sitting in an easy chair with a book in our hands, and yes, yes, this is a human story, a marvelously lovely and overwhelmingly sad but all too human a story.

There has never been a Wapiti Mennonite Church; Thom Wiens never literally lived, nor Deacon Peter Block, nor Elizabeth Block. After fifty years of trying, of writing, fiction, I know only too well the many weaknesses of that first novel; but after two hundred pages of it I hope that the reader is convinced by young Thom's very active and often desperately striving/searching Christian character, and by Peter Block's as well, the traumatic past which Block thinks he has overcome and from which he thinks he has hidden himself and his fellow Mennonites in the boreal forests of Canada. That they are believable as human beings; that after the horrific damage Peter Block has experienced with his daughter, he is nevertheless all too humanly believable when he tries to convince Thom in that winter hayfield:

"... we have to know about evil just enough to be repelled by it and be happy to live our secluded lives. We are not of the world, the Bible says. We have to live separated to prepare ourselves for the world that is coming. Our knowledge and attitude therefore creates a certain distance between us and — the breeds [the Métis] for example.... In a compromise it is truth that suffers.... Our fathers always said that they had to maintain a certain distance from ungodly people. So must we... You, Thom, will undermine this community completely by trying to bring breeds — and Indians will naturally follow — into it.... to have breeds members of our church? Can you imagine it? They're not the stuff." (*Peace* 202, 205)

Block asserts this, fully aware that his own life is "a living lie ... But his action had been right!" (204). Everything he has done was done in order to protect his community.

As for racist superiority: well, historically speaking, Mennonites hardly invented that. Think of the deeply Christian English of the nineteenth century and their "white man's burden" to "save the world" with their elitist, often ruthlessly brutal British Empire.

So, by the end of the book the leader of the Mennonite community is in profound moral trouble — at least as deep as any beer-drinking Métis, if not more-so. But the social conflict, the all-too-human infighting is already there in Wapiti as in any other isolated community, no matter how superior it may believe itself to be to the surrounding, slovenly "breeds and Indians." Conflict is already there in Chapter 2, when the happy neighbourly events of fishing at Poplar Lake and a school picnic and sports day turn into a furious confrontation, very nearly a violent fight, between Thom Wiens and Herb Unger. After that, Thom just wants to get away, and he goes to look for his 8 year-old brother Hal, to give him a chocolate bar. But Hal has left the picnic; he's been in the woods watching beavers — "we saw three biggest ones!" — with Hankey, a Cree Indian boy. The two little boys come out of the woods together, a Cree and a Mennonite boy side by side, talking, and Thom cuts the single chocolate bar he has for Hal — chocolate such a rare dream during wartime — cuts it in half for the boys to share.

Then Thom looks up and sees Hankey's father, Two Poles, a tall man in denim standing beyond the ball diamond: "It was startling to see him there with the falling sunlight on half his face, without a stir of his coming, like a spirit materializing." And the strangest thought forms itself in Thom's mind, the strangest thought he can imagine: "Perhaps it would be better living in a community with a man named Two Poles than with a man named Unger" (*Peace* 38–9).

Strange indeed. In 1944 Canada to face Native Cree people: the Russian Mennonite village equivalent of the Turkic steppe people, the Bashkirs. Is it possible for a Mennonite safe in Canada to be attracted to living with Cree?

Perhaps possible: for small boys, born here, watching beaver together.

But adult Thom has had the thought; and the novel has just begun.

FOURTH PERSPECTIVE: *a realistic novel about recent Mennonite history and Anabaptist principles.*

So, Thom and Deacon Block and Elizabeth — tragically flawed, totally imagined — are Mennonite characters; in a *novel*. The word "NOVEL" is the 4th word on the book's dust-jacket! Nevertheless, people did literally ask me, "Where in Canada is the Wapiti Mennonite Church? I've never heard of it."

And I answered, "Of course you haven't. I made it up."

"But sounds a lot like the church in —" but I'd interrupt quickly, "Like, like, okay, in some ways 'like,' but it *isn't* that place you're thinking of — and certainly not any people you're thinking of either."

That being said, incidents in novels can be based on actual events; in fact, incidents in novels are often "inspired," their writers say (admit, confess?), by historical happenings. A large number of mine are — that's no secret to my readers. But during that controversial spring of 1963, an article in the *Mennonitische Rundschau* did a classic misreading of that very common fictional process. Let me explain.

In 1951 Peter P. Dyck published *Orenburg am Ural*, a history of the Mennonite colonies founded on the steppes north of the Russian city of Orenburg in 1893. In it he describes the massive starvations that took place in and around them during the winter 1921-22. My parents came from Village No. 8 in Orenburg Colony; with three small children they lived through those horrific times, and they of course bought the book, and I read it at home; I have that copy to this day. Chapter 28 (133-44) is called "Konflikt um das Wehrlossein" (Conflict about Being Non-resistant). Dyck describes at length how in 1922 hunger drove people to steal from each other; how Mennonite villagers caught neighbouring Bashkirs stealing food hidden in Mennonite barns; how such thieves were always beaten before being turned over to authorities, and over some months twelve food thieves were beaten so savagely that they died. At least two Mennonite men aided the Bashkirs, to get a share of the food; the two were caught, beaten, and eventually starved to death in prison.

In the novel, the fictional Wapiti Deacon Block grows to manhood in Orenburg; he is involved in these 1922 starvations, and they shape his life and thinking forever. Even 22 years later, harvesting a fine Canadian wheat crop, his memories of his personal violence to save his young family from starvation overwhelm him.

The title of the German *Mennonitische Rundschau* article is "Wir koennen nicht schweigen" (We cannot remain silent). It is written by "we brothers from Orenburg," and they state that in *Peace Shall Destroy Many* the claim is made that Deacon Peter Block of the Wapiti Mennonite Brethren Church (it is clearly MB because on page 53 the baptism is *Flusstaufe*, stream baptism), so, according to the novel, in 1922 in the Orenburg settlement of Russia an MB deacon had beaten a Bashkir to death.

The article continues: "Dieses ist aber fuer uns Orenburger ganz neu; wir haben bis jetzt nicht einmal davon gehoert." (For us, from Orenburg, this is something completely new; until now we've never once heard of it.)

The article then goes on to describe exactly what Dyck reports in his history book (quoting details from the 1922 report of the violence by CF Klassen, brother of the 1963 editor of the *Rundschau*), the very same reports I of course used to create Block's memories in the novel. The article does not deny that Mennonites as such beat 12 Bashkirs to death; no, it is documented they did that: the *Rundschau* point is that no member of the Mennonite

Brethren Church was involved. Specifically, no MB deacon killed anyone.

It was a long, analytical article, full of minute historical details and arguments. Unsigned of course.

What a way to read a novel. No Mennonite Brethren.

But. There is a very large "but" here, which the novelist must face.

On the one hand, literature is not accounting. A novelist is not an accountant, and a novel is not a balance sheet of assets and liabilities that must be dead accurate down to the last factual penny of historical memory. My point is, a realistic novel, that is, one that is life-like in its portrayal of people (not fantasy like *Harry Potter* — nothing wrong with fantasy, it's simply a different kind of story), a realistic novel, by inventing characters that take part in historical events, tries to get you deeper into the lasting effects of those events, deeper into the consequences for the novel's characters.

But — let me come back to my "but." Though I say the novelist is not an accountant, nevertheless, because he has published, that is, has "made public" his story — he expects to have readers, and therefore he must recognize the public will react to what he has written. Indeed, he wants it to react. That goes with the territory of publishing. And some of the public may react very positively, even praising what he has done (many in 1962, and after, have done that); others may dislike it intensely, for many reasons. I could cite a long list of why readers have disliked *Peace* but, more usefully, let me conclude with two letters I received half a century ago, letters from ministers in my church who were truly important in my life.

The first is from Rev. B.B. Janz, the venerable Coaldale elder who in the 1920s helped mastermind the emigration of over 20,000 Mennonites out of the Soviet Union. Janz and I knew each other well, especially after I graduated in 1953 from the high school he founded and was granted a provincial scholarship to attend the University of Alberta. In September 1963 Janz sent me (then in Goshen) a copy of the letter he had written to Rev. H.H. Janzen about *Peace*. By this time Janz was 86, had moved to Vancouver and was being treated in the last year of a long, difficult illness. He notes he is most disturbed by this "*dringende Angelegenheit*" (most urgent, pressing matter) regarding the book "von Br. [Brother] Rudy Wiebe 'Peace Shall Destroy Many.'" I translate a few sentences from his classically complex German:

> ... new and startling phase...the press announcement by the *Free Press Prairie Farmer*... to publish in its pages in the near future this book... [and thus] portray to the Canadian nation the entire Mennonite community in the worst possible light. I enclose the printed announcement... You will recognize the far-reaching consequences [*Tragweite*] [of such publication]. Not only that the reputation of the whole community is drawn into the dirt [*Dreck*], [but also] future emigration will, for the general public, be made seriously more difficult... by stupid/ ignorant [*Dumme*] opposition. It concerns not only the reputation of the MB [Church] but of all Mennonites.
>
> (personal letter, 1963)

Janz then asks that Janzen contact the Conference leadership to convince "R. Wiebe" to refuse to allow the publication in the weekly newspaper, after all "*gilt er doch als unser Bruder*" (he is known as our brother).

Revealing again the remarkable person he was, Janz sent me a copy of this typed letter. And also added along the left margin, in his own Gothic-script handwriting:

"*Mein Lieber: Auf solche Wendung haette ich nicht gerechnet. Sehr zu bedauern.*" (My dear one / My dear friend: Such a turn of events I had not expected. Much to be regretted.)

Such a hard official letter; such warm, personal words. I don't think Janz ever read the novel, and John B. Toews, his biographer (*With Courage to Spare,* 1978) agrees with me; but he certainly was told a great deal about it. I wrote Janz a long letter in reply, trying to explain what I thought I had done. And that very evening the editor of the *Free Press*, Bruce McDonald, phoned me in Goshen and told me, "It would not be advisable at this time to run the book." He confirmed the decision by letter (September 23). A delegation of Mennonite church and business leaders had visited the *Free Press* — I don't know who they were, but was told later that my former supervisor H.F. Klassen, editor of *the Rundschau*, was one — but I have no doubt Janz's letter influenced them to go. So, in 1963 a condensed version of *Peace* did not appear in several hundred thousand Canadian homes for possible reading. (Note: five years later, beginning in November 1968, the *Free Press* did run the serialization. I never heard one negative word about it then, from anyone.)

I will conclude. With Rev. H.H. Janzen, the minister who married Tena and me in the Basel Mennonite Church, Switzerland, and in 1963 was lead pastor of the large MB Church in Clearbrook, BC. In January 1963, when the controversy about *Peace* was building, I wrote to him and asked his opinion of the novel. On February 4 he replied with a 1 ½ page letter in English, commenting that as a literary work it was "good...I am very happy and grateful to the Lord to note that he has endowed you with the gift to write."

However, he continues: "The spirit of the book from the first page to the last is a purely negative one. You pointed out some of the dark spots in the history of our people." After several more paragraphs of that, he notes, "The same (negative) spirit one can notice in editorials and in the mail bag of the *Herald* . . . I notice there is a strong attitude of resentment against you building up in our constituency . . . it would be wise on your part if you would resign your position, because it will be hard to correct the wrong done . . . May the Lord guide you . . . give you grace to use your talent in the service of the Church of Christ to the edification of His body. In Christian Love, Yours, Henry H. Janzen."

At the time, I thought this classic MB politics: get rid of the trouble-maker, the best is he resigns and we continue with the status quo. Actually, those are standard political tactics everywhere. But Janzen was also a Christian brother: shortly after this letter, he gave me practical support as editor by sending me a fine sermon to publish in the Easter issue of the *Herald*: "The Resurrection from the Dead" (April 11, 1963).

I was encouraged by many people who appreciated *Peace* and my work at the *Herald* to stay on, to "fight it out." But, I was not fired: I resigned before that could/had to happen. And as Tena and I have often reminisced since, leaving the "church family" conflicts of Canada for the unknown United States in August 1963 was the very best turn our lives could have taken. To better understand one's home world, distance can be more than helpful; it can nudge, explode your imagination into human landscapes you could not have dreamed, before.

Enough now to say: that first novel crash taught me, in no uncertain ways, that *Words are Power*. Especially when they are published — made public — in a black and white and red (read) book.

2010

ON THE TRAIL OF BIG BEAR

For the story teller there is only one problem of historical recon-
struction. A.M. Klein has described it exactly in his poem,
"Portrait of the Poet as Landscape":

> Sometimes, depressed to nadir, he [the poet] will think
>   all lost,
> will see himself as throwback, relict, freak,
> his mother's miscarriage, his great-grandfather's ghost,
> and he will curse his quintuplet senses, and their tutors
> in whom he put, as he should not have put, his trust.
> (Klein 331 – 2)

The poet trusting "his quintuplet senses"; the story teller, too, has
been trusting them, yes, tutoring them to be his guide through
the maze of life and imagination. Through the smoke and darkness and piled up factuality of a hundred years to see a face; to
hear, and comprehend, a voice whose verbal language he will
never understand; and then to risk himself beyond such seeing,
such hearing as he discovers possible, and venture into the finer

labyrinths opened by those other senses: touch, to learn the texture of leather, of earth; smell, the tinct of sweetgrass and urine; taste, the golden poplar sap or the hot, raw buffalo liver dipped in gall.

This trust of the wayward though beloved senses: that is the problem of the story teller. The facts: all the facts he will ever need to know, and many more besides, they are very easily and often pleasantly found.

For, unless they are very carefully handled, facts are the invariable tyrants of story. They are as inhibiting as fences and railroads, whereas the story teller would prefer, like Big Bear, "to walk where his feet can walk." A hundred years ago Henry James said of story telling: "What is character but the determination of incident? What is incident but the illustration of character?" (*The Art of Fiction* 3). In terms of history I suppose that means that if we knew absolutely everything a person ever did, we could know his character absolutely. This theory has helped beget in literary circles the so-called laundry-bag-slip school of biographers (as you might expect, its finest example is Leon Edel, biographer of Henry James), and it may have begotten similar historians and, taken with temperance, such theory may even be useful. However, since not even laundry bag receipts can reveal everything a person ever did, let alone thought, it is obviously silly to hope by the simple massing of facts to arrange for art.

Therefore, when I decided to stick to historical incidents and characters in writing this novel about Big Bear — it is impossible for me to speak of writing a novel that way. For I believe in "story" as a fact beyond and outside the entity of its maker. Michelangelo's beautiful (perhaps apocryphal but no matter) statement that he studied the rock for the shape that was inside it and then used his chisels not to create that shape out of the rock but rather to release the shape from all encumbering rock around it — that has always seemed to me profoundly true to the storymaker's art also. At least of my own attempts. In the summer of 1968 I was working on one of the final versions of *The Blue Mountains of China*, but I was already probing about, wherever, for a large story beyond that novel. Somewhere during the winter of 1967–68 (we had returned to Canada in the summer of '67 after four years in the USA and I was feeling the goodness of the land where I belong) I stumbled on William Fraser's fifteen-page article, *Big Bear, Indian Patriot*, first published in *The Alberta Historical Review* (September 1966). This revived a nudge of imagination from the late '50s when, while writing *Peace Shall Destroy Many*, I first read William Cameron's *The War Trail of Big Bear* (1927). It may be that I was again looking up Cameron's book and discovered Fraser's new publication in the library card catalogue beside it. Anyway, it was when reading Cameron in the '50s that I first realized that bush homestead where I was born in northern Saskatchewan probably was traversed in June 1885 by Big Bear and his diminishing band as among the poplars they easily evaded the bush-clumsy military columns of Strange and Middleton and Otter and Irvine pursuing them; that I first realized the white sand beaches of Turtle Lake, where Speedwell School held its annual sports day with Jackpine and Turtleview Schools, right there where that brown little girl had once beaten me in the grade four sprints, a race in which until then I was completely invincible: perhaps on that very beach Big Bear had once stood looking at the clouds trundle up from the north. Of course, thanks to our education system, I had been deprived of this knowledge when I was a child: we studied people with *history* — like Cromwell who chopped off a king's head, or Lincoln who freed slaves — but I can see now that this neglect contained an ambiguous good. For in forcing me to discover the past of my place on my own as an adult, my public school inadvertently roused an anger in me that has ever since given an impetus to my writing that I trust it will never lose. *All* people have history. The stories we tell ourselves of our past are by no means merely words: they are meaning and life to us as *people*, as *a particular* people, as *specific* persons. The stories are there, and if we do not know of them we are simply, like animals, memory ignorant, and the less are we human.

Anger, even imaginative anger at one's own ignorance, is hardly enough emotion to sustain years of work. One of the first things I noticed about the person of Big Bear was the contradictory feelings he aroused in people; this was true for Whites as well as his fellow Cree. To William Cameron and Teresa Gowanlock, held as prisoners in his band for two months, he is an admirable old man, yet to Commissioner Irvine of the Mounted Police he is simply a troublemaker, always demanding and never agreeing. Lawrence Vankoughnet of Indian Affairs, Ottawa, orders him either to take a reserve or starve, yet Lt. Governor Edgar Dewdney gives him a character reference (albeit carefully unofficial) at his trial. He is spoken of as "the head and soul of all the plains Indians" (*Saskatchewan Herald*, March 24, 1879), and soon thereafter has a personal following of over two thousand, an incredible number among the buffalo-hunting Cree. Yet at Frog Lake Big Bear, this orator, this leader who has a power bundle given him by the Great Parent of Bear, has no influence at all over his own warrior band of Rattlers, led by his own son Imasees. He stands helpless, his great words falling into nothing as the white men he has personally pledged to protect are disarmed, sported with, and shot before his eyes. Big Bear, I found, lived these contradictions, contained these extremes of greatness and pathos. Beneath the giant slagheap left by the heroic white history of fur trader and police and homesteader and rancher and railroad builder, somewhere, beneath and in all that, is the story of this singular life. Can I dig it out? Will I dare to look at it once I have, if I dare, unearthed it?

When my mind is tumbling story possibilities about, a process that inevitably takes years sometimes — even for short stories — I write down nothing except very occasional notes to myself. A note dated January 19, 1969, begins:

Themes for a novel / setting Edmonton, possibly Klondike days...

and ends:

People: modern business man? triangle? just fucking around?

Evidently that didn't hook very deep (I can still see why) because the next note is dated just over a month later (February 28, 1969) and this one I'll quote completely:

Big Bear. A novel of historical Big Bear, the greatest chief of the Plains Cree — defied whites and their treaties for the longest time — treated in tragic-farcical manner and tone — there is undoubtedly farce in it (especially re attack at Frog Lake).

But I find the next note dated a year and a half later, September,

1970. After two summers of working on the historical Big Bear, it still begins

– novel: present day Indian…

and ends

just out of jail, as Big Bear is heading into jail – they [i.e., "present day Indian" and 19th C. Big Bear] live out each other's lives (apparently some ninety years apart) in a kind of reverse?

It seems I am still, in September 1970, struggling to get Big Bear's story unearthed so I can face it, so it will not disintegrate in our polluted modern atmosphere. But seven months later (after *The Blue Mountains of China* was published in October 1970), I have reached some conclusions. The page is almost empty, just marked,

The Temptations of Big Bear

and underneath a single line:

title thought of on my way home from U of A – passing Aberhart San[atorium]. March 8, 1971.

To take the problems of following Big Bear's story to its final version, I can do no better than to quote part of an original introductory chapter, since dropped. It contained a sort of Henry Fielding *Tom Jones* narrator who hints at explanations in case his readers (whom I think he basically does not trust) don't catch on.

This sometimes coy narrator was one of the reasons the chapter did not survive, but there are a few things in it I very unwillingly let — well, here are the relevant passages:

> There are some stories into which the reader should be led gently, and I think this may be one of them.
>
> I quote Hugh MacLennan's opening line in *The Watch that Ends the Night* because it says exactly what needs saying here. This story is another one of those that demands a gentle leading into. Factually, so that everyone is quite clear about some things, at the very beginning. Anyway.
>
> To begin with, every individual who will appear in this story is an historic person. Not one name has been invented. Every person (and a fair number of the animals) who has a part was once, literally, a living being and there is documentary historic evidence available for each, if you care to look for it. Of course, the evidence varies widely: books, sometimes several, by or about a person; three to four feet of letters and papers in archives; an "X" at the bottom of a treaty or a courtroom confession; a name mentioned in newspaper gossip: a smudged face on a photograph with perhaps a pencilled name on its back followed by a question mark that could refer to the spelling of the name or the identification itself — or, more likely, both. Usually, there are a great many, but always there are at least two points of historic reference to help us believe that those people actually breathed; that they were once born and, after their allotted time, like us all, died.

The author — I hesitate to over-use the pronoun "I" in the first short chapter of what promises to be a lengthy novel; the reader will understand the gentle circumlocution — the author, I say, has never physically met any of these people. (There is only one exception to that statement and it will be noted in its place, which is not this story.) That is so because this story's events all took place before January, 1888, and the more it emerged out of the vacuum called history, which in Western Canada is no vacuum at all but rather the great ocean of our ignorance as horizonless as the prairies themselves, the more it became impossible to invent a non-historic person to act as guide into and through it. For if one is once willing to understand that he is beyond doubt thoughtlessly treading water on his ancestral past, on the past of his place, and will dare to plunge in, reckless of life and eyes wide open, he finds in that ocean a teeming of wildlife and tamelife and every other kind of life that takes his ordinary breath away anyway; he drowns in happiness, into a new life altogether.

I believe: Let that life itself be its own guide.

That said, it remains clear that a certain minimum of historic "facts" are needed to make comprehension, recognition, possible.

I then give paragraph summaries of the lives of the main persons appearing in Section One: There are, among others, Wee-kas-koo-kees-ay-yin, translated Sweetgrass, Alexander Morris, John Kerr, James McKay, Pakan and John McDougall, ending with:

Mis-ta-ha-mus-kwa, translated *Big Bear,* Plains Cree chief whose vital statistics in the Admittance Record Book of Manitoba Penitentiary at Stony Mountain are given as

Prisoner #103

Received: Sept. 29, 1885 *Born:* Northwest Territories

Age: 60 *Race:* Native Canadian *Religion:* None

Married: Yes *Height:* 5 ft. 5 1/4 *Complexion:* Dark

Eyes: Black *Hair:* Black *Trade:* None

Crime: Treason-Felony

He may have been born near Fort Carlton. In the summer of 1875 he was warned in a letter by the Reverend William Newton, first Anglican missionary to venture into Saskatchewan Territory, and as soon as he arrived there: "To the Cree Chief, Big Bear: I am a priest of the Queen's religion. I have learned that thou art a turbulent and seditious fellow and I admonish thee to put aside such vain practices, as you shall surely...etc." (Personal files)

So far my dropped introduction; I have concentrated on these imaginative problems in finding Big Bear's story, which is what being "on the trail of Big Bear" means to me, because that is the novelist's largest concern. The question for the novelist is not "Will I find the facts?"; it is rather, "Will I dare to fully contemplate with all my quintuplet senses the facts that I do find?"

For the facts themselves I go to mostly the same places as historians:

People: if there are any alive, matching one muddled memory against another. There was only Duncan Maclean left, age 94 in Winnipeg when I met him in June 1971, and now he too is gone;

Books and pamphlets: always trying to recognize the personal biases of writers, even those biased by their seemingly unbiased scholarliness. The list is long, and includes George Stanley, William Fraser, Joseph Kinsey Howard, John P. Turner, William B. Cameron, Robert Jefferson, David Mandelbaum, Leonard Bloomfield. Alexander Morris, John Donkin, John McDougall, Charles Mulvaney in total, and many others in bits;

The Sessional Papers of the Parliament of Canada: which include the annual Mounted Police and Indian Affairs reports, and the 1885 trials (but not, strangely enough, Big Bear's address to the court at his sentencing, although all the other major chiefs' responses are there. So, with the help of Cameron, who testified at Big Bear's brief trial, I have to write that one myself);

Diaries, notes, speeches, personal letters, memoirs, interviews: all those miscellaneous treasures to be found in archives in Ottawa, Winnipeg, Regina, Saskatoon, Calgary, Edmonton, and even in Duck Lake or the cemetery at Ft. Qu'Appelle or Batoche or the marker at Frog Lake or the depressions in the soil on the Poundmaker Reserve, Battle River, Saskatchewan. And best of all, Big Bear's power bundle itself, intact in a canvas bag and tied with binder twine, in a place where one would expect it to be. Not anywhere in Canada of course, but taken away long ago to a museum in New York City. That's a story complete unto itself ("Bear Spirit in a Strange Land," *River of Stone* 163).

It is in these searches that I discover those details that make the past sing in my ear with sweet songs, and wild songs, and with the contradictions that all historians I am sure must, when they discover them, love. A small example: at the Indian trials only four months after the fact, not one of the witnesses who was at the sacking of Fort Pitt can agree on what day it took place. Four possible dates in April 1885 are suggested; yet six men are hanged for their actions there.

But, in my idiosyncratic and certainly unscientific approach to historical research there are a few points I must emphasize:

The necessity of calendar: In writing this novel I found myself becoming almost psychotic about dates; I had to know whether something happened on Monday or Tuesday! In the 1970 Fraser Valley Telephone Directory (I had retreated to the seclusion of a BC hillside to write) I found the page that saved my sanity: it was called "Calendars 1776 – 2000" and contained all 14 possible calendars plus an index for any year from 1776 to 2000. Marvelous.

Newspapers: often not too helpful with absolute facts but beyond peer in presenting contemporary opinion. *The Saskatchewan Herald,* 1879 – 88, with its opinionated editor P.G. Laurie, and the *Regina Leader,* beginning in 1883, are beyond price. One example will suffice. As I mentioned, the Sessional Papers do not record Big Bear's defence speech before his sentencing and, though I spent a week in Ottawa doing little else, I could find no trace of it in either the Archives or the Department of Justice. So there is nothing left but William Cameron's summary of what Big Bear said, and he concludes with Richardson's answer:

"Big Bear," said Justice Richardson, and his tone was not unkind, "you have been found guilty by an impartial jury. You cannot be excused from all responsibility for the misdoings of your band. The sentence of the court is that you be imprisoned in the penitentiary at Stony Mountain for three years" (Cameron 225).

That's written some forty years after the fact; this is Nicholas Flood Davin's report in the *Leader,* October 1, 1885:

> First came Big Bear, who made a long address to the Court, in the course of which he frequently used such language as, "when we owned the country" and he drew the Court's attention to the fact that he being in prison, who was to protect his people.
>
> Judge Richardson in sentencing him told him that they never owned the land [,] that it belonged to the Queen, who allowed them to use it, that when she wanted to make other use of it she called them together through her officers, and gave them the choicest portions of the country and that, as to his people, they would be looked after as though nothing had occurred. He was then sentenced to three years in the Penitentiary.

How time smears the edges of memory; even for Cameron, who in 1885 must have heard the judge officially tell Big Bear: "[You Cree] never owned the land...the land belonged to the Queen, who allowed [you] to use it!"

Pictures: I don't really need to tell any researcher the value of pictures; how, far clearer than the sharpest observer, they give so much of certain kinds of information, as it were, quite incidentally. For a fiction writer working on a convincing illusion of life, it is often their tiny details that make his story work best.

Maps and places: Old maps, with the Indian names for topographical features, and what remains of those old places to this day. Strangely, considering the decades of industrious pioneering, some bits of the world crucial to Big Bear can still be seen, a few are not even greatly disturbed. One of the most enjoyable experiences of writing that novel for my whole family was visiting every place where it was recorded Big Bear had been. His life was lived approximately along what is now the Alberta-Saskatchewan border, from Cold Lake in Alberta to the Missouri River in Montana, west and mostly east of that line several hundred miles. It is an immense world, especially when you think of walking and riding it.

As my family and I travelled this world, we took such pictures of it as we could, and sometimes I would look at them again as I was writing: the North Saskatchewan River near Carlton where Big Bear was born (It is now agreed that Big Bear was born northwest of Carlton, beside Jackfish Lake — see Dempsey 11, Wiebe, *Big Bear* 1); the buffalo lands at Sounding Lake and Cypress Hills and Milk River; The Forks of the Red Deer and South Saskatchewan where the Great Spirit of Bear gave him his vision, his song, his power bundle; the sad sequence of Frog Lake and Fort Pitt and Frenchman Butte and Loon Lake Crossing, and Regina and Stony Mountain Penitentiary; then the Battle River on the Poundmaker Reserve, where we met Mary Peemee, Horsechild's wife now 89, and Elder John Tootoosis showed us Big Bear's grave, which is more or less exactly on the site of his last thirst dance held the summer of 1884 when his power was still too strong to permit his young men to wipe out Crozier and his Mounted Police, but no longer strong enough to unite his People. And finally, the wind-moving surfaces of the Great Sand Hills. Simply seeing these few pictures, I think, you would recognize how necessary it was for me to travel this world in order to find his story.

To conclude. In the National Archives I discovered some English observer notes of a speech made by an unnamed Cree chief in the summer of 1884. From the internal evidence I felt certain that the chief was Big Bear, and I discovered later that historian George Stanley, who saw the notes long before I, had come to the same conclusion. In any case, I used those sketchy notes to construct Big Bear's speech to the Carlton area chiefs in Part III of the novel, and I would like to conclude with one paragraph of it here. He is speaking particularly of his People and the buffalo, but in a strange way it seemed to me I had to understand what he was saying, understand it for myself, if I were to truly follow his trail, if I were to dare contemplate his story.

"My brothers!" Big Bear's deep voice lifted to a great shout that shivered the lodgeskins and rolled out into the afternoon heat, "the Whiteskins have brought all this evil on us, but we trust them. Who does not have a white friend? Who has not received good things from them? What Person was ever shot by police? The buffalo has been taken from us. On this earth he was our life, and how can he return except The One who took him from us return him again? I see his track in the deep paths he wore to sweet water, and at river crossings where wind moans through his wool hung on the low bushes, I see his shape in the wallows, the print of his tongue where salt gleams like frost in the Scattering Moon, I hear the thunder of his running under the Tramping Lakes, and at Sounding where the Giver Of All runs the great herds still and they graze the soft spring grass and lick their little calves. Eiya-eiya-a-a-, where have we gone, where, where." (*Temptations* 200)

1974

WHERE THE TRUTH LIES: EXPLORING THE NATURE OF FACT AND FICTION

There is no simple or easy way to deal with the overwhelming dominance of words in our lives. Many of us may not consider ourselves professional writers, but most of us are certainly professional talkers. Clearly, if we did not have language, this building would not exist, nor we in it. In fact, human beings as we now are, and the world we live in, are unimaginable without language. *Words.*

For our exchange of words this evening I have offered you the title, "Where The Truth Lies." I liked that title as soon as it flickered in my mind. *Where the truth lies.* I'm sure you all instantly notice the various, and quite different, thoughts these four small words evoke about the immense subject human beings call "truth." This is possible because the tiny sound "lie" in our language can mean so many things: *The Oxford English Dictionary* actually has 6 pages of definitions for "lie." I'll discuss only two.

There is the *physical* meaning of it as a verb: "to lie" as in, "I lie on my bed," this is my place, this is where I rest. Regarding truth, the meaning of the title then is: "This is the place of truth, this is where truth rests, lives, i.e., here, look at it: This is *The Truth*."

But of course in English "to lie" has not only a *physical* but also a *moral* meaning. "To lie" means, oddly, not only to "be in place" but also "to utter a falsehood"; used as a noun, "I tell you a lie," I state something that is *not* The Truth.

Obviously, then, my punny title contains at least two contradictory images: this is the place of truth; this is where truth is falsehood.

I want to discuss these contradictions with you. Because in all writing the contradictory "truths" of what human beings literally do are forever staring you in the face — truths pleasant and amusing but sometimes also extremely unpleasant and disturbing — human truth daring you to look at it, factual truth you might never have wanted to see, but there it is, slipping past you while looking over its shoulder and laughing at your clumsy attempts to avoid it. To be brief: in relation to my own writing, I try to use the word "truth" as little as possible. Nevertheless, in reality, an imaginative writer wrestles with "the truth" all the time, whatever he is writing, fiction or (so-called) non-fiction.

I'll return to those words, "fiction" and "non-fiction." My point now is, a writer has nothing but language with which to explore "the truth." Language: this incredible cooperative ability — every human group on earth has it, no matter how isolated — a totally unique way of making sounds with our mouths that cause precise new combinations of images or ideas to arise in each other's minds. Just puffs of air, clicks of our tongue, our glottis: they make reason and morality possible. Who could ever have imagined such a simple, such an endlessly complex matter: the first sounds a baby utters will eventually make it possible for us to walk on the moon, to converse about love or hate, to think eternity.

Let's be clear: human language makes complex thought possible because it is not a *sign* but a *symbol*. All animals use signs to indicate food, danger, etc., as do humans: we stop when we see the sign of a red light. A sign is something noted or expected in experience, and it always means the same thing. On the other hand, a symbol does not necessarily announce *the presence* of the object, but it *brings the object to mind*. In other words, as philosopher Suzanne Langer explains it, "a sign causes us to think or act in the face of the thing signified, whereas the symbol causes us to think *about* the thing symbolized" (Langer 96). No animal, as far as we know today, has a "language" in this symbol sense, an agreed system of sounds that will free it from its immediate sensate world to think about what has been, what is, and what is not. Language as symbol makes memory, morality, logic, imagination — in fact, human beings — possible.

One reason I have worked at being a writer all my life is because I grew up using three languages. My first, my "mother tongue" was Russian Mennonite Low German: *Plautdietsch*, a superb language for plain, exact speaking, which is what *plaut* means: "clear, understandable." It also means — the doubleness of language is everywhere — "flat, low," which has nothing to do with "degraded" or "poor" but indicates it was the language spoken by people along the North Sea Lowlands from Flanders to Poland.

Low German is what our family, immigrants from the Soviet Union to Canada, always spoke at home. The linguistic roots of Low German are in West Germanic, which is where modern English, Dutch, High German and Yiddish started as well. As a child I also heard and grew to understood High German when

I was taken to church (we used the Luther Bible) and eventually, as a teenager, I learned to write it, but I was born in Canada and when I started school I of course learned to speak, read and write English. The marvel of a child learning three — in this case closely related — languages by age six is that I have no memory of having to learn any of them. As by instinct, I learned how different languages can express shades of thoughts, images, ideas in their own distinct and evocative way to particular people: marvelous training for a writer.

In my autobiography, *Of This Earth: A Mennonite Boyhood in the Boreal Forest,* I tell stories of growing up in a small, isolated Canadian homestead community, but nevertheless inside a wonderful polyglot world of languages. Oral people often speak several languages. The Mennonite writer Magdalene Redekop's comic description of her linguistic/biblical childhood fits mine very well: "When I was a child, I assumed that although the Holy Ghost spoke in tongues and God probably spoke High German, Jesus, being the Son of Man, surely spoke Low German; only the scribes and Pharisees spoke English" (97).

We could easily spend weeks talking about the marvels of the Germanic languages, or the some 7000 different languages (thousands more have disappeared) spoken in the world, their staggering variety. The majority have no written form. In Canada alone about 50 aboriginal languages are still spoken (at least 15 have vanished in the past century), and those 50 belong to 11 language family groups unrelated to each other. Some are languages without nouns (everything is expressed in terms of action), or nouns without gender; others have verbs without tense, others are agglutinative, stringing flexible syllables together into enormous clusters of meaning.

But I had best avoid telling stories about that. All my life I have worked most of my waking, and many sleeping and dreaming hours at trying to be a writer. So:

Let me tell you: The fact is, I think of myself as a fiction writer.

And you say: So what? What does that mean?

And I answer you: *Fiction is the narratives you and I make out of the facts of our lives.*

Such a statement is, of course, fraught with ambiguities and contradictions and perhaps, if you insist, nonsense. In fact (excuse me!), it is exactly the kind of thing that only words themselves can create: a construct of the human mind that, though it may be of profound significance to us, may have no discernible, no *sensory* existence anywhere *except* in the human mind. I am quite certain that none of you will go out the door and expect to see an act or an object, or hear a sound, or smell or taste or feel anything that could be described as being a *fiction-is-the-narratives-you-and-I-make-out-of-the-facts-of-our-lives*. Such a cluster of words may or may not have meaning, but in either case that meaning is outside, *beyond* the grasp of our physical senses. Nothing in the world but words can create such meaning; any meaning it has can only exist in our minds as a symbolic — not a sign — concept constructed by words.

Perhaps it is because words can create these infinitely complex meanings that human beings have such a relentless appetite for them. For example, in one of the narratives in the biblical Gospels, there is a character named Satan. What do we know about him?

Or is he a she? New Testament Greek, and also English and German, think that gender distinction is very important; their pronouns simply force you to decide which it is, before you can speak it — is Satan a male or a female? Greek and German even add a third possibility: neuter. However, if my first language was Cree, like it is for novelist and playwright Tomson Highway, I would not have to make this decision because Cree has no gender forms. "According to [Cree language] structure," he writes, "we are all, in a sense he/shes, as is all nature (trees, vegetation, even rocks) as is God...." (Highway 197)

No gender for God — or Satan; marvelous. Unfortunately, I cannot speak Cree, and so my earliest understandings of the concept of either was, unlike Highway's, limited to "He."

Okay, in a Judean desert a character named Satan is told by a character named Jesus that human beings shall not live by bread alone, but by every *word* that proceeds from the mouth of God (Matthew 4:4). What can such a desert story mean?

The Judeo-Christian tradition as recorded in the Bible actually uses the image of "word" to try and explain some of the most difficult concepts humans can grapple with, like, where did all the stuff of the universe come from, in order that, what modern scientists call "the Big Bang," could happen?

(Was that thirteen billion years ago? Do you comprehend what that sound means: "thirteen billion"? We celebrate a person who lives to be one hundred.)

The Bible discusses these barely thinkable issues quite matter-of-factly. Not only does it speak of a state before matter and space and time, as when it declares: "In the beginning was the Word and the Word was with God, and the Word was God" (John 1:1) but, with a slight shift of the same image, Genesis "explains" the origin of the universe, the earth and everything it contains, as having been made by the Word of God. For the biblical story makers — whoever they were, we could really only call them "poets" — it seems that all that *is* began as Word or, more precisely, Word was before everything, and Word brought into existence everything that we today physically experience as world. There is that majestic repetition in Genesis 1: "And God said... And God said..." — and behold, everything that is spoken is there, all creation is there — the earth, water, land, plants, the sun, the stars, animals, all exist when Word speaks them.

I find this a story of imaginative brilliance beyond fathoming. Even if scientists could, for example, build a machine that enabled them to look so far (those are the words they use, "so far,") a telescope, say, that could look "so far" back into the universe so as to actually "see" that point of origin, the instant where the Big Bang happened — the next question that would immediately face them would be: "What was there the instant *before* the Big Bang?"

It would seem (for now?) only words have the power to take us to that instant. Not science — words. And there's another story in Genesis, told after the creation story, which notes this incredible power. Genesis 11 (Revised Standard Version):

Now the whole earth had one language and few words.

And as men migrated from the east, they found a plain in the land of Shinar and settled there. And they *said* to one another, [Note: people can make complex plans, because they can talk] "Come, let us make bricks, and burn them thoroughly." And they had brick for stone and bitumen for mortar. Then they *said*, "Come, let us build ourselves a city, and a tower with its top in the heavens, and let us make a name for ourselves, lest we be scattered abroad upon the face of the whole earth."

And the LORD came down to see the city and the tower, which the sons of men had built. And the LORD said, "Behold, they are one people, and they have all one language; and this is only the beginning of what they will do; and nothing that they propose to do will now be impossible for them. Come, let us go down, and there confuse their language, that they may not understand one another's speech."

So the LORD scattered them abroad from there over the face of all the earth, and they left off building the city. Therefore its name was called Babel, because there the LORD confused the language of all the earth.

Notice that in this story the LORD recognizes that, if all human beings have only one language (that is, one common symbolic system of sounds), then "nothing that they propose to do will be impossible for them." Language makes everything — anything — possible. Language is so powerful the Creator himself fears it.

Let's return to the relative simplicity of the Big Bang story. If words allow us to think back to the point just before the universe we know existed — that is, before matter, energy, time and space came into being — then words can certainly deal with my infinitely simpler statement: "Fiction is the narrative we make out of the facts of our lives."

At least we can start a discussion.

That discussion can only be created by words, so we must define what the key words — fiction, fact and narrative — mean. That those definitions perforce require the use of other words is, ipso facto, part of our difficulty, but it's the only way in which we can proceed: once we are inside them, words are necessarily a closed system. Contemporary English words often grew from the cobbled together usages of earlier language forms, frequently Latin, so etymology is a good place to begin.

Our English noun "fact" comes from the Latin verb *fac(t)-ere*: to do, a thing done. As in *manufacture*: to make. An early English meaning for "fact," obsolete now, is simply "action." *The Oxford English Dictionary* explains that the present predominant meaning of the word "fact" is "something that has really occurred, a particular truth known by actual observation...as opposed to what is merely inferred...a particular datum of experience as distinguished from the conclusion that may be based upon it."

So: I lift my hand to my head: you saw the fact of my action. At least, those of you who were looking.

Fact, then, "the thing done," implies both an act of *witnessing* — remember that word, it's important to this discussion — fact is an act of witnessing *and* an act of remembering: after all, every action immediately becomes a thing of the past, or a thing *now* — that incomprehensible instant of present which separates past from future.

I've stopped lifting my hand, but you remember — I think!

All right. The word "fiction" is a variant form of the Latin *fictus*, derived from *fingere*: to fashion, to form. (It is not related to the Germanic word "finger.") "Fiction" has the same root as the English word "feign": to fashion or to shape, also the technical word used in making pottery, *fic'tile*, which is what clay is in the hands of a potter: moldable. The basic meaning of "fiction" is, therefore, a thing made or shaped out of words.

"Fact," then, is a thing witnessed as being done, or experienced in the past and held as memory, and "fiction" is what is made with words out of that witnessed, that remembered experience.

"Narrative" also comes from Latin; the word *narration-em*, a noun of action which means "that which is suitable to be spoken, giving an account [of facts] in speech, making a story."

Ergo, my original statement: Fiction is the narratives, the stories we make with words out of the facts of our lives.

With these definitions in hand, the statement may seem rather simple; don't be fooled. To begin with, we should not get confused by the typical and very narrow literary definition of fiction: that fiction is merely narrative writing drawn from the imagination of the author rather than from history or fact. Or, even worse, get confused by the word's colloquial meaning as "something made up," and often used by novelists for shock value, when they say "I write fiction, nothing I write ever happened, all fiction is *a lie.*" You have, no doubt, all heard some novelist say, with a grin, "I made it all up, I'm really a liar."

Personally I find such comments vaguely silly; at best, jokes. The facts you and I live every day, the things we do and witness, we also recast into words every day. Whenever someone asks you, "How are you?" or "Where were you?" or "Why did you do that?" or "What are you doing after this talk?" and you answer with words, then you are making a fiction, that is, making a narrative, shaping in words whatever you wish to recount concerning the facts of what happened, or whatever facts you remember happened, or (even more interesting) making a narrative to suit the facts you expect, or hope, will happen in the next minutes. Or years. These are usually not lies per se. We honestly speak hundreds, thousand of such words every day and in-so-doing we tell hundreds of stories every day, stories big and little, and in a very real sense we live by them because we are time-bound creatures and it is only by means of words that we can deal with past facts, or contemplate future facts, which, of course, haven't happened yet. But when we make words, in speech or in writing, future facts can happen: in our imagination. And very often we do then physically act upon that anticipation we have shaped by making words.

To say it plainly: A story is not necessarily "a thing made up"; in fact it almost never is. More often it honestly recounts in words (rather than, for example, in pictures or music or in actions like mime or dance) what happened or what we expect to happen to us, to you, to those people long ago. So, whenever we talk we are shaping certain basic facts about ourselves into words, that is, in actuality we are, in the strict definition of the term, making fictions about ourselves.

For most people, the primary story they have to tell is the story of their own life; life-telling is particularly important in our media-dominated civilization where persons can become "world-famous" in one technological instant. The empty media epics of Monica Lewinski or Bernie Madoff (can you remember them?) are merely two of endless news examples: if someone commits acts the media can sensationalize, we are expected to be endlessly interested in these stories made about very ordinary people or greed-driven frauds. Even people as insignificant as writers, when they get involved in a public act like publishing a book, get asked innumerable questions about their place of birth, ancestry, education, childhood bed-wetting problems, loss of faith if any, psychic traumas. Why? We want to know *the truth* about them. Why?

I don't know. Usually writers have lived lives no different from anyone else; the one thing that makes them different from most people is, perhaps, their adeptness with words, their obsessions with solitude, perhaps their verbal imaginations, and when interviewers think that a writer has lived only one life, well, that merely proves the interviewer's impoverishment. Every person actually lives many lives; these include the factual lives we live, or endure, but also the many other lives we all live, even momentarily, as we remember or anticipate what has or will possibly, hopefully, happen to us. Many people, especially imaginative writers get tired of telling the same old limited stories of their own lives — notice how carefully I put that in the plural — and at a certain point of "fame" may well tell an interviewer to go online to Wikipedia that professes to give "the bare facts" (the naked truth?) of a life.

Truth, it seems, must not be covered with anything; it must parade around naked. But then total public nudity is against the law, so there's fun in words!

Some years ago I became bored with repeating certain facts about my life, and when an interviewer approached me with the usual questions, I agreed to answer them as my verbal imagination wished, at that moment, to approach them. Here is one brief excerpt:

> INTERVIEWER: Maybe you could begin by telling me where you were born and where you grew up.
>
> WIEBE: There's a story around that I was born in Saskatchewan, Canada, to a Mennonite family, but that's not the truth. I was really born in Alberta, quite near Edmonton, a tiny hamlet that has now disappeared. [You have to cover your tracks.] My father was the son of the Inspector General of the British Army and he came to Alberta to homestead when my grandfather got tired of him sitting around home [in England]: he was 19 years old, so Grandfather said, "Go out to the colonies and see if you can make something of yourself."...

INTERVIEWER: How did a Mennonite end up a general in the British army?

WIEBE: There was no Mennonite. I'm not a Mennonite.

INTERVIEWER: You aren't?

WIEBE: I'm British, I'm racially English. I never had anything to do with Mennonites; that's a fiction I made up because of course in western Canada there's much more point to being racially ethnic than to being English.... I had the races of the world to choose from and I made a really bad choice; I should have chosen Jewish, which would have given me a magnificent literary heritage and contacts in ways I can never have as a Mennonite — Mennonites generally don't read, and never buy, books. At best they borrow them from non-Mennonite friends — but really, I'm English.... ("Blindman River" 346 – 47)

You may have noticed how in starting to tell the particular story of my life (it goes on for 11 pages) I have invoked that most trusted of modern narrators, the eye witness: *I* was there, it happened to *me*. How much more trustworthy can you get? Even skeptical news reporters, the judicial courts administering legal justice invariably accept an eye witness story, correct? Interestingly enough, neither the Greeks nor the Jews, who between them invented all our major western literary forms, except perhaps the novel, neither have much interest in eye-witness reports. There is almost no first-person writing in pre-Roman narratives. The Greek historian Thucydides (5th century B.C.) was a soldier in the Peloponnesian Wars between Athens and Sparta, but when he comes to write his massive history of those wars he makes no direct mention of personal experience or observation; he stresses only his authority as a "histor," the authority of the investigator rather than the witness to his own, personal experience.

In the same way, the Greek writer Luke tells the stories of the life of Jesus and the early church, not by stressing his own personal involvement; it would seem he never met Jesus physically, but it appears certain he experienced some of the events he recounts in The Acts of the Apostles. Towards the end of Acts he occasionally writes, "We set sail," etc., but he never says "I" in the Gospel except in his brief introductory statement. Rather, he stresses his authority as an investigator. In his gospel Luke writes concerning

> the traditions [that is, the practices of the community, the agreed upon memories] handed down to us by the original eyewitness.... And so I, as one who has gone over the whole course of these events in detail, have decided to write a connected narrative for you, so as to give you the truth about the matters [concerning these people and events] of which you have been informed. (Luke 1:2,4)

In moving from my personal story to Luke's we have moved from an insignificant narrative to one of incomprehensible greatness. Jesus is one of the most influential human beings in history, and yet, what can we know about the *facticity* of his life? Nothing at all, it would seem, if we do not accept words. There are no fingerprints, no images or signatures, no physical descriptions, absolutely nothing DNA testable. What we have is the Jesus narratives in the New Testament and a handful of references in secular histories. All written down several decades, perhaps up to a century "after the facts" of his lived life. Words carried for decades in the memories of narrators before they were, at last, fixed in written texts. Always, only, words.

For Christians this Jesus narrative is, of course, contained within the even larger and more complex narratives of the Bible, an enormous compendium of stories that begin with the very creation of the universe, progress through shreds of Jewish, Middle Eastern and other histories to end with a "new heaven and a new earth" to replace the first one so badly messed up by human beings that only total destruction and a "new creation" can resolve its problems. Strange, ancient stories that suddenly, in an age of nuclear warheads and environmental destruction and religious/racial hatred sound incredibly contemporary. Where does this immense biblical story compendium, attempting to overarch all history, come from? From what authority? Who is the narrator?

For millennia Jews and Christians have been taught to say "God." It cannot be denied that much of the Bible was first spoken orally, carried in the human memory for generations, until at some point, after the very long and gradual development of writing, it was written down. Very ancient manuscripts do exist in bits and pieces, though no original, "first," documents. A few writers are named in the texts, and some can be verified from other historical records as having lived; some seem to write as eyewitnesses, others as "histors" – investigators, searchers, sifters of fact after the fact (sometimes very long after) – while still others write as if their verbal constructs came upon them very much like the New Jerusalem is described in the last book of the Bible, coming down whole and complete from heaven itself to touch down on each of us. Indeed, historically some Christian believers insisted that, though God may not have literally written the text down, every biblical writer, known or unknown, was certainly inspired by him. In Greek the word "inspired" means "breathed into" — interesting, since words, as we speak them, are made by breathing, particular sounds carried *on* the breath as well. Thus, the Bible writers were *breathed into by God* so that every fact in the biblical text is divinely right and consistent.

The written Bible assumes that "God" is a given, that every person who can read/hear these stories knows that "the One God" *is*. Today, many people on earth would say that they know no such thing. The Hebrew text gives no explanation for or of God, and the one time that God declares him/her/itself in the text, it is simply a statement of the Hebrew verb "to be": "*I am. I am who/what I am*" (Exodus 3). Which leaves us with mystery; belief or disbelief. Marvelous inferences, but no repeatable facts. Only words and, scientifically speaking, factual ignorance.

Animals have a powerful sense of awareness, but human beings go beyond awareness into a profound sense of *self*-awareness. People look around, see other humans distinct from themselves; they see, hear, touch, smell, taste the facts of a physically experiential world and eventually ask: "Where did all this come from? Why is it the way it is? Why am I — you — the way I am — the way you are?" We do not yet know whether animals ask themselves these questions, but human beings certainly do, continuously, and they deal with them most intensely by talking.

Every race of people on earth has language, and in every language they tell stories about these very questions. I'm sure you all know several, so let me tell another. The creation story once told by the Tetsot'ine people who once lived along the Mackenzie River below the Arctic Circle in what is today Canada, a people we call Yellowknife Dene in English, a people now gone, wiped out by European diseases and tribal warfare 150 years ago. This is the creation account of a nomadic people who lived mostly by hunting caribou in a land of overwhelming cold for six to eight months of the year, where in December and January the sun never appears above the horizon. So don't expect gardens, fruit trees or snakes.

An Elder named Old Soul told one Dene story of the creation of man and woman to the English explorer, Richard King, in 1834, and I adapted it for my novel, A Discovery of Strangers:

[The Elder Keskarrah said,] "There was no human woman yet...and man was alone, and lonely; he had only berries and roots and leaves to eat [because he didn't know how to cook anything the way a woman would have], and when winter came he grew desperately hungry. He sank deep in the snow as he watched rabbits and caribou and ptarmigan travel so lightly on it, that finally he dreamed his feet were much bigger, and he was running over snow everywhere as easily as the animals, as swiftly as wind smoothing it, whispering among the birch. So at last he turned to the trees, he peeled the white, thin birch and bent them into large hoops. He stepped inside them, and he knew his feet were in the right place — but he didn't know what to do with the centre; there was no woman to see the strings of babiche possible in animal leather and so weave the webbing to hold his feet inside the wooden frames he had made.

"The bent birch lay there, empty, and every day he traveled, hunting. But in the deep snow every animal ran easily from him; every day he returned with nothing, and always hungrier. Then one day he heard a noise in his shelter, so he ran as fast as he could and a ptarmigan [a grouse-like bird] flew up out of the opening at the top before he could get inside. The next day he hunted until dark, and then from a distance he saw smoke rising from his shelter. He rushed there and the beautiful ptarmigan flew out again, but inside he saw a fire burning and his snowshoe frames drying beside it, their sad emptiness half woven over with babiche.

" 'The ptarmigan has done this,' he said, amazed as the fire warmed him.

"So next morning before leaving he covered the roof opening and did not go far; he returned early, breathing as quietly as he could, sinking deep in the snow. And there he surprised the ptarmigan starting the fire again in his lonely shelter, the snowshoes lying almost complete with babiche webbing. The bird darted around, tried to fly out but could find no way to escape, and when he caught it, between his hands it turned into what he had often dreamed: someone like himself but o so different!

"Woman, yes, who made everything beautiful happen, fire to cook meat and tanned hides for clothing and lying together hot as bears and children for ever, because she alone could weave the leather webbing into the frames he had dreamed and bent. She changed when he held her, but her holding changed him as well: frame and woven centre, when she fastened the snowshoes to his feet he became a bird, flying over the soft, deep snow everywhere in the beautiful world, and she prepared the animals he captured, and they ate together, and lived. Long ago my mother told me this story of beginning," sings old Keskarrah. "O my mother, long ago my mother," he sings. (*Discovery* 90 – 91)

I have traveled and lived, briefly, in the arctic lands of the Tetsot'ine. I can understand why this kind of sacred story would be told only in winter darkness, as people gathered around a fire in a lodge, only in the long, total winter darkness. But what is it: fiction or non-fiction? There is a great deal of facticity in it: hunger, hunting for food to live, sinking in snow, wood and webbing for snowshoes, running on snow instead of sinking, especially the warmth of people holding one another – in such a climate human beings must live cooperatively, lovingly together, or they perish. Where does "the truth lie" here?

Or consider a more personal story, one from my book *Of This Earth: A Mennonite Boyhood in the Boreal Forest*, a bit of my memories of World War II, which happened in Europe while I was four to ten years old in Saskatchewan, Canada.

> *War,* Tjrijch [in Low German], the very word hissed. Our parents said it was like the Communist Revolution in Russia, men killing each other, as many as they possibly could to see who had the most dead first; then that one lost...
>
> ... Our parents repeated, it was Germany that said in December, 1929, Come, come to us out of that Stalin hell in Russia, Germany gave us refuge then, fed us for three months, made us healthy enough to pass the Canadian doctor tests every time till the CPR could bring us here in 1930...but now Germany was so horrible, and Churchill and Roosevelt were calling Stalin their friend, his devil's schnurrboat, *mustache,* smiled on the front page of the *Free Press Prairie Farmer* with them. And the Americans had even built a highway thousands of miles long across

Canada to Alaska and were hauling guns and food to help him — what had happened? In a few years?

"It's the war," Mam said. "War turns everything good up-side-down. Suddenly in war good is evil, evil good."

My brother Dan said, "Hitler never got us into Germany."

"Was it Mr. Churchill?" I asked.

Pah guffawed, without amusement. "Huh! All de groote Manna," he said. "Wann' et doa'ropp aun tjemmt, saje de bloss, 'Itj sie fe Dootscheeten.'" *Huh! all those big men! When it comes right down it, all they ever say is, "I'm for shooting them all dead."*

But what if Stalin had converted and was now, really, good? God could do anything, the Bible said that He could even change a heart of stone — so steel would be easy, just heat it a little like Sam Heinrichs in his backsmith forge. And Stalin was fighting Hitler, who they said had started this latest of world wars. So, had the worst Communist in the world been saved?

There was a late summer evening, after the mosquito season, when I brought our small cattle herd home from their slough pasture, and I looked beyond them to the barbed-wire gate that opened our yard to the road allowance, with the spruce black, spiky across the road behind them; almost as though they were a great wall, hiding us from the Big World of Groote Manna forever killing poor people in some new, more horrible way. I watched our scrubby cows... trail to the water trough to drink....

And it came to me: okay, war and Big Men twist the world up-side-down, so what if a big touring car suddenly appeared and turned in at our gate, a long car with the top down, all yellow with black trim and Josef Stalin sitting in it. And he would stop in our yard beside the buggy and from under his mustache offer my father his land again in Orenburg, Russia, if he wanted it back. I knew my father was forty-one years old when they fled Russia and that he had never owned land there…but Communism taught that everyone should share equally, so if Stalin — what would my Pah answer? It struck me he would laugh, incredulously; wordless as he often was. Or say he would think about it, the way he tried to avoid direct decisions and then ask my Mam when they were alone, what is to be done? Or maybe he'd just smile a little, and mention that perhaps Stalin had a lot of people on his famous memory, what about them?

But my mother would know what to say, instantly, absolutely: "Niemols. Wie komme nie tridj." *Never. We're never coming back.*

And, since she had Stalin right there smiling in her yard, face to face, she'd lay it on him: "Now you tell me, Josef Vissarionovich, where is my brother? Johann Knelsen, the teacher in Orenburg, Number Eight Romanovka. Woa hast du dem omm'jebrught? *Where did you murder Johann Knelsen?*"

And Stalin's smile would slowly freeze into the steel of his name. For he would certainly know my uncle Johann Knelsen. They said Stalin never had to write anything down, he remembered everything his Bolsheviks ever did, and to whom, every single name. God gave him that living hell, my mother said, to be able never to forget, anything. (*Earth* 178, 223 – 6)

Can these stories, in some way, be called "true"? The ancient creation story of the arctic Tetsot'ine, my sixty-five-year memory of World War II, my memory-vision of Stalin driving into our bush farmyard? Are they, to use standard literary terms, fiction or creative non-fiction?

More significantly: could they be called *The Truth*?

To help us understand what is going on here, we need an image. Imagine the infinite variety of possible word stories as an enormously long line — stretch out both arms as far as possible — to represent the endless continuum of word forms. At one end lie pure facts — waggle RIGHT — everything that can possibly be done, and at the other end of the continuum, as far away as possible — waggle LEFT — lie the farthest reaches of fantasy, that is, things that are so far out that no one has ever yet imagined that they could be done. Both extremes are, essentially, unknowable to human beings. We might say of them, "Only God Knows," as we sometimes do, but the essential point is that all word-constructed narratives lie somewhere on this continuum, from the baldest statement of simple fact only — "I touch my hair" — all the way to what to me seems one of humanity's most imaginative ("far-out," if you will) verbal constructs — "In the beginning was the word."

Let me say that again, with a slight change: "In the beginning was the Word" — capital W — the Word, before the Big Bang. And then, amazingly, I realize that if "Big Bang" is the farthest, most absolute *fact* science can uncover, and "Word" is the farthest, most absolute *non-fact* science cannot even imagine, then, in terms of the Bible story, one begins, begets the other, Word and Fact come together — bring out-stretched hands together — in a circle! Why?

Because in terms of the Word story, when Word (the unimaginable) speaks, all that is explodes in the Big Bang, and thereby begins time and all the originating physical facts of our world; a line forever explorable by means of human logic and science and mathematics, and therefore a line of fact lengthening endlessly throughout human history.

From my words, can you imagine it?

In "Big Bang" terms our diagram is an on-going straight line, but in originating "Word" terms, our line is actually "Circle." Can you imagine?

Don't get confused: a circle is an endlessly connected continuum and therefore difficult to imagine verbally, so I'll return to my simpler image of the straight line. Again, I suggest that all the spoken and written human verbal forms, from the most detailed court reports or histories to the most magnificent lectures to the greatest novels and poems, lie somewhere along the line in a continuum between fact — that which is or has been done — and fantasy — that which can be imagined — some tending more towards one end than towards the other, but all, at their very best, reaching for both extremes. For me this is a useful image, the linear fact-to-fiction continuum: worth pondering.

To return then to our original question, where does the truth lie?

After what we have considered:

— We might say the truth lies, somehow, in the present. Here, in this place where I physically am, in the now which is the instant split between past and future: "Now" — gone even as I say it, already memory;

— We might say the truth lies in our memory, which can include experiences felt and thought beyond the conscious ordering of words;

— We might say the truth lies in our words, which is how we order and shape our memories, both for ourselves and for others. As novelist Thomas King says: "Stories…help keep me alive" (King 119).

That is, we can understand our life most clearly when we can arrange words to "think things through." This necessity for specific words to help us understand is most obvious when we experience something not quite describable in the language available to us, and so we make a new word to grapple with our experience. This is what Raphael Lemkin did in 1944, when the world was forced to struggle with what was being done in Nazi death camps: Lemkin created a new word, *genocide*, from Latin "genus," race, and "caedere," to kill: genocide, to kill, to try to exterminate an entire race of people. Sadly, we have needed that dreadful, horrifying word all too often in the past 70 years.

Okay, the endless line of fact to fiction. But I haven't really explicated the disturbing physical and moral pun of "Where the truth lies," have I? Perhaps marginally? Perhaps enough to nudge your never-satisfied, ever-reaching imagination? It's a comfort to know the pun doesn't work at all in French, nor in the two Germanic languages I know; it doesn't even work in English when you shift into the past tense; you have to differentiate: "I lay down"; "I lied to you." I'm not sure any logical ordering of words could explicate this "lie" conundrum. However, I do think I've explained that the closest I can come to "where the truth lies" is by arranging words into stories. As my generation, my country Canada has given me the opportunity to do: a lifetime of writing. None of my ancestors in Europe, as far back as I can find them, were given this amazing gift of time and opportunity to write stories. My first story published in a national magazine appeared in 1953 — now, millions of words later, fiction and non-fiction in many different forms — everywhere on the line of words continuum.

As a closing conundrum, here is poet William Cowper's comment:

> And differing judgments serve but to declare,
> That truth lies somewhere, if we knew but where.
> ("Hope" 1. 423–24)

This couplet emerges in a very long poem called "Hope." Hope indeed. As I contemplated these words, I remembered the profound motto of my Anabaptist/Mennonite forbears as recorded in a huge book called *The Martyrs Mirror* when it was first published in Dutch, Dortrecht 1660. On the title page is the emblematic picture of a man digging with a shovel in the earth, and circled over his bent body is the Latin motto "Fac et Spera" — that word "fact" again, to do! In English this motto is usually translated as "Work and Hope." Truly, all I as a writer can do with truth is dig for it with words, dig into words for it, dig for it wherever it may lie: work and hope.

2007, 2010

PLACE IS A STORY

IN THE WEST

If landscapes do not start to be real until they have been
interpreted by an artist, so, until they have been written about,
societies appear to be without shape and embarrassing.

V.S. NAIPAUL, "Jasmine"

To grow up in a prairie Mennonite home as I did in the 1930s and
'40s was to speak Low German first and English third. At that
time there lived a literary genius in Manitoba named Arnold
Dyck. He invented a kind of spelling for oral Low German and,
in a hilarious series of stories about two farmers, evolved what
might be called a Mennonite literature of the Canadian West.
His farmers, Koop and Bua (*Koop enn Bua op Reise,* Steinbach, MB,
1942) always got themselves into the farcical situations of simpletons who are wise as only simpletons can be; with them, Dyck
poked fun at both Mennonites and the dominant Anglo society
that controlled our Canadian world.

In *The Blue Mountains of China* I tried to capture both the
contorted language and self-deprecating folk humour of prairie

Mennonites in a narrator named Frieda Friesen. When I read parts of Frieda's monologue to Canadian Mennonites, they laughed themselves silly. However, the reviewer in *The Globe Magazine* (January 2, 1971) found the language impossible. It was enough, as she wrote in an inimitable phrase, "to make out-group of us all." That was the fall when *The Joys of Yiddish* was raved about on every book page in the country.

Presumably book reviewers reflect the preconceptions of the dominant society. The fact that Yiddish and Low German are both Germanic languages and sometimes so closely related as to share a common vocabulary is irrelevant. Canadians rightly enjoy Yiddish because it has a marvelous North American literature to establish it. Why, ten years ago a publisher flew me to New York first class to tell me that, if only I was writing as well about Jews as I did about Mennonites, I could be a best-seller. No doubt if I had known I would want to be a writer, I would have chosen my parents more wisely.

As it is, I do not complain; I am simply giving a Canadian example of what Naipaul discovered in Trinidad. He, of course, has with the power of his writing destroyed the "embarrassment" about Port-of-Spain, something I have not yet achieved with, for example, Steinbach, Manitoba. And if you smiled at that statement, you proved what I am trying to explain: in the fictional worlds of Canada, certain societies are still not really acceptable.

A few prairie fictions are by now relatively acceptable in the central Canada that dominates all of us: the sturdy, suffering but indomitable pioneer found in Frederick Philip Grove and Margaret Laurence, coming West from Ontario or an acceptable European country like England or Sweden; the sensitive person with artistic leanings found in Sinclair Ross or Laura Salverson or John Marlyn; the child alert and vital with nature found in W.O. Mitchell.

These writers created such powerful fictions about the West that central Canada now seems to believe there is nothing but that world out here. I sometimes get the impression that *As For Me and My House* actually *made* the Depression on the prairie, yet Barry Broadfoot's tape-recorder ramble through the same period proves there were many places without dust and even more without a minister's wife who could not forget that she might have been a concert pianist. Nevertheless, the fiction of longing to escape the dusty prairie persists, especially among the thousands of prairie-born people now in high media positions in Vancouver and central Canada.

But there are societies on the prairie beyond those created by the best-known works of the best-known western writers. There are people who love the prairie, and their love has nothing to do with cowboy boots or grain elevators or even oil or potash or gas. It should not be surprising to central Canada that in the emerging prairie fictions of the 1960s and 70s Sir John A. Macdonald (born in Scotland) becomes a conniving bastard and William Aberhart (deserting Ontario) a saviour, that William Van Horne (born in Illinois) is an exploiter, and Louis Riel (insisting he is a Red River Métis) has become a saint. For telling our story on the prairie *is* different from telling our story in the Maritimes or Ontario or British Columbia.

To a large extent we have always known this about Quebec — its language forces our recognition — but somehow the prairies are still assumed to be a literary (to avoid politics altogether) colony of the dominant central society. Therefore, to create a heroic character named Jerome Martell (*The Watch that Ends the Night*) is to write in the tradition of high realism, but to try to create a heroic character named Big Bear one is expected to write in the (to me ridiculous) romantic tradition of the "noble savage"; the bloody black Irish (*The Donnellys*) of Biddulph Township, Ontario, are now recognizably the subject of fine (and almost endless) high art, but the Ukrainians of bush poverty Alberta (*Hungry Hills*), though certainly accepted everywhere as dancers in decorated pants and blouses, are literarily still mere "ethnics." An older word for that, as every Ukrainian and Mennonite knows, was "bohunk."

I am not trying to hammer anyone: I am trying to illuminate. As Robert Kroetsch once commented to Margaret Laurence: "In a sense we haven't got an identity until someone tells our story. The fiction makes us real" (*Creation* 63). There are still large elements of prairie society that *must* be made real.

For Canadians this is no academic problem. For every society, small or large, is created and destroyed by myth, and since our large Canadian society that includes Quebec now appears on the verge of breaking apart, it's urgent that we ask ourselves: Where, o Lord, were our fictions inadequate to sustain us?

1978

ON THE CIVIL RIGHT TO
DESTROY CANADA

On the Thursday afternoon after the Quebec sovereignty referendum (Monday, October 27, 1995) I drove Alberta Highway 2 from Edmonton to Calgary. As hundreds of thousands of us do every year at cruise-control speed, watching the brilliant daylight of sun and sky shift, change, the aspen parkland gradually transform itself into prairie and mountain horizon. And I realized that this, my country that I love and cherish and have written about all my life, was very nearly ("No" vote: 50.58%) destroyed by 2.3 million voters in Quebec.

Not the land of course. It was here before the first humans arrived, and will certainly be here still when we are all dead. No, not the land, but the nation, the human society we have all slowly built together, on and with that land.

The "leaders" of Quebec kept telling Quebecers, "We will decide our own future." And the "leaders" in Ottawa told those of us living outside Quebec to just keep quiet, say nothing, it will be all right. Well, it wasn't all right at all, and without that enormous outcry of "ordinary" Canadians in Montreal a few days before the vote it would have been wrong beyond any disaster anyone wants to imagine.

What I realized while driving, what I finally understood in my very body like a boot in the gut and a plank smashing my head, was that if Quebec had voted for separation, the vote would have *destroyed my country*. And I would have had not a word, or a vote, to say about it. What kind of democracy is that?

We Canadians have been so confoundedly civil that we don't even know our own civil rights.

Logic tells me that the very act of voting to destroy one's country must be, ipso facto, unconstitutional. Unless there is a clause providing for such a vote in the constitution — and it wasn't in Canada's the last time I looked. Therefore, to call for a referendum in one province to break up our entire nation can only be seen as an illegal act, *n'est-ce pas?* And especially so if called for by politicians elected under that very constitution.

In Canada, illegal acts are dealt with by the law: those who commit them are brought to court. Therefore, instead of allowing the "Big Three" to travel around Quebec, their every word recorded and reported, their every temper tantrum and their latest injured sensibility revealed in close-up TV detail, they should have been taken to court to have the legality of their behaviour judicially evaluated. It strikes me that in this case our vaunted Canadian civility has amounted to not only a profound ignorance, but also an incomprehensible, and very nearly disastrous, stupidity.

In an honourable democracy the legitimate needs and aspirations of all citizens, especially a minority, must be cared for. Since half the voters in Quebec are deeply unsatisfied with Canada as it is, significant changes must be discussed and made. But no civilized "leader" has the right to say to the citizens of Canada:

"I won't talk to you about our common country — I talk only to Quebec." Nor can a small minority of our citizens have the right to say, "We will unilaterally solve our problems by just making our own country." The majority of a nation has powerful rights as well, and such minority actions will destroy the nation all have built and the vast majority want to continue.

Surely no country, no matter how stupidly polite, can allow that. If a nation is to be broken up by ballot, then *all its citizens* must have the right to vote for such breaking up.

So, what can the people of Quebec, Canada, do? They can continue to work for change within our nation. As they have with such outstanding success in the past thirty years. Or they can begin a campaign to convince all Canadians to vote Yes to their separation. However, they cannot unilaterally vote to destroy the Canada we have mutually built. Not in a democracy. If the changes which will now, hopefully, be made are still not enough to satisfy certain Quebec citizens, then eventually such citizens may have no alternative but to leave Canada. Tens of thousands of Canadians — and their descendents, who include me, now number in the millions — at one time had to leave their beloved homelands because life there, for whatever reasons, was impossible for them.

But before any Quebecers leave Canada, I would invite them to spend a few days exploring Alberta Highway 2; or any of a thousand other highways outside their province. To stop and contemplate the land, to stop and talk with a few "ordinary" Canadians. To especially avoid all so-called leaders. There are profound reasons why other people call this, our home and native land, the best nation on earth.

1995

LAND, LANGUAGE AND LAW

It would seem a fortuitous accident of English linguistic development that the words "land," "language," and "law" have the same initial sound and spelling. But I hold that there is a much deeper relationship between these three words that is not accidental at all; rather, it is axiomatic. Let me explain:

Land: all human beings live on land, they are nourished and sustained by what it provides. Without land, human life as we know it on earth is impossible.

Language: all human beings on earth speak a language, that is, by making sounds with their mouths, they can, as linguist Steven Pinker explains it, "reliably cause precise new combinations of ideas to arise in each other's minds" (15). This is what we are trying to do here this afternoon, together, "cause some new ideas to arise in each other's minds," and as far as I am concerned this common ability all people have is the greatest, and most continuing, miracle of the human race. In fact, the Judeo-Christian story of the creation of the universe is based on this unfathomable power of language. In the Book of Genesis the story of creation begins, "And God said, 'Let there be light,' and there was light" (Genesis 1:3). Just like that: it is said, and it is. The ineffable power of spoken language. Every person does that: create, innumerable times, every day.

Law: a word which may derive from prehistoric Old Norse *lagu.* However, *The Oxford English Dictionary* points out there is an Old Icelandic strand to the word *log/lag* that some modern scholars, like James Sakej Youngblood Henderson at the University of Saskatchewan, now suggest may be rooted in an Aboriginal Greenland word "something laid down or fixed," and may well have come to Old Norse from Iceland (personal conversation). How very strange indeed, if our English word for "civilized order" had come from what Europeans have traditionally considered the "lawless" civilizations of the western hemisphere. In any case, *OED*'s primary definition for "law" is "The body of rules, whether proceeding from formal enactment or from custom, which a...particular community recognizes as binding on its members," and if this term is etymologically Greenlandic, then there may be a closer connection between Aboriginal concepts and English law than we had heretofore imagined.

If we go backwards through these three words, we recognize their deep connection. We live in communities, we order our social relations between individuals within those communities by agreed-upon behaviour, that is, rules or laws: this is acceptable, this is totally unacceptable. The whole spectrum of these agreements about behaviour within any group, from the one extreme of "Yes, this is very good" to the other of "No, this is absolutely bad," is of course worked out in the shifting context of living and, particularly, talking — by *continuously talking*, because every society and the conditions within which it lives is continuously changing.

The laws, then, of a community, that is, its acceptable rules and customs of behaviour, are agreed upon and framed in the living context of that community's language. And since the land where a people live is what feeds them, the agreements and customs they have concerning land are fundamental to their very existence.

Such agreements, though often in conflict, are there in every human society on earth, even those that, within the sometimes rigid Eurocentric traditions, at first glance seem to be structure-less. Perhaps we have Thomas Hobbes to thank for the strength of our prejudices against those peoples Europeans first labelled savages. In his *Leviathan* (1651) Hobbes gave a "sound-byte" description of what he calls "the natural condition of mankind" as having "no account of time, no arts; no letters; no society; and which is worst of all, continual fear and danger of violent death; and the life of man, solitary, poor, nasty, brutish, and short" (Pt. 1, 13). That is mankind's natural condition, Hobbes says, when they "live without a common power to keep them all in awe" (*ibid*); only fear and force, he believes, will overcome each individual's personal self-interest. Now it is true that Hobbes's thinking was strongly affected by the social chaos created by the English Civil War, but if we consider the attitudes of Europeans upon first encountering the inhabitants of the western hemisphere a century before Hobbes was born, we find exactly these evaluations. The mostly naked creatures Columbus met on his first voyage lived "in a state of nature" and, as St Thomas Aquinas (1225?–1274) had expounded centuries before, "the law of nature, in its first principles, is the same among all men" (Q. 94, art.4). The question was, since they appeared to be, in Spanish eyes, so unbound by any discernible strictures of a society, appeared so poor, so nasty, above all, so *brutish*, need these creatures actually be considered human beings?

This was a crucial moral question. Before the Reformation Spain was, after all, the world's most powerful Christian nation which, in its moral theory and in much of its practice, held that the whole earth belonged to the God as taught by the Holy Catholic Church. Therefore, if these newly discovered creatures, though they obviously had human shape, were animals, then they could hold no *sovereignty* over their lands; rather they merely *inhabited* their territories after the manner of wild beasts of the forest and consequently the newly discovered lands could be possessed by Europeans, using force if necessary, without any moral question or debate. On the other hand, if they were human, they came under the authority of God, whose representative on earth was the Pope in Rome; therefore, the papal court could argue it was for the Pope to decide how Christians should behave towards these previously unknown people.

Columbus first touched land in the western hemisphere on October 12, 1492; he subsequently landed on several other Caribbean islands, including the largest now known as Cuba. He returned to Spain on March 15, 1493 and told the astounded Spanish court that he had returned from "another world." As visual proof of his voyage he displayed both florae and faunae. Within six weeks, on May 4, 1493, Pope Alexander VI had seized the opportunity to underline his global authority by issuing the first papal Bull concerning this "another world." In *Inter caetera divina* he listed the territory described by Columbus and then declared:

You [that is, King Ferdinand and Queen Isabella of Spain] have purposed...to bring under your sway [law] the said mainlands and islands with their residents and inhabitants and to bring them to the Catholic faith... And...we, of our sole largess and certain knowledge and out of the fullness of our apostolic power [note the accumulation of heavy power language] by the authority of Almighty God conferred upon us in blessed Peter and of the vicarship of Jesus Christ, which we hold on earth, do by tenor of these presents, should any of said islands be found by your envoys and captains, [we] give, grant, and assign [them] to you and your heirs and successors...forever.... [We] make...you and your said heirs and successors lords of them with full and free power, authority and jurisdiction of every kind.... (Green and Dickason 5)

Pope Alexander then divided the new world by "drawing a line from the Arctic pole...to the Antarctic pole" 100 leagues beyond the Cape Verde Islands and assigned all new lands found west of that line to Spain and east of it to the competing seafaring nation of Portugal. The 100 leagues was in 1494 changed to 370 leagues, which is one reason why Portugal got a foothold without war in the western hemisphere in what is today Brazil.

Such politically definitive language from God's assumptive authority laying down acceptable rules of conduct on earth was all fine and good as far as the eager "discoverers" of the Iberian Peninsula were concerned; the other European nations would, of course, never agree, and this in itself was one of the many causes contributing to the sixteenth-century social and religious revolution we now call the Reformation. To discuss that would require an impossibly long talk. A more practical question interests me regarding land, language and law: how does one, actually and legally, take possession of "new" land?

Columbus thought he had found a way; he reported that:

> I caused a high cross to be fixed upon every headland and have proclaimed, to every nation I have discovered, the lofty estate of your highnesses and of your court in Spain.... [These] lands... I, by the Divine will, placed them under your high and royal sovereignty.... (Green and Dickason 7–8)

It seemed necessary that a mark denoting possession had to be made and, for the European nations, a cross with a coat of arms, perhaps a display of flag and voiced proclamation fulfilled that necessity, at least as was meaningful amongst themselves. Who knew, or cared, what the local denizens thought, if they thought at all. Cabot for England (1498), Cabral for Portugal (1500), Cartier for France (1534), all performed similar acts of what can only be called a very attenuated "symbolic sovereignty," since they no more than Columbus had slightest physical control of any kind over the land they were claiming, nor indeed had the remotest conception of the enormous territory upon which they had, by fortuitous accident, momentarily stepped.

On July 26, 1576, the English navigator Martin Frobisher first saw the Arctic headlands of Baffin Island and he, like Columbus 86 years before him, hoped fervently, and sometimes could even convince himself to believe absolutely, that he was seeing Asia. However, facing Frobisher was:

so great store of ise [after all, this was not the Caribbean but the Arctic] all the coaste along, so thicke togither, that hardely his boate could passe unto shore. At lengthe, after divers attempts, he commaunded his company, if by anye possible meanes they could get ashore, to bring him whatsoever thing they could first find, whether it were living or dead, stocke or stone, in token of Christian possession.... Some [on their return] brought floures. (Collinson 75)

Flowers become the "token of Christian possession" in what will eventually be Canada's immense north. I like that, very much. Instead of a raised and planted cross, that grotesque Roman instrument of prolonged torture and excruciating execution, you gather from the tundra the random and fleeting summer beauty of flowers. I doubt if Frobisher, as avaricious and brutal as any Elizabethan high-seas pirate ever was, who sailed into the Arctic hoping to find the riches of new trade with Asia or, much better yet, to simply find gold he could shovel up by the ton, I doubt if Frobisher actually recognized what this action could signify in "Christian" terms. It was, after all, Jesus who taught that people should not concern themselves with wealth and power, Jesus who rendered that teaching in one indelible image: "Consider the lilies of the field, how they grow. They do not toil or spin. Yet I tell you, that not even Solomon in all his splendor was dressed like one of these" (Matthew 6:28).

But to return to our original line of thought: what if the inhabitants of this "another world" were so "brutish" as to not be fully human beings? In 1493 Columbus forced ten Natives from Hispaniola to return with him to Spain, and six of them actually survived the voyage. It seems all six were baptized in Barcelona; it is clear from that, and also from the papal Bull just quoted, that they were obviously considered to be human. I cannot here elaborate on the decades of discussion that evolved on this question, for, as Olive Dickason notes, "It was the Spaniards, with their traditional concern for the rights of man within the framework of the law, who hammered out the theoretical case for Amerindian rights" (Green and Dickason 185). But let me mention four of the many questions that arose as ships poured west over the Atlantic and more and more of this "strange new world that has such creatures in it" was encountered:

1. Concerning the matter of *Clothing*: The practice of "Christian" nations in fifteenth-century Europe directly contradicted Jesus' profound distinction between "the lilies of the field" and "Solomon in all his splendour." For Europeans, human dress itself, clothing, made visible the wearer's status, power and authority; from the simplest cloak to the most elaborate military uniform to the ultimate regal dress extravaganzas of the king/queen and their court. (Have you noticed how contemporary police or the military dress? Power figures. Or what about the present pope? I have never seen him clothed like anyone else on earth, thereby, may I cynically presume, emphasizing his extraordinary, supra-earthly authority?) In contrast, not only did the Amerindians go about largely naked, in their natural skins like animals do — or, if you will, like the lilies of the field — they often decorated their nakedness with glittering objects made of gold and pearls. Nevertheless, they seemed to place no economic value on these metals and jewels that "civilized" Europeans held to be of such enormous importance. In the Americas, even the most highly developed societies,

like the Aztec or the Mayan, still remained so "uncivilized" as to use not gold but plants such as cacao beans for their currency.

2. Concerning the matter of *War*: The art and knowledge of war, which in European eyes was primary evidence of high human attainment, indeed — was abysmally under-developed in the "New World." Otherwise, as some writers noted, how could a handful of Spaniards have conquered so quickly such numberless savages, including the huge, highly organized Aztec and Inca empires? Such commentators forget, as Ronald Wright in *Stolen Continents* has pointed out at length, the decisive role of European diseases in the conquest, waves of communicable diseases that decimated populations and, most obviously in the case of the Aztecs, destroyed that nation's leaders who had stopped the Spaniards dead in their armour for several years.

3. Concerning the matter of *Cannibalism*: Our English word "cannibal" comes from one of the variant group names for the Caribs — it may simply be a matter of hearing "carib/canib" — a fierce people who inhabited what is now Haiti and Puerto Rico. Columbus first recorded these names; their practice of eating human flesh (especially that of their defeated enemies) was particularly repugnant to Europeans. At the same time, of course, Europeans ignored the fact that the central ceremony of sixteenth-century Christianity involved, as Church doctrine absolutely affirmed, the ritual eating of the literal body and the drinking of the literal blood of the human incarnation of God.

4. Concerning the matter of *Human Sacrifice*: A number of peoples in the Caribbean area had elaborate religious rites that culminated

in the sacrificial killing of a person, followed by ritual dismember-
ment and/or burial in a sacred place such as a temple vault or a
high mountain. The best documented were the annual rites of
the Aztecs. Such human sacrifice was abhorrent to Europeans,
and for many philosophers it provided the clearest indication of
the inhuman condition of these creatures. In so doing, they were
again ignoring European practice, where not one person but endless thousands of them could be quite legitimately slaughtered on
a battlefield for the presumed good of church or state, or both —
persons who died in agony, their violated bodies hacked or blown
to pieces — with no shred of considered, realized religious ritual
or ceremony to give some larger meaning to their deaths.

It seems to me that, ignoring all the avarice and overwhelming
greed Europeans displayed upon encountering the immeasurable
riches of the western hemisphere, the practice of human sacrifice, which was by the conquistadors so often cited as justification
enough for conquering the Amerindian societies by violence and
forcing them to submit to the rules of Christianity upon pain of
death, could be considered the symbolic core of the moral problems of first encounter.

Mexican novelist Carlos Fuentes discusses exactly this question in his superb story "The Two Shores" (1994). In it there is a
scene where the book's narrator, a Spaniard who can speak Aztec
and therefore is Cortes' translator, tries to explain to the Aztec
priests, whom he ironically calls "popes," that Spaniards, since
they are Christians, do not want human sacrifice.

> I said it and bit my tongue because I saw in my argu-
> ment a justification of the Christian religion I hadn't
> noticed before. The popes exchanged looks, and a chill

ran down my spine. They realized what I realized. The Aztec gods demanded the sacrifice of men. The Christian God, nailed to the cross, sacrificed himself. The popes stared at the crucifix raised at the entrance of the house taken over by the Spaniards and felt their minds collapse. In that moment, I would have been delighted to change places with the crucified Jesus, accepting His wounds if this nation did not make the invincible exchange between a religion that demanded human sacrifice and another that allowed divine sacrifice. (28)

I have dwelt in some detail on the Spanish encounter with America not only because it was the first and therefore indicated European surprise and possible direction in dealings with it, but also because the Spanish were truly concerned about human rights. Their theologians as well as their rulers, particularly the humane Queen Isabella who decided first to support Columbus in his seemingly demented voyage, and also the subsequent Holy Roman Emperor Charles v, were, it seems to me, deeply concerned about humane justice. At the same time, of course, the behaviour of the Spaniards in the far-away "New World" was so often inhumanly violent, from the enslavement of whole peoples and working them to death in mines and plantations, to the indescribable, revolting conquest of the Incas by Pizzaro. This atrocity was taking place in distant Peru (1532) at the very same time that the Dominican theologian Bartolome de Las Casas in Spain began his inspired public defense of the Amerindians. Not one war, he argued, that Spain had fought in the "New World" had been a just, legitimate war; every one was a violation of the humanity of the Amerindians and their natural right of *dominium* over the lands they lived on, rights that were enshrined in both natural and canon law. Twenty years of exhortation by de Las Casas culminated in 1551 when the Emperor Charles V ordered a moratorium on all "New World" conquest until a full scale debate could resolve the problems that threatened the very souls not only of the conquistadores (most of whom were too preoccupied with wealth to remember they presumably had souls) and also the authorities who permitted their behaviour. The conclusions of The Council of the Indies at Valladolid were indecisive: both sides claimed victory, but contemporary scholar Sharon Helen Venne concludes that

> The Council's decision was that Indigenous Peoples were [human beings and that they were] to be converted to Christianity. Any unbaptized Indigenous person could be killed by Christians. [As a result a] spiritual battle for the souls of Indigenous Peoples emerged as an objective for states to continue to deny legal rights to Indigenous inhabitants of colonized lands. (7)

Nevertheless, it seems Emperor Charles V could not find inner peace. He was concerned enough about his own soul to divide his empire between his son and his brother and in 1555 retreat to a monastery where he died three years later.

A brief personal aside. It would seem Charles' son, Holy Roman Emperor Philip II, learned little from his conscientious father. Philip became the aggressive, ultimately violent defender of Roman Catholicism during the next half century of the Reformation, using the religious power of the church courts and the secular power of his armies to try and enforce religious belief. My own ancestors were Dutch Anabaptists, later called "Mennonites"; in the 42 years of Philip's reign his officials executed thousands of them in the name of a pure Christianity, mostly by torture and burning. In my more historical moments I can suppose I have Philip to thank that my sixteenth-century Wybe ancestors fled Friesland, going ever east, first to Danzig, then two centuries later to the steppes of the Ukraine, and after another hundred years to eastern European Russia, only to be forced to leave there also — it was the ultimate power of Stalin they were fleeing then — to finally arrive on the opposite curve of the world in 1930 so that I could have the unimaginable destiny of being born in the aspen and spruce and willow bush of Saskatchewan, Canada — just north of where we sit today. Best place in the world. So far.

Well, that small aside brings us right here, this place of learning in the city of Saskatoon, which we have built on this land we hold to be ours, where we can — to give a legal description of it — exercise all our rights as human beings: the first and primary one of which is, of course, that we can live here. A life, here. How did we get this right?

By looking at you, I gather that most of your ancestors, like mine, were European. So, how did we get this land? By what act of possession? By the mere fact that four centuries ago an ancestral European actually made it across the storm-ripped North Atlantic and shoved his boat through the immense ice all along the shore — lovely image of Canada, that, protected by the everlasting Arctic ice — our ancestors struggled through storm and ice onto this land, and then gathered flowers?

I do like that. I like it much more than stepping on shore and instantly chopping people to pieces with the cross of the sword. The way all too many did. Still, it sounds a bit slim as a convincing

legal basis for asserting *dominium*, for saying "This is mine, forever." Especially when the people who silently watch you tear up
one flower after the other have already been living there for hundreds of generations.

Generally speaking, neither the English explorers in the Arctic
or Virginia nor the French explorers sailing into the immense
river maw of Canada they called the St. Lawrence dealt with the
inhabitants and the land, as the Spaniards did, by means of military
conquest. They knew they were not militarily strong enough to
overpower the inhabitants, so they generally reached a negotiated
agreement concerning limited land use for habitation and culti-
vation, usually in exchange for trade in manufactured goods and
support in intertribal warfare. In that way the French in Quebec
became the allies of the Algonquians, but over the centuries lost
the advantages of that alliance because that automatically made
France the enemy of the powerful Iroquois Confederacy, which
then of course had every reason to side with the English, as they
did. It seems to me the fall of New France to the English in 1759
had far more to do with the relative strength of their Aboriginal
allies than with any other military factor, including Montcalm's
poor strategy or Wolfe's "heroic" death on the Plains of Abraham.

For the land where we live, the great landmass of the centre of Canada from our southern border to the Arctic Islands,
European possession had no basis in military achievement: it
was all trade and local agreement. Trade and treaties, that was
the English way. And for all the land drained by rivers flowing
into Hudson Bay, which includes much of present-day Quebec,
Ontario, all of Manitoba, most of Saskatchewan, Alberta, and a
good deal of the Northwest Territories, a trading charter from
the English King Charles II in 1670 gave all that vast territory

to one mercantile organization, now the oldest still active in the world, the Hudson's Bay Company. Two hundred years later, after long negotiations between London and Ottawa, on October 1, 1869, all of the company's rights and privileges were transferred, for 300,000 English pounds plus various scattered bits of land, to the new nation of Canada.

There is a scene in the CBC television mini-series, *Big Bear*, that succinctly focuses the problems the Aboriginal peoples had with these political machinations in distant capitals they had never seen. The scene is based on the diary Edgar Dewdney kept during his first journey to the prairies in 1879 as Sir John A. MacDonald's new, handpicked Indian Commissioner. Dewdney travelled west up the Missouri River by paddle steamer and on June 26 arrived overland from Fort Benton, Montana, at the NWM Police post of Fort Walsh in the Cypress Hills, North-West Territories. There, on June 30 he first meets Big Bear, with other Cree leaders, and for some days talks Treaty with them. His diary entry for July 4, 1879 includes:

Had long interview with Big Bear but no results. The same — talk but would not take the Treaty. Parted good friends.... (Dempsey 1983, 7)

"Long interview with Big Bear" — that's enough factuality for any informed writer of fiction. Let me briefly quote from the dialogue in *Big Bear*, telecast nationally by the CBC on January 3, 1999:

DEWDNEY: Since you are here [at Fort Walsh], perhaps you should now consider signing the treaty.

(Big Bear does not bother to hide his contempt.)

I am only trying to help you live so you will not go hungry. We can set aside a piece of land for you.

BIG BEAR: Land — always there is land.

(Changes directions swiftly.)

Tell me, why did Government pay the Hudson's Bay Company almost two million dollars for our land?

(Dewdney is startled; he had no idea Big Bear knew this.)

DEWDNEY: Well... the money was payment for trading rights.

BIG BEAR: From whom did the Company get these "trading rights"?

DEWDNEY: From the king... there was a king then.

BIG BEAR: And from whom did your "king" get the rights?

(Dewdney is in difficulty; he deflects the question with a laugh.)

DEWDNEY: Well, how can I explain the "laws of the nations" to you?

BIG BEAR: If the Company received that much just for trading rights, how much more should we receive for giving up the whole land?

(Dewdney cannot answer. After a moment Big Bear continues.)

Since before I was born, this land was my home. When the sun rises over it, the shadow I cast is longer than any river.

Who was this Cree man, Big Bear, and how did he understand white history and politics so well? He was born in 1825 on the shore of Jackfish Lake, just north of the present North Battleford, and when I first learned of his existence — I was going to university at the time — one of the first things about him that caught my interest was that I was born near Turtle Lake, no more than 30 miles away from Jackfish. In other words, he and I, though we were born over a century apart, saw the very same natural world growing up, because the log house where I was born was built by my parents and siblings on homestead land where, we were told (even the official land title written in the name of the Crown told us that) no one had ever lived there before. Oh, the stories we tell our children about ourselves, stories distorted and contorted so usefully to suit our adult ignorance.

The long, complex history of Big Bear's struggles with the Canadian government are now explicated in numerous books; the most comprehensive are Hugh Dempsey's biography *Big Bear: the End of Freedom*, 1984, and my own *Big Bear, Extraordinary Canadians* (2008). But when I began writing *The Temptations of Big Bear*, the only insightful study on him was the article "Big Bear, Indian Patriot" by William Fraser in *Alberta Historical Review* (Spring 1966), and I gladly acknowledge that it was Fraser's bibliography that helped me begin my research. For me, Big Bear's refusal to sign Treaty Number Six, and thereby give away "the tract of land embracing an area of one hundred and twenty thousand square miles, be the same more or less; to have and to hold the same to her Majesty the Queen and her successors forever," can be summed up in two profound imagistic statements.

Big Bear made the first to the Reverend George Mac-Dougall, who was sent across the prairie in the summer of 1875 to "tranquillize" the Cree in the light of the coming treaty negotiators. Big Bear told this devoted Methodist Christian missionary, who came to him as a hired Government messenger: "We want none of the Queen's presents: when we set a fox-trap we scatter pieces of meat all round, but when the fox gets into the trap we knock him on the head" (Morris 174). And the second statement he declared to the Canadian chief treaty negotiator himself, Alexander Morris, at Fort Pitt on September 13, 1876: "When I see him [the Governor] I will make one request. There is something that I dread. To feel the rope around my neck" (*Temptations* 18). That is my interpretation of his words as recorded by Morris (240). Dempsey devotes an entire page (*Big Bear* 74) to explicate the problems of translation and what Big Bear may literally have said, but he comes to the same conclusion as I: Big Bear is talking not of the White punishment of hanging, but of being led around, powerless, like a horse on a rope. In that regard, I hold Fraser's 1966 evaluation of Big Bear to be absolutely valid:

> Big Bear foresaw the humiliating subjugation of his people and made a tremendous effort to prevent it. History made his failure almost inevitable, but left him no honourable alternative other than the course he took. His name belongs with those Canadians who have resisted tyranny and opposed injustice, for Big Bear was not only a great Indian, he was also a great Canadian. (Fraser 13)

To return to the crucial legal question in my television scene, in which Big Bear asks of Indian Commissioner Dewdney in 1879: "From whom did your King get the trading rights to our land, so he could give them to the Hudson's Bay Company in 1670, and they in turn could sell them to the Canadian government 200 years later?"

Dewdney evades, pleading the difficulty of explaining "the laws of the nations." I'm not sure if Dewdney himself knew the "laws of nations," but if he had had L.C. Green's legal expertise to help him, he might have explained, as Green does in *The Law of Nations and the New World*:

> The international law concerning title to territory was evolved by the European countries and has been accepted by all countries in the world [Green can only mean "European nations" here — I doubt, for example, if China or Japan would have agreed].... Insofar as international law is concerned, there can be no doubt that the title to the land belonged, in the first instance, to the country of those who first discovered and settled thereon. Subsequently, the title thereto passed to the state which defeated the first sovereign in battle or acquired the territory from the latter by treaty. (Green and Dickason 125)

That explanation would hardly have made Big Bear any happier. What did the words "discover" or "settle" mean in this context? Had the Cree not discovered and settled the land after the glaciers melted off it millennia before Europeans, in their own way as a nomadic, hunting people? Clearly, this understanding of so-called international law was formulated without consulting the Aboriginal nations most affected by it, the ones that had lived for hundreds of generations on the very land under discussion. As Olive Dickason points out in her counter argument to Green in the same book:

Although European colonizing powers were committed in principle to the rule of law and the universal right of access to that law, in practice none ever seriously doubted its right to assert unilaterally its dominion over the lands and persons of Amerindians. In the words of Henry Wheaton (1785–1848), American jurist and diplomat, it became "a maxim of policy and of law, that the right of the native Indians was subordinate to that of the first Christian discoverer, whose paramount claim excluded that of every other civilized nation, and gradually extinguished that of the natives." (Green and Dickason 143)

As Dickason, with great scholarly restraint (she herself has predominant Amerindian ancestry) points out: "This challenged and even contradicted concepts in legal thinking that had been evolving since the twelfth century" (143), that is, since before St Thomas Aquinas' *Summa Theologiae*.

To illustrate how such thinking has carried on into our century, let me quote a paragraph from what has been the most widely used university text on western Canadian history since it was first published in 1936:

The gravest problem presented to the Dominion of Canada by the acquisition and settlement of Rupert's Land and the North-West was the impact of a superior civilization upon the Native Indian tribes. Again and again, in different places and in different ways, the problem has unfolded itself at the contact of European and savage. Too often the advent of the white man was led to the moral and physical decline of the Native. In Africa,

Melanesia and America, the clash of peoples in different stages of development has spelled disaster to the weaker. The European, conscious of his material superiority, is only too contemptuous of the savage, intolerant of his helplessness, ignorant of his mental processes and impatient at his slow assimilation of civilization. The savage, centuries behind in mental and economic development, cannot readily adapt himself to meet the new conditions. He is incapable of bridging the gap of centuries alone and unassisted. Although white penetration into Native territories may be inspired by motives of self-interest, such as trade and settlement, once there, the responsibility of "the white man's burden" is inevitable.

Different methods have been adopted by different peoples in dealing with primitive races... (Stanley 194)

"The savage, centuries behind in mental development" indeed! This condescending "white man's burden" crap was standard scholarship when I attended university in the 1950s. The book I quote from is, of course, *The Birth of Western Canada: A History of the Riel Rebellions*. It was published in 1936 and is still used in universities, not one word changed, and the author George F.G. Stanley, a Rhodes scholar from my alma mater, University of Alberta, became a much-honoured history professor who late in life was named Lieutenant Governor of New Brunswick.

No doubt George Stanley is a brilliant scholar, so why did he, in his obviously carefully researched history, write that "the savage cannot readily adapt himself to meet the new conditions"? Did he not know that, with the arrival from the north of trade guns in Hudson Bay after 1670, and the felicitous conjunction of the horse arriving from the Spanish south only a few decades later, that the Aboriginal prairie peoples rapidly undertook an adaptive change of their society that amounted to a social and cultural revolution? Did he not know, for example, that within less than half a century many of the Woodland Cree people changed from a small-group canoe-and-trapping-and-stalking-solitary-animals people to become incomparable horse-riders who hunted buffalo in large, precisely organized groups, where the behaviour of each hunter was ordered and assigned? The Plains Cree hunted the enormous buffalo from camps on the open prairie that numbered into the thousands of people. Does this indicate the Cree were "incapable of bridging the gap of centuries alone and unassisted"?

To get back to the Plains Cree leader, Big Bear, and his question, "Where did the Hudson's Bay Company get the right to trade on my land?" As far as the Plains Cree were concerned, the right could not come, as Indian Commissioner Dewdney implies, from the King of England. Whatever so-called "international laws," or the specific laws of England, or the King, or the Company had to do with organizing an expedition of ships into Hudson's Bay, only the Cree themselves could give the company the right to trade. And when the Cree or Chipewyan peoples offered their goods — pelts, food, knowledge of the land — to the English and accepted their iron knives and kettles and needles in trade, then they established that agreement: by this very act, we give you the right to trade with us. And when they took a gun, which they had received from the Company in exchange for 14 beaver and travelled inland for days and eventually traded it to the Blackfoot or Dene people for 50 beaver, or one hatchet which they had received for 1 beaver and then traded for 6 beaver (Milloy 19), they were not only proving themselves sharp and competent businessmen in the best "civilized Christian" sense of the world, but they were legitimizing the English presence in their land. There can be no question that, on the whole, for some 200 years a healthy more or less balanced symbiotic relationship existed between Aboriginals and Europeans in western Canada. Big Bear knew this as well as anyone ever did, and said so plainly in his speech in the Regina courtroom on September 25, 1885:

> Before many of you were born I ran buffalo over this place where you have put this building, I ran buffalo over this place and white men ate the meat I gave them. I gave them my hand as a brother; I was free, and the smallest Person in my band was as free as I because the Master of Life had given us our place on the earth and that was enough for us. But you have [now] taken our inheritance, and our strength. The land is torn up, black with fires, and empty. *You have done this.* And there is nothing left now but that you must help us. (*Temptations* 398; cf. Cameron 223–24)

Big Bear, in his wisdom, struggled for six years before he agreed to sign the Treaty, albeit under the duress of starvation. Many other chiefs signed Treaties much more readily, and it now seems that often a kind of soft, romantic halo surrounds the Treaty signings, a kindly, wholesome aura perpetuated by both White and Aboriginal Canadians. For example, Crowfoot's Treaty No. 7 speech of acceptance is often quoted, which includes his magnificent tribute to the North-West Mounted Police:

> If the Police had not come to this country, where would we be all now? Bad men and whiskey were killing us so

fast that very few, indeed of us would be left today. The Police have protected us as the feathers of the bird protect it from the frosts of winter... I am satisfied. I will sign the treaty. (Morris 272)

This is all fine and good — no one can say that First Nations statesmen do not make superb speeches — but why, for example, is the parallel speech of Button Chief never quoted? Granted, he was a lesser leader than Crowfoot, but it is a well-known political strategy to leave the heavy negotiating to under-officials before the leaders step in and risk their status. Here is Button Chief negotiating for the Blackfoot on Oct. 19, 1877, the day before Crowfoot speaks:

> The Great Spirit sent the white man across the great waters to carry out his (that is, the Great Spirit's) ends. The Great Spirit, and not the Great Mother, gave us this land.... We want to be paid for all the timber that the Police and whites have used since they first came to our country. If it continues to be used as it is, there will soon be no firewood for Indians. (Morris 270)

Chief Negotiator David Liard simply rejects Button Chief's arguments; he will change nothing. Big Bear tried to negotiate for six years, and he never got a single Treaty word changed either, nor did any other Native before or after him; so we do not know what Big Bear might have achieved if his idea of a united political stand by the Prairie People had been realized. Perhaps something like what is developing in the Arctic now at the end of the 20th century, Nunavut. Such an event was unimaginable by Whites a hundred years ago, though it may well be that Big Bear dreamed it. Sadly, sometimes a century of nightmare has to pass before a dream can begin to be realized.

My topic of "Land, Language and Law" is too enormous — one could say it is as large as the land itself — and the Canadian law that has over time grown around it does not reside only with the Treaties; the law is also defined by the federal government's Indian Act which, as historian J. Rick Ponting explains, "is of great importance because it touches, and not lightly, virtually every aspect of Indians' lives" (19). In the nineteenth century the Aboriginal peoples of our land knew something about the Treaties, and what they knew worried them. Also, it is now clear that they did not understand or interpret the Treaties in the same way that federal officials did; this became particularly obvious during the Treaty Eight Centennial Commemorations of June, 1999, at Grouard, Alberta. And beyond that, the Aboriginal peoples knew nothing about the Indian Act, perhaps not even of its existence in a far-away House of Commons in Ottawa; nor did they know that, unlike the more-or-less public treaties, the Indian Act could be changed at any moment, at any whim of any government, as it has been altered hundreds of times since first enacted in the 1860s and greatly expanded in 1876. All I can say to historian Dr. Stanley is that, if he thinks Aboriginal peoples cannot adapt to new conditions, he should have tried to live as a Native in Canada, both on and off a reserve, for the past 100 years. He might have discovered something historically very important, especially as it applied to his exercise of his human rights.

There are, however, significant signs of progress, and it may well be that today the Supreme Court of Canada is leading the way. This is perhaps a disturbing development, that tens of thousands of Canadians must drag themselves through long and expensive court cases in order to be given very fundamental rights, but any positive process is preferable to the status quo. As Stan Persky writes of one ruling:

> From the moment of its release…on December 11, 1997, the Supreme Court of Canada's decision on aboriginal title in the case of *Delgamuukw v. British Columbia* was immediately recognized as a landmark judgment. The Court ruled, unanimously and more forcefully than ever before, that Native people in Canada have a unique claim to their traditional lands, that provinces don't have the power to arbitrarily extinguish aboriginal title, and that future courts must accept valid Native oral history as a key ingredient in proving such claims. (1)

Peter Russell agrees fully. In his balanced, detailed world survey, "High Courts and the Rights of Aboriginal Peoples: the Limits of Judicial Independence," he concludes that "*Delgamuukw* [is] as progressive a decision on Aboriginal rights as has ever issued from a common law court" (Russell 275).

It's all there in that decision, land, and language, and law. Especially impressive is the weight the decision places on Native concepts of history: for the first time oral tradition is ruled to be as significant in legal matters as written documentation. One is inevitably reminded of Genesis, and the enduring power of the spoken word, the *power of the word to create*. And *Delgamuukw* has already borne fruit: it is the basis on which in 1998 British Columbia reached a land agreement with the Nisga'a People.

Supreme Court Chief Justice Lamer wrote the 186-paragraph decision with extraordinary care and perception. He ruled that "the aboriginal rights recognized and affirmed by s. 35 (1) [of the Canadian Constitution], including aboriginal title, are not absolute. Those rights may be infringed, both by the federal and provincial governments." However, any such infringement must be restrained by the necessary duties of consultation, and of fair compensation. He concludes:

> Ultimately, it is through negotiated settlements, with good faith and give and take on all sides, reinforced by the judgments of this Court, that we will achieve...."the reconciliation of the pre-existence of aboriginal societies with the sovereignty of the Crown." Let us face it, we are all here to stay. (Persky 122)

Absolutely right: we *are* all here to stay, in what for me is, despite our problems, the best of all countries on earth. So we better keep on talking and figuring out how to live together, in peace, and with justice, and respect for each other's human rights. It's about time.

2000

THE ELUSIVE MEANING OF "NORTH"

What do we mean by "North"? I think Dorothy Livesay said it too simply in 1972: "North is from wherever you are looking." In a time of national confusion, both cultural and political, Canadians need to discuss such a poet's evocation, and several recent books by women could help us begin.

The word "nordicity" does not appear in *A Dictionary of Canadianisms* (1967), but Louis-Edmond Hamelin explains it at length in *The Canadian Encyclopedia* (1985). Nordicity is "a concept developed in Canada from the 1960s that refers to the perceived state or degree of northerness of high-latitude situations." Each of ten "Polar Value" factors (climate, biogeography, geography, psychology, etc.) is evaluated and given up to 100 points; they are then added together for a total nordicity value called a VAPO index.

A few examples make the concept clear: the Extremest North of the North Pole has the maximum VAPO index of 10 × 100 = 1000; in the Far North, Resolute is 775; in the Middle North, Yellowknife is 390, Red Lake (Ontario) 220. "North" is then, measureably, not merely a matter of latitude, cold and tundra; it also embodies the attitudes humans have about it.

During the Age of Discovery, Hamelin notes, Canada was considered to be *all north* — because it was believed to be so inhospitable and cold. One of the strangest things about Margaret Atwood's book, *Strange Things: The Malevolent North in Canadian Literature* (1995), is that it reflects so much of that ancient attitude. Though her lectures, first delivered at Oxford University in 1991, are sub-titled *The Malevolent North,* a great deal of the literature she discusses happens in "Base Canada," areas with a VAPO index of zero.

She begins in the Far (not Extreme) North and moves steadily south: "1: Concerning Franklin and his Gallant Crew" explores the continuing saga of Franklin's disastrous third (the naval) Arctic expedition. "2: The Grey Owl Syndrome" satirizes those persons (mostly travellers from afar) who still aspire to imitate an imitation. "3: Eyes of Blood, Heart of Ice: the Wendigo" discusses the legendary cannibalistic spirit that haunts the mythology of the Algonquian-speaking peoples. "4: Linoleum Caves," a striking image borrowed from Alice Munro, illustrates how women's work differs from that of men when they write about the North.

Atwood's style and ideas are invariably evocative; nevertheless by page 116 I experienced a major problem. After a strong beginning, North finally comes to mean simply variations on "Indian" and "wilderness." Indeed, in chapter 4 the Indian is a southern Mohawk (Pauline Johnson) and the wilderness that of Moodie, Traill and Marian Engel's *Bear.* These texts all happen somewhere below the 46th parallel — which is a very long way south of Oxford itself.

The lectures received their direction, Atwood writes, when she was "struck" by the "great...inspiration" that "the English were very fond of cannibalism." I laugh of course, as I did long ago when we personally talked about this subject, but it seems her tongue-in-cheek gradually takes over: the book becomes not so much a grappling with a Canadian literary North as it is a witty concession to the presumed gastronomic deviance of her donnish audience.

And as such Strange Things, despite its wide-ranging and often brilliant discussion, tends to affirm Oxford's conceded ignorance: in Canadian writing, any character not on a city street is in the North and therefore either lost, or freezing, or starving to death; or all three.

Victoria Jason's book, Kabloona in a Yellow Kayak (1995) was not, of course, available for Atwood's consideration. Unfortunately. For though its style may plod, the amazing character it creates in a Far North (VAPO 5–750) experienced over years through the total, unmitigated immediacy of paddling (and occasionally dragging) a kayak for some 5000 kilometres is utterly astonishing. It is accurately sub-titled: One Woman's Journey Through the Northwest Passage.

Jason's improbable journey required four summers. The first two stages, from Churchill to Repulse Bay (1991), and to Gjoa Haven (1992) were made in the company of Don Starkell, well known for his book Paddle to the Amazon. The romantic notion of the Arctic is that it needs conquering by powerful, usually self-sacrificial, males. Starkell generously allows Jason to accompany him, but it is he who proves himself unfit to paddle the ice-and-tide-and-shoal-ripped coast of Hudson Bay. He is stubborn, overbearing and totally egoistical. When edema forces Jason to remain at Gjoa Haven, he continues alone, and two months later the RCMP find and rescue him near Tuktoyaktuk. He loses all his fingers (he carried no gloves!) and most of his toes to frostbite, heroic trophies he displays in full colour in his inevitable book.

Jason, alone and unmutilated, completes her journey from the opposite direction: Fort Providence, NWT to Paulatuk (summer of '93) and Gjoa Haven ('94). Absolutely alone, in a tiny kayak along 2000 kilometres of Arctic coast that destroyed so many men (she skirts King William Island where Franklin's ships were crushed). She meets, with pleasure, many northern Canadians, she experiences the beauty of landscape and sea/ice vistas, the enjoyment of waiting for ice and weather to change, of being always surrounded by land and water animals and birds. They teach her how to live with a land that demands strength and quiet, resolute patience, but defies "conquerors." An improbable journey, an amazing woman.

Atwood's lectures could have discussed Aritha van Herk's "geografictione," *Places Far From Ellesmere* (1990). The Ellesmere in question is the island of the Extreme North (VAPO 900), and the book makes an imaginative leap into sheer "northernness," which is astounding in its perceptions and implications.

Beginning with a constructed, elaborated fiction of her own life, van Herk uses the structure of a hiking trip around Lake Hazan, the northernmost lake on earth, to explicate why Tolstoy's heroine, Anna Karenina, "should have escaped to Ellesmere." Because Ellesmere is what it is, beyond the usual "north" of weather and no food, beyond male order and rules where the "no choices" Tolstoy allows Anna have no meaning. The "puzzle ice" in the lake, the hare, the book in hand, the Peary caribou, these exist; and so do the immense glaciers, and sleeping on the tundra in the three-week nightless summer held by permafrost. Ellesmere is "as far as it is possible to get away."

And into yourself. And out of your self. Into and beyond, the true, imaginative contradiction of North. Where you will be so small you may be gigantic. Malevolent? Well...not if you can, like van Herk most certainly can, unread the unreadable North on Ellesmere.

When I look at Canada, I see a country capped by enormous North; perhaps only North holds our disparate regions together. Jason in her amazing physical journey, van Herk in her beautifully written and even more evocative psychic journey, tell us this. It is time that Canadian writers grappled with more than European anachronisms when they look in that direction. Perhaps they should even venture travelling there; the North has a lot more to tell us than mere weather.

1996

THE WIND AND THE CARIBOU

The Dene Elders say, "Who can know the way of the wind, or of the caribou?" On the open tundra beyond the tree line — fully a quarter of Canada — the movements of the clouds in the sky and the animals on the earth remain as mysterious as they have always been.

If any human beings understand this mystery, they are the Dogrib Dene who live north of Great Slave Lake. Always nomadic hunters, for thousands of years they have known that, in the months we call August and September, the immense caribou herds will return again from where they have spent their summer, north to Bathurst Inlet on the Arctic Ocean. So September is the time to hunt them, to prepare dried meat and fat and hides for the long winter.

But in September 1995 there were no caribou where they usually are, flowing back into the boreal forests around Snare and Roundrock Lakes, 230 kilometres (as the Twin Otter flies) north of Yellowknife.

So where were they? Six Dogrib men with all our equipment flew northeast to look for them near Jolly Lake. Shortly after eighteen more of us were in a second plane, following them by radio. Within an hour and a half we circled down out of the clouds north of the tree line, round and round over a terrain more water than land where the other plane was below us, skimming over a large, nameless lake.

Our plane roared its pontoons back into the sandy shore and when I climbed up the bank, the people out before me were already staring into distance over the rock-strewn tundra. There against a ragged ridge were caribou.

Forty, perhaps fifty of them. Moving slowly, steadily south, their greyish-brown bodies blending into the rocks, but the massive white collars of the bulls hung indelible as snow. And their antlers: through binoculars they seemed too immense to be believed. Great branched lyres, as high again as their thick bodies, the arctic wind whistling in our ears as if they were making music for our arrival.

And as we all stood motionless, watching, they disappeared. A disappearance so gradual, so without hurry, as if their vanishment were simply the inevitable nature of their movement, and then they were gone. The greatest land travellers on earth, always travelling. In August, 1820 the English sailor and artist Robert Hood saw them and wrote in his diary; "We had at last penetrated into the native haunts of the reindeer [caribou], whose antlers were moving forests on the ridges of the hills" (Hood 142).

Within two hours I had seen four caribou shot. One, a bull, took four direct hits from 30.06 bullets before he went down. He was shot by Ian Robins, an Australian Canadian teaching at the Chief Jimmy Bruneau School at Edzo, NWT, who cut the meat up in the careful Dogrib way, as he had learned on previous hunts. After a time John B. Zoe, who was finished with his cow, came to help Ian and together they bundled the meat into a tight, solid pack. John is head of the Dogrib Treaty 11 Land Settlement negotiations; as he washed his bloody arms he laughed at his soft "office hands," though they seemed plenty tough to me. Ian had no tumpline, so John fashioned one for me with cord and his towel for a head strap.

On a straight lift I could just raise that pack to my waist, but it felt good on the small of my back with my legs standing fixed. The problem was moving, and the tumpline. That holds the load in place very well as you walk bent forward, neck and back straight, but this towel was a bare padding, the four strands of rope bunched together, tough, tough. My neck creaked, squashed together by dead weight; in ten steps I felt I had been compacted two centimetres. But, I argued to myself, this is a good way to begin; every load I carry after this will seem so much easier with a proper, broad head strap.

Through spongy muskeg, tussocks, over boulder fields, up the rocky ridges among the erratics sitting on the skyline every- where like shattered houses: balance is the other big problem. There are superb caribou trails cut into the ground everywhere, always leading over the smoothest paths, but never in the right direction. As John pointed out when I rested, my pack high on an erratic, the best way to walk to a tundra camp is not necessar- ily the most direct route. But from the ridge I could see our white tents against the indigo lake.

When John took up the pack and I carried his rifle, I couldn't catch him. He moved at almost a trot, bent so low, eyes on the ground, feet seemingly always certain on the treacherous, ever- changing ground.

And how do caribou walk here anyway, run in massed herds on such ground as I saw them run? How is it possible they don't break their hooves, their legs, on such brutal stones? They have four legs to place and never watch a single one of them. Perhaps they have eyes in the hard scoops of their hooves.

John hoisted the pack onto my back again and walked away with his rifle. I had thought the weather cold, but soon I realized it was warm, no, positively hot. Previously unacknowledged parts of my creaking body declared themselves, argued with my split, aching head. I compacted another two centimetres.

At the fire between the tents Terry Douglas had bannock waiting as she would have food ready all weekend. "You'll feel it in your neck tomorrow," she said cheerfully. Actually, I already did.

The caribou had let us find them, and then about midnight the wind sought us out. We were all comfortably bedded down in the two big tents — twenty-four of us: two Elders, two boys, seven Dogrib leaders from the community and the Chief Jimmy Bruneau School, and also twelve white teachers, there to learn more about Dogrib culture. When the wind hit, it was with boxer combinations, boom! boom! boomboom!

We were in an excellent canvas tent, sewed in Fort Mc-Pherson, NWT. During the night the stovepipes crashed over the stove; someone had gone outside, was pounding the pegs down deeper, but came in and said that only the corners were holding. Sometimes I awoke; a giant outside was kicking my backpack through the canvas wall, kicking me in the head. By morning we had to shout to make ourselves heard over the wind. Two men were holding down the windward corner of the tent with their sleeping bags; when someone zipped up the flap, we saw the streaking snow outside just before the wind got a muscle inside and threatened to heave us with the tent out over the lake running whitecaps.

In the larger tent everyone had bundled up their packs, piled them around the centre support and with their body weight were trying to hold the tent on the ground. No fire was possible in the stove. Camp boss George Mackenzie told us: "It can't hold, so we move."

A new site had already been chosen: a hollow with a small grove of tiny tundra trees. In whipping snow we let the tents collapse over our equipment, fought to roll them up, and began to dismantle the camp.

Into the teeth of snow and wind, but calm, orderly, not a single order given that I heard. Everyone simply worked, carried poles, stovepipes, packs, food boxes, everything, as much as they could, trip after trip. Meanwhile some cleared and levelled the site for one tent and the Elders built a fire, set kettles and hung racks of caribou ribs on sharpened sticks over it. The low density of tiny trees was amazing shelter; when we had drunk tea and eaten as many roasted ribs with cold bannock as we wanted, the snow and wind had dropped and we put up the biggest tent. All twenty-four people moved in, the barrel stove blazing its thick wood heat — wood we brought with us on the plane. The moss floor spread with spruce boughs no larger than a hand looked wonderful.

The lake whipping waves was large, but nameless; apparently not even the Elders knew of a name. This was a particular problem for literature teacher Blake Wile. He pored over detailed maps but could not recognize the lake's shape. Finally someone suggested the name Blake Lake, which he liked until a general consensus decreed that, in order for the name to be valid, he must somehow die here, preferably in great pain. It seemed a high price for a name.

When we came out, John, whose naked eyes were better than mine with binoculars, saw a single bull grazing lichen against a far skyline. The afternoon wind was steady and fierce; it was time to hunt again.

The hunters I was with did not shoot that caribou: he moved too fast for us. But I followed John as he circled down to a peninsula and started five other bulls from their ruminations; as they ran past us in their usual orderly line, he dropped the last one. The other four circled uneasily, out of range, then moved up the corridor between the hills where our companions waited. They shot all four.

I went to watch Robert Mackenzie cut up those animals. A master with a long, thin knife, not a single gesture wasted, the thick saddles of back fat seeming to slip free stroke by stroke from those muscled rumps. One could write half a book on the intricacy of muscle sheathing bone in a caribou's leg.

The next day Robert skinned a two-year-old bull who still had velvet covering his antlers. After cutting off the head, he slit the hide and peeled it off from neck to rump like a body stocking. In sixteen minutes the animal was totally disassembled and wrapped again into its own hide, tumpline attached and ready for carrying.

Which everyone did. The four women teachers did not use rifles, but helped skin the animals and every day they carried meat packs for kilometres to camp. Cutting up and carrying, a living ritual as old as humanity on the tundra. And though we might wear Gore-Tex instead of caribou skins, the actions of our bodies remained exactly the same.

That evening the Elders told stories. And we listened circled on our bedrolls inside the tent, not a whiff of wind moving it.

Dogrib Elder Joe Susie Mackenzie told of ancient footprints around this lake, of the hard life he lived on this land always moving to feed his family. In summer by canoe, sled dogs running along the shore, fifty-seven portages in a month of travel from Rae to Courageous Lakes with children and elders; of hunting accidents and near death; of how men of the first Franklin expedition died here because they did not show the proper respect for animals. And John interpreted his singing Dogrib words, compounding the human mystery of language and memory with that of translation.

Elder George Blondin from Great Bear Lake told stories of the legendary leader Yamoria, stories told to him by his grandmother. (Many more are recounted in Blondin's book, *Yamoria, the Lawmaker: Stories of the Dene*, NeWest Press, 1997.) And also of traditions of medicine power. He said people lived to be so old in the days "when the world was new" because they had power for everything: for weather and animals and water and sun and sickness and even their own aging. For years he has tried to define medicine power to me, and in the stories he told us it is both a spirit and a gift. All the great power died, he said, when the last medicine men fought among themselves at Fort Norman in 1926; today no one has any. And though he tells many stories about it, and has written and published several books, sadly he says that he himself has none either.

So he said. But I have listened to him often, and watched others listening, and I doubt that. A person with real medicine power will, of course, never talk about it.

Snow, but no wind Sunday morning. Elder Joe Mackenzie led the morning worship of prayers inside the tent while facing the sun rising on the canvas. Then we went out to bring in the last of the meat. Twenty-four animals for twenty-four people: a fitting number. The meat was repacked, to distribute between hunters and people back in the community. George Mackenzie had been on the radio regularly, and afternoon planes were coming in with fifteen students to continue the hunt, and to learn with the Elders, over the coming week.

But just before the planes arrived for us, the caribou came again. Appeared at the same spot where they had vanished when we first stepped on shore; it seemed the same number, the same animals, coming back. But much closer to us than before, of course, because the wind had forced us to move camp. We all stood motionless around our fire, watching them come closer.

And then they began to run. Across in front of us as they always do, the mass of them breaking into tremendous speed, running right behind a ridge and then emerging again, running back left across the tundra and up among the erratics until their antlered bodies walked south there, a moving forest high against the wild, cloud-driven sky.

1996

ON BEING ON THE
TOP OF THE WORLD

We three are on the spine of an unnamed nunatak rising out of an unnamed glacier, and we are having a conversation about the age of rocks. Here, June 28 in the last year of the millennium, is a blazing blue twenty-four-hour day, the temperature at noon is four degrees Celsius, and we sit on our backpacks in a virtual ocean of black mountain peaks and snow a little less than a thousand Canadian kilometres from the North Pole. I have questions, always endless questions of the kind only writers have who, since they always need to know more, will persist with in a kind of indefatigable and shameless ignorance:

"How can you talk like that, 'older rocks,' 'younger rocks'? A rock, the earth, is what it is, what it has been, from whenever, from wherever."

Ulrich, the senior geologist, breaks the brown bagel he has taken from his lunch bag and bites into it, says nothing. We have had this conversation more or less since the first time we met, most recently on the Twin Otter as we flew north between the cliffs lining Grise Fiord. He told me then, he told me earlier, "Geology isn't so much a mathematical or chemical science, it's mostly history. Just try to think in somewhat longer terms, millions, billions, of years." On the plane his eyes rolled away from me, unhopefully towards heaven. "Oh," and he grinned, "we have work to do on you."

But now Keith, the younger geologist, responds: "The earth is never just 'what it is,' it's always changing. Volcanoes, floods, earthquakes are quick and obvious, but there's always erosion, you walk on this scree and start a small landslide. Everything changes, rocks do too, they just take longer."

"But their elements have always been in the universe, how can you call them 'older'? Even if a meteor from space slams into the earth, it's not as if something 'new' has actually been made, so how is 'older.'"

Even as I say this, I realize it sounds a good deal like the explanatory notes in the Scofield edition of the Bible I once had, where at the head of Genesis chapter 1 the date of the creation of the universe was affixed as 4004 B.C. For a child that seemed sufficient time.

Keith interrupts, "You could say that about yourself too, the elements of your body have been around forever, in just a different form. If change doesn't count, then…"

"Okay… okay." Logically he's dead right: "young" and "old" are our time designations for particular states of matter. If the elements contained in the universe are a closed system, as probably even the truncated Scofield insisted, then every newborn baby is simply a re-assembled form of original, irreducible elements. Fundamentally we are, every one of us, as old as the universe.

•   Ulrich, Keith and I are part of a Geological Survey of Canada team located for six weeks of 1999 at Carl Ritter Bay on the northeast coast of Ellesmere Island; we sit in stunning sunlight on the tenth largest and, together with its companion Greenland, most northerly island on earth. Here, among unglaciated mountains unending as an ocean, the brain cannot truly comprehend what in every direction the open eye must see: there are no margins to help you frame or focus, your glance seemingly cannot stop moving because at every edge of seeing — left, right, down, up — there is merely more depth, more distance; the lure of overwhelming space. You begin to understand that human eyes, fixed as they are to peer relentlessly ahead as if nothing except forward mattered, your eyes should really be set on either side of your head and equipped with multiple focusing lenses so that you could comprehend, simultaneously, every direction and every depth and height, the full round bulge of existence all at once. Like any eagle.

But 81 degrees north is too utterly North for eagles. This is the depth down to the toe of that glacier and that river braiding itself gray down the broad, round valley, the width of unccountable mountain peaks domed around us with ice fields, the distance of the Nares Strait beyond Carl Ritter Bay smashed white with ice and the long, layered plateau of Greenland rising flat out of that, so close a polar bear could amble over in a day.

•   Traversing, studying, recording rock formations, in eight hours we climb and descend five undulating shoulders of mountains and arrive high above our pick-up point at the foot of another glacier. This final slope of the day is a long ride down scree tilted precisely to the angle of repose into a slender, still frozen, lake. We have seen occasional fist-sized clumps of moss and

purple-blooming saxifrage, a few prints of musk oxen, the weathered scat of caribou, foxes, ptarmigan, hares, but not a single living
creature. Soon the giant steps riding me down the scree make my
knees and thighs ache bitterly. I sit down to stop; the tiny figures
of my companions appear and vanish far below.

Utter silence. Even the sound of white water over rocks has
vanished. I hear my ears straining to hear.

Suddenly a fly loops by, returns slowly, and settles on my
knee. Amazing, a fly buzz in a world of soundless rocks. The fly
probes, twitches, the smell of my sweat no doubt luring it, and
Emily Dickinson murmurs:

> I heard a Fly buzz — when I died —
> The Stillness in the Room
> Was like the Stillness in the Air — ...
>
> ...And then it was
> There interposed a Fly —
>
> With Blue — uncertain stumbling Buzz —
> Between the light — and me —
> And then the Windows failed — and then
> I could not see to see — (223–4)

There is such imaginable Stillness here. The endless noise of contemporary living batters us until we ignore almost everything, but
in the Arctic a tuft of moss is an event, a fly a blue companion.
You watch, and listen. Hear silence.

•   The left front seat of a helicopter is a sky-box seat in the
stadium of the world. The geology you have hoisted your body
over all day, at times driven to a life-terror concentration on the

next placement of your boot, your body running sweat and your lungs exploding with too much oxygen, that geology shifts itself away as easily as a hand, turning; collapses into spectator sport. You do nothing but sit and stare; rejoice. Vertical escarpments are momentary uplifts; slit canyons with rock walls folded tight as wadded paper are slight tilts, are imperceptible movements of Mark's hands and feet on the controls; water channels scooped out of rock into razors now become a splendid carpet you could, obviously, walk along barefoot with enormous, sensual pleasure.

An abrupt white blob under us leaps apart into two long arctic hares stretching for opposite distances. In my earphones Mark chuckles at them, "Sorry about that!", then adds to me, "Summer's short, they've gotta do it while the doin's good." After a tiny turquoise lake and more cut valleys he tilts us right, above cliffs and over the braided stream that leads to our camp. Across the flat valley, on the long lateral moraine left by the glacier's melting eons ago, I can see the muskoxen. Tiny black burrs on an immense brown, grey land pushed up vertically into the blue sky by straggles of snow and black and tan and startling red streaks. I saw the animals first when the Twin Otter bringing us circled down out of clouds into this valley three days ago.

"They're always on the move," Mark says, flying along the right mountains not to disturb them. "Seven... or eight of them, they should get to camp, they graze in a kind of circuit."

I've never met a muskox. I've been told that, unlike the curious caribou I've tried to approach, they won't run away and circle back to have another long look from a wolf-safe distance. But I know where these are, and in three days they've moved about ten kilometres along the valley peaks; if they don't come lower past camp, I can climb out to them.

•   The valley opens even wider, flatter, its gravel and braided stream bed twisting towards the distant curve of Carl Ritter Bay and the Nares Strait, both choked with crushed ice and icebergs drifting from the north. The tents and fuel barrels of the Geological Survey of Canada 1999 camp are an almost unnoticeable sprinkle of white and a touch of orange against a snow-crested mountain that rises over it with gigantic strata of rock folded into a lop-sided W, both tips vanishing into sheer overlay. Here till the middle of August live eight Canadians and six or seven Germans — five women and nine or ten men — the "Carl Ritter Bay Hilton" as Monica the camp manager calls it — complete with individual-bedroom tents, a walk-through kitchen and attached three-table dining and radio room, a bathroom fitted with washtub hot water, a tin basin and a rope-elevated shower in a plastic bag. Alone at some distance, facing a mountain, is the tent unambiguously named "the shitter," complete with a movable red tag to indicate occupation; the men's urinal is any distance 360 degrees all around.

Dorothy could certainly cook at any Hilton she wanted to. Despite the mountains, after three weeks I'll have gained two kilos on her morning muffins and five and six-dish suppers. But she prefers cooking in the Arctic summers, and when she isn't at her home near Ottawa she's teaching English in Hong Kong. The first time I see her, she's reading a book of poetry by a Canadian writer she knows personally. She tells me:

"This camp would be the perfect setting for a murder mystery, à la Agatha Christie."

It certainly would; but I see a problem: "Fourteen people is too many, too much work to create character and tension."

"So," she's basting a mound of beef that fills the propane oven end to end, "okay, kill three or four quick."

"Well…let's talk about it at supper. We'll need corpse volunteers."

"No," she says. "We draw lots."

• July 1, and Mark settles us soft as a feather, but much, much noisier, on a mountain peak overlooking the snow domes and glaciers of the Victoria and Albert Range. We crouch; hold down caps and equipment as he hurricanes away. I awoke at 3:15 am: it was the sun blazing above the shoulder of the folded mountain directly north, welcoming me to Canada's 132nd birthday. The light was too stunning, I couldn't sleep again, but now I see other illuminations about rock ages. In this outcrop are embedded masses of sponge and algae trails and bodies, the hollowed spoor of worms, the blunt tracks of pebbles moved by currents in the silt at the bottom of a shallow sea: all turned into sedimentary rock in one of the oldest reefs in the world. Precambrian era, Middle Proterozoic period, somewhere between three to seven hundred million years ago.

"The first forms of life so far found on earth," Ulrich says.

Here in a sea of unnamed mountains on the last land of northern earth; older, and much more primitive in structure, then the Burgess Shale creatures found at the tops of the Rocky Mountains west of Banff. Six hundred million years older than dinosaurs.

"How come the oldest rock is on top of mountains?"

"Some force under the earth's crust pushed it," Keith says, "thrust it up and over other rock. Or a crust shoved under, and lifted it."

I hammer off a piece and hold it in my hand. Learn to see what you are looking at. That is how geologists know the age of a rock.

And I remember a story told about Big Bear, the Cree leader who died in 1888. It would seem he told a story about rock, a story told in many versions by most of the first peoples of the western hemisphere. It happened that a certain person began a long journey, searching for eternal life. Finally, after perhaps a lifetime, this person arrived in the presence where such a request could be made. And the request was granted; the person "was transformed into rock. Rock gives us the pipe by which we pray to The First One, for rock is the grandfather of all, the first of all being as well as the last" (*Temptations* 314).

•   The day after Canada Day (which we celebrated after work with everyone wearing red and a Maple Leaf flag covering the office tent roof, fireworks, extended libations of every kind and beverage, shrimp and escargot baked in flaky pastry, New Brunswick lobster and barbecued Alberta beef steak very heavy on the garlic) the muskoxen are above the camp. Six of them on the high saddle between mountains. What marvelous serendipity: Pete, our resident mechanic, is working on the helicopter; it will not carry any geologist to work anywhere today. I arm myself with film and paper.

Two muskoxen graze below me, unaware, on a ledge above a stream that cuts its canyon down into the immense valley with our tiny camp, the sprawled, milky river, the distant bay between whose framing capes of mountains lies the dazzling ice, a tip of Hans Island cliff, grounded icebergs, and the broad, humpy band of Greenland closing the horizon in blue. To stand in such a place on earth; the widest possible camera lens is basically a silly little thing. With the warm, beautiful animals who live here, the mind drops, bottomless.

For half an hour I work my way downwind towards them, keeping out of sight as much as possible in the crumbles of the ridge. While I do, the largest, the one on the right whose excess winter wool flows in long, grey shags around his (her?) black body, lies down facing the river cliffs to ruminate; gradually three, then four, five others appear from behind a lower outcrop. All six are within fifty metres of each other, nosing continuously for moss or sprigs of grass, and when I straighten myself out of a depression above them, the one on the left instantly lifts her head. She stands motionless, facing me, and the two largest in the centre shift to stare at me as well. After a few moments Big Shaggy far on the left hoists his body up, bends his head around ponderously. Four facing me, motionless as placed hassocks with the gorgeous sheen of their black-brown wool draped over them long and thick to their white-stockinged hooves: like any over-grown shaggy dog, they simply must be petted. Only the double boss of horn shaping their foreheads, the downward swoop of horn tipped outward, as it seems, with complete ineffectiveness to either side, would even make you hesitate.

Moving more slowly than is imaginable, they coagulate together toward a lower flat above the canyon where the two smallest — yearling calves, I think — have already gone. Whenever an adult moves a little, at least two others stand facing me. When they retreat, I step forward, they step back. Eventually they are all on the ledge and I'm closer than I dare: on an outcrop high enough to see the creamy light saddles behind the humps on their shoulders. They shift into a row, two adults on either side flanking the calves, considering me. Abruptly Big Shaggy rubs his head against his legs and snorts. The sound is explosive, but strangely puny in this spectacular world dropping away and rising everywhere around us in mountainous silence. They shuffle their positions, the now nervous calves always surrounded, and I am close enough to recognize that their eyes, set so high on the outer edges of their heads just inside the heaviest down-curve of their scimitar horns, their faces are positively malignant.

Another adult lowers its head, rubs, grunts, and they shuffle again. On and on during the next fifteen minutes, changing positions with the two smallest often hidden. They seem like a mirage in a dream: wild animals that will not run. Finally the calves disappear altogether, the adults are so tightly compacted they have become one massive black animal with four white saddles and seven visible legs, its four heads facing outwards in three directions. Only one vicious head confronts me, and it would surely be enough. But they do not move from their narrow place, and neither do I from mine.

Then, gradually, their concentration starts to slip aside, their movements loosen. One, then another adult ignores what is, perhaps, happening and moves aside to nose among rocks. I sit down, scribble, eat part of a sandwich I have made from the table of food Dorothy sets out every morning: today it's lettuce, tomato and thick pastrami on light rye, easy on the mayo. The calves amble on the cliff, skipping a little, they might like a taste of tomato if there was some way I could get it to them. But Big Shaggy still faces me, glowering head low, his peeling winter skirts rise in the wind like gossamer. The first two adults eddy around rocks, down towards the valley, and soon the calves bump and bound away after them; Big Shaggy is the last to forget about me.

I go back to where he (she?) lay down overlooking the canyon, and sure enough, I find swatches of *qiviut*. The shed winter wool, easy to spot because it is the only thing on the ground that moves, a clump of wavering light on the wind. The warmest natural fibre on earth grows here in the long darkness of bitterest storm and winter to protect *oomingmak*, the bearded one. When human beings first came to the Americas from Asia, *oomingmak* had already been living here continuously for seventy-five thousand years.

It is not yet noon, and the muskoxen have vanished down around the shoulder of the mountain. I follow them.

• Franz, the organizer of the German geological team with us, is a large man with long grey locks of hair and beard. He has been a researcher for the German Federal Institute for Geosciences and Natural Resources all over the world, including Siberia and Spitzbergen, and most recently for years in the Antarctic. We discover that we have a bond beyond the German language: the castled medieval town of Tübingen. We both attended university there, I several years before him. Geology, he tells me, is not an exact science; when physicists study it, they despair because in geology there are always too many unknowns to make any exact formula possible.

At various supper tables Franz tries to explain things to me: "Geology is more like the investigation of a crime. You gather every bit of evidence you can, any way you can, to try to put together the story. What happened, who did what to whom, who is what, who moved where, when. It's very difficult, the evidence is often covered by mountains of rock, what you do find can be accidental, but you try to compose the scene of the crime. And sometimes you can be predictive, for example you drill for oil on a geologist's calculations, and you hit it. Then you're 100%, but usually 50 or 80% is all you can get. So the theories, the stories keep changing, as we try to interpret more of the evidence we gather."

And then he laughs. "In geology you can never close a case completely because the 'criminal' will never confess everything."

Despite my initial impressions, geologists are starting to sound a lot like writers. In the Arctic, however, their story evidence is gathered more labouriously. Carmen, a young Canadian student geologist, spends her day hanging, as it appears to me when we helicopter by, on a massive cliff over the Nares Strait. The cliff is conglomerate, rocks pressed so tightly together that there is almost no matrix between them. To get some statistical concept of its composition, she drapes the various faces of the cliff out in measured squares and then, with unbelievable concentration, counts the pebbles of a certain size within each square. After her count, Oliver breaks out chunks of limestone which he will ship in pails to his laboratory in Germany, crush and dissolve in acid, and in this slurry try to discover irreducible, microscopic sharks' teeth. If he can find them, he will be looking at what remains of earth's first fish, and so be able to date the rocks in the Ordovician period around 500 million years old.

"If you can be within five to ten million years," Oliver says, "that's very good."

Carmen tells me about the seals who sun themselves all day on the drifting ice below them. It is July 7, and the strait is opening, its deep, deep blue a startling contrast to the turquoise water that pools on the ice pans as they slowly drift south. And one day, while waiting for the helicopter to pick them up in the valley, she and Oliver face off with a muskox bull, grey, solitary and totally irascible, who will not allow them to walk wide around him. They simply have to wait him out — twenty-six minutes.

At 8:30 on July 7 Ulrich and I step onto the peak of a nameless mountain where no human being has ever stood. We make a long traverse across loose rock tipped half a kilometre down into a green, frost-patterned lake, and take a rock sample from an outcrop. The Global Positioning System instrument, which fits into my hand, finds three satellites, and that triangulation places us at

Latitude: North 80 degrees, 58.442 minutes

Longitude: West 68 degrees, 37.079 minutes

"It's not dead accurate," Ulrich tells me. "The U.S. military always throws it off a bit, though they could be precise within a metre." He has worked in the Canadian Arctic every summer for twenty years, and he studies long and carefully the formations tilted upright from this mountain to the next, and next, across valleys, in synclines and anticlines, trying to identify them by name — Cape Phillips formation... Eleanor River... Bauman Fiord... Ella Bay — the names given them from locations where they were first identified. The formations this morning seem to be ordered "backwards," a geological confusion that highlights this part of Ellesmere Island: whereas Greenland across the strait is as flatly layered and ordered as a Black Forest cake, these formations on the Judge Daly Promontory less than forty kilometres away seem as wrinkled and confused as a squeezed English trifle.

But Ulrich is undeterred by the "Nares Strait problem" — trying to explain the physical/mechanical relationship between Greenland and the North American plate — that has been, to use Franz's image, "under criminal investigation" throughout the twentieth century. Ulrich sits above this astonishing world overloaded with pyramidal peaks and stares through his stereoscope to get a three-dimensional view of the aerial photographs that have been made of every inch of Canada. Then he draws coloured lines of formations he identifies in rock onto the photograph, erasing and refining them as we clamber down the mountain, hike across valleys and up again. He says his particular job is to map. "It is for other people to explain 'why'; I walk over this land, and I describe."

To judge from the lines he draws, there are times when we step across a hundred million years in one stride.

• On the day of the muskoxen, when I see them again they are tiny specks several kilometres closer to Carl Ritter Bay and the ocean, climbing up the slant of the mountain north of camp. Hard slogging. Eventually I reach the ledge above them; the tents are below me in the wide, flat valley and the six animals lie on what must be the humped middle of the lop-sided W I saw from below folded into the mountain. Big Shaggy is aware of me first, they all heave to their feet, move away to bunch together where the ledge turns into steep rockfall. I get directly above them, perhaps twelve metres up a cliff too rough for them to charge. But they look up and back away; several turn to face me.

A rock ptarmigan, then another, more white than brown, walks slowly away from me to pose on the cliff. I find the muskoxen, the camp below, the ptarmigan in the miniscule lens of my camera.

After some time, one by one the muskoxen turn away and lie down on the rock-strewn ledge. An adult whose front leg seems bent awkwardly under her against a stone hoists herself up, front and back. She noses a spot of moss, then turns a slow circle and a half very much like a husky settling in snow, and eases herself down in a curl facing the air of the immense valley far below.

The ptarmigan have stepped behind rocks, the muskoxen rest; perhaps they sleep. I lie back against a boulder in the blue sunlight. In this perfect, brilliant air there is such stillness with wild animals, they are so calm and exact in their movements, untroubled by anything within themselves. A pair of snow buntings, the male black and white and the female slightly greyer, waft over me and vanish below the cliff. I have watched buntings as they fly low along the ground, or hop picking seeds from sparse plants; there are few birds at 81 degrees north, and these are the only ones that have a song rather than a cry or a scream. And now, suddenly, the male rises from below the cliff, lifts straight up, sings its dazzling little song and drops straight down again. What a beautiful way to sing, bouncing on the spring of an enormous happiness.

On the ledge below me overlooking the valley, all the musk-oxen are lying down; perhaps they are sleeping.

The pyramid tent where I sleep is a triangle far below me; I have written down its exact global position, and I have dreamed there of the names that bother me, this surround of English and Norwegian and American and yet more English enduring, icicles growing forever longer out of their explorerly correct but-very-bad-for-icing-up beards, all suffering by the century. Hall Basin, Cape Isabella, Kennedy Channel, Lady Franklin Bay, Trold Fiord, Sylvia Mountain, Sverdrup Inlet, Kislingbury River, Ellef and Amund Ringes Islands, Jones Sound — a forgettable City of London alderman in the seventeenth century. So, who was Judge Daly, who Carl Ritter? Rising up to cut off my view of the strait to the south is Cape Leopold von Buch, who was the foremost German geologist of the nineteenth century; I suppose I should have studied his portrait in Tübingen, where he taught; and might have if in 1958 I had thought to enter the Geological Institute.

And this island, named Ellesmere in 1852 for the gold braid of an English admiral. There must be a truer Inuktitut name for this extraordinary polar desert land.

•   Today people live in three distant spots on Ellesmere. Alert, at the northeastern bend of the island, closer to Moscow than to Ottawa, and Eureka, on a mid-west-coast fiord, are weather and military stations where temporary southern Canadians rotate in and out. Grise Fiord (Aujuittuq: "the place that never thaws out") on the south coast is a permanent hamlet, population about 150, begun in 1953 with the controversial (most would say forced) movement north of eight Inuit families from Inukjuak, Quebec, and Pond Inlet (Mittimatalik) by the Canadian Government. No contemporary Inuit have ever lived on Ellesmere of their own free will.

But millennia earlier, when this land was a good deal warmer — ice-free summers and milder winters that cooled from about 1200 CE into the "Little Ice Age" of 1600 to 1850 — different peoples lived here, from the Thule People and the Dorsets to the variously named Arctic Small-Tool cultures that spread across this continent from Asia in separate migrations and lived in small hunting camps throughout the High Arctic as early as 5000 years ago. During the time of the Egyptian and Roman empires they developed a technology to successfully hunt the great whales and other sea mammals, and so on Ellesmere their ancient living sites can be most easily recognized along the coastlines.

When I ask Ulrich about this, he shows me what to look for; as we fly back to camp along the Nares Strait shore outlined by rotting ice, he spots a site almost immediately. Mark drops the helicopter down, hovers for the best view. An irregular ring of brownish stones on the jagged black gravel. And we see two more sites before we round the cape into the river valley. After lunch I hike back for an hour to reach the nearest.

Stones a good size to lift with both hands, to carry against your stomach, to lay down on a tent's edge against the wind. Ten days ago I walked this shoreline and didn't see what I was seeing: so much like a prairie teepee-ring, though this one is not as large and not at all overgrown; not a sprig of green anywhere on this rock floor. There is also the adjacent stone scatter of a possible food storage site directly above the drop of the gravel beach. I search for possible artifacts, but I don't really know what I'm doing and don't wish to disturb anything: what I find are two jagged pieces of weathered bone inscribed by tendrils of moss — how ancient? — one of which is broken off and possibly sucked out for marrow. I look about, at the eroded cliff above me sloping up to the cape's peak, at the ice and open water and Hans Island and the endless shimmer of Greenland across the Nares Strait, the sun gleaming on its snow as far as can be seen either south or north. Then I recognize another site on the narrow bench to the left; two other rings of stone even more clearly laid out on the black gravel. And in front of them the most intimate structure of all: between the tent rings is dug the hollow of a family hearth, three stones placed open to the sea.

Archeologists tell us these people lived a life of extreme meagerness; it would seem that the things they carried were infinitely less in number and complexity than what we apparently need to live in comfort. But around the warmth of this hearth, with family and friends and food, and such astonishing beauty, they must also have known happiness.

If human beings had existed forty million years ago, we might have lived on this last fringe of land before the North Pole as comfortably as we now live in central France. For reasons still unexplained, at that time the earth's temperature at the poles was much the same as it was at the equator, and temperate zone plants flourished on the Arctic islands now dominated by perpetual ice. With Franz and Kersten, his assistant, I find petrified wood and beech-like leaves veined in rocks on the saddles of Tertiary period mountains. Even more amazing is the unique "Fossil Forest" in the Geodetic Hills of neighbouring Axel Heiberg Island, discovered in 1985. The trees in this incredible place grew up to two and a half metres in diameter, and their colossal remains are not petrified: they are mummified in up to nine-metre-long trunks frozen in permafrost; they will still burn in a campfire! I am told these Tertiary period forests were roamed by huge rhino-like mammals called brontotheres, and crocodiles, garfish, and tortoises, like those still living on the Galapagos Islands, swam in its waters.

It comes to me that, in order to write true fantasy fiction, one should move imaginatively backward in time, not forward. And North.

• On July 15 I hear the name I have been dreaming about. On the sandy shore of Lake Hazen, a thermal oasis in the Arctic desert of Ellesmere Island National Park. The final chapter of Aritha van Herk's superb fiction, *Places Far From Ellesmere*, happens here; on its cover the island becomes a woman floating over the apocryphal edge of the continent; she kneels bending forward, her hands are clasped on her thighs, her hair streams above her.

"The name is 'Quttinirpaaq,'" Pierre, the Inuit park warden tells me. He prints it on a piece of paper and helps me pronounce it syllabically: Qu-ttin-ir-paaq. "It means…you can't translate it exactly, but it's close…it means 'On the Top of the World.'"

•   On the sun-and-smoking patio of the canvas Carl Ritter Bay Hilton, Kerstan explains that the oldest rocks in the world have been found just north of Yellowknife. Radiometric dating, four and a half billion years old. So, I conclude, according to the rocks and if you accept the Beringian migration theory, then both in land and human settlement, Canada is the oldest country in the western hemisphere.

"Don't forget Alaska," Franz says; then laughs. "And usually, eventually, rocks are always found to be older in the United States."

Laughter all around.

"So what?" someone asks. "Where does that get you, oldest... first?"

"I don't know," I say. "Maybe as far as the UN gets us, calling us the world's number one country six years in a row."

"I don't like it," someone else says. By the accent, it's a Canadian. "They're blowing our cover."

"Yeah," says someone else. "We've been so careful, complaining and complaining about weather, taxes, Quebec, cultural destruction, weather, Quebec... they keep this up, soon everybody in the world will want to come live here."

Yes; come; even by the desperate, rusting, shipful. We sit in the eleven pm sunlight; we ponder the ultimate existential Canadian problem.

•   Leaving Quttinirpaaq you fly south over mountains and floe ice and open water, across giant Devon, Cornwallis, Prince of Wales and Victoria Islands before you reach the mainland. As we do so, the haze clears and suddenly I recognize the edge of the continent with Bathurst Inlet below, the Burnside River angling itself in from the south, the Hood River trailing west into the evening horizon. Where the Hood plunges from its inland plateau there hangs the white halo of the Wilberforce Falls. This inlet, long and spectacular, which from ten thousand metres I see at one glance; in 1821, mapping its intricate shoreline doomed over half of the First Franklin Polar Expedition, including young Robert Hood, to miserable death on the tundra. I can see that tundra too: all I have to do is shift my head.

A few hours by First Air from my home in Alberta, from all of us millions crowded in cities along the southern edges of our country, it seems to me again that Stephen Leacock, that most Canadian of all Englishmen, still has us dead right. In 1936, after sixty years in this country he wrote "I'll Stay in Canada," which concludes:

> It's the great spaces that appeal. To all of us [in Canada], the vast unknown country of the North, reaching away to the polar seas, supplies a peculiar mental background. I like to think that… an hour or two of flight will take me over the divide and down to the mournful shores of the James Bay…. I have never gone to the James Bay; I never go to it; I never shall. But somehow I'd feel lonely without it. (212)

1999

ACCEPTANCE SPEECH, GOVERNOR GENERAL'S AWARD CEREMONIES

Your Excellencies, ladies and gentlemen:

It seems most appropriate to be accepting this award for the novel *A Discovery of Strangers* in Montreal. Because *A Discovery of Strangers* tells the story of the first encounter of the nomadic Dene peoples of today's Northwest Territories with Europeans in 1820–21, and that encounter was made possible by French Canadian voyageurs, men who literally paddled and carried the English officers of the First Franklin Expedition from Hudson Bay along Canada's northern rivers into the land of the Yellowknives. For this enormous service, nine of the eleven, including the one Mohawk voyageur, died a miserable death. Our land has many stories that we need to hear.

A Canadian prime minister once said, foolishly: "Canada has too much geography, and too little history." Even one of our finest poets has written that in Canada "it's only by our lack of ghosts / we're haunted."

I find these statements ludicrous. We are not haunted by a "lack of ghosts." People have been living in our country for at least eleven thousand years, people have been living in our country for more than five hundred and fifty generations. I would say that, if we are haunted, we are haunted by our ignorance.

We know too little about ourselves. In this enormous, beautiful land we inhabit, we seem to have no eyes to see, no ears to hear, the stories that are everywhere about us and clamouring to be told.

I say, only the stories we tell each other — about ourselves, about each other — can sustain us, because only the stories we tell each other about ourselves create us as a society, as a nation.

Only the stories we tell each other can create us as a true Canadian people.

1994

WHERE I LIVE

WHERE THE BLACK ROCKS LIE
IN THE OLD MAN'S RIVER

I

It is bright spring, and we have been travelling an Alberta circle
from Calgary to Lethbridge for three days. The brilliant accumu-
lations of cloud and sun loop us east first, to the Red Deer River
cutting out its long swath of badlands between the Hand and the
Wintering Hills (on the north side of which we can discern, very
clearly as soon as it is pointed out, the hollow of The Old Man's
Bed), and then circling around north through Cochrane and the
lands of the Stoney People to the Rocky Mountains. The low, grey
sky begins to whiten with snow; wet flakes splotch the windshield
like the splayed hands of spirits that would certainly stop us if
the nerveless automaton of our wipers did not swish them aside.
Gradually we bend west on black, gleaming pavement, lift over
foothills and the overcast opens suddenly, very high, just where
the Bow River breaks between cliffs. And there is the immense
front wall of mountains repeating itself into every discernible
distance, massifs row beyond row both north and south, shining

like crimson icebergs in the last evening light.

At the hot springs on the slope of Sulphur Mountain, snow rims the pool, but the falling snowflakes vanish before they can touch our heads afloat on the steaming water.

Next morning we circle again, but south. Following the Highwood River between the nunataks of the Highwood Pass, and then down to the Sheep River and Willow Creek, south along the foothill valleys of the Porcupine Hills until the Oldman River breaks white beside us through the Livingstone Gap, curves past the great stones where Napi, The Old Man, played, and over to the Crowsnest River cascading away from all the semi-sleep of coal towns barely breathing and the granite castellations of Crowsnest Mountain thrust into the blue sky again. Then we swing east, past the white, blasted face of Turtle Mountain, fast as the prairie flattens down step by giant step into horizon until I turn off on the gravel road I know and there's the house at the lip of the Oldman cliffs; a prairie house not yet strewn east up the coulee by the relentless wind. I find the hidden key and unlock the door. Two of us remain on the deck overlooking the deep bend of the river, the eroded cliffs and gigantic cottonwoods below turning pale May green, thunderheads piling higher over mountains in the west.

"It's really not fair," says the woman from South Africa — or is it Kosovo, or Afghanistan or Sierra Leon or Cambodia or North Korea or Colombia or Bosnia or Iraq or Somalia or Palestine or a country we have not yet heard of in Canada — this gentle woman says, "It's not fair."

"What?"

"You just drive us around for days over this incredible land, anywhere you please, and no one stops you with machine guns hanging on their shoulders and you never have to show papers to anyone or explain a word about where you're going or with whom and you come down a track to this isolated, beautiful house and there's no seven-foot steel fence with electrified barbed wire along the top or guard dogs or bars at the windows or bullet-proof glass, just birds singing while the river runs and all the grass and the trees grow."

"There's a thunderstorm coming, over there, with the wind."

She laughs aloud. Her companion leans out over the balcony rail above us.

"No, it certainly is not fair," he says. Into that sudden hush before the wind bends the trees along the river below us with a roar. "To be able to live in one of the rarest places on earth."

And momentarily, all around us in this delicate spring, there seems to be nothing at all in the world but weather.

II

The first time I saw Lethbridge must have been a late spring Friday in 1947. I read in my sister Elizabeth's Five Year Diary (five narrow lines for each day) that my mother, father, she and I arrived in "our new home" in Coaldale "about 7 o'clock" on Thursday, May 15, 1947, and that next day the same businessman, Mr. Voth, who had come in his car to Saskatchewan to bring us to southern Alberta, "took us to Lethbridge" and we "got some nice furniture."

Lethbridge, the Irrigation Capital of Canada, 1947 population 17,807; it seems I cannot find it in my memory, not that first time. We must have driven the ten miles from Coaldale on the new gravel of Number Three Highway then being built to parallel the CPR tracks, past the two red Broxburn elevators, because the old highway route led two miles south from Coaldale before turning west and that would have taken us between the Experimental Station and the 1911 fortress of the Lethbridge Provincial Gaol, where, as Mr. Voth would certainly have told us, fourteen men had already been hanged over the years and no doubt more were inside waiting. Such facts would certainly have remained hooked into me; I was twelve.

As it is, I do remember that I sat in the back seat, tight against the right window, and just north of the intersection where the highway bent into the city there appeared for a moment seemingly endless rows of ugly rectangular two-story buildings. Lethbridge Internment Camp No. 133, as I did not then know to name it, flat roofs level as the horizon above what looked like double rows of grey posts and close strands of barbed wire, which I had known all my life of course, but until then had only seen used to control the movement of animals. Prisoner-of-war camp, Mr. Voth told us, lots more prisoners in there than people in Lethbridge, maybe twenty thousand inside that wire for the whole war, they'd never say exactly how many, men only and fed as good as any Canadian soldier. Fed a lot better than anybody else in the whole country, and five of them hanged just before Christmas in the Lethbridge Gaol back there behind the trees for strangling a fellow prisoner who had, it was said, yelled something against Hitler.

Barely five months before, December 18, 1946. Three of the five attempted suicide with smuggled razor blades, but they were patched up and then hanged. One of them, while climbing the gallows, had shouted in German, "My Fuehrer, I follow thee!" Everybody inside that barbed wire spoke German as exact as printed books, Mr. Voth told us in Mennonite Low German.

The flat camp on the flat prairie at 5th Avenue North —
maximum capacity 12,500 men — was empty and the barracks
being torn down when I first saw it, the watchtowers and main
gates already gone. The last war prisoners had been shipped
back to Halifax and Europe on the CPR and the camp closed, by
strange coincidence, also on December 18, 1946. Six thousand
POWs, as they were called, from all over the land had requested
to remain in Canada, but not a single permission was granted.
Four decades later a professor of English in Graz, Austria, would
tell me stories about Camp No. 133; he was a short stocky man
who in 1940 at age eighteen was perfect for submarine duty,
the "sexiest," as we would say now, of all possible services in the
German military. "When we walked down the quay in Kiel,
every girl smiled greetings at us," he told me. Sexier and safer
than the Luftwaffe, he thought then too (wrongly), leaving the
beauty of Austrian mountains for what he discovered was the
silent, explosive violence of the depths of the sea. On his very
first tour of duty their sub was blown out of the water; from
a crew of sixty-five, he and five others survived to be picked
out of the North Atlantic by the British-Canadian convoy they
had been attacking. He told me that beyond the Government
Elevator and the low houses of Lethbridge, where he arrived in
December, 1942, he could see the crest of Chief Mountain under
snow on the south-western horizon, mountains like his memory
of his homeland, but all around the circle of open land such as
he never seen or could truly imagine before. "My war was very
quiet, absolutely safe on your immense, beautiful Canadian prairie. I never got closer to your mountains, I worked in beet fields
and learned English." When we compared locations, we discovered he and I probably had thinned and hoed the same beet

fields, he no more than five years before I, and certainly under the same windy sun.

As I said, I remember nothing about my first glimpse of Lethbridge itself. I read in my sister's diary that while we were buying furniture for our small new house in a store on Third Avenue "we met a nice man," but I do not remember him either.

What does remain is the pavement the construction crews laid next summer on the highway from Coaldale, west over the crest of land towards Lethbridge; laid down as slowly, carefully, as if they were engendering an unending strip of thick and priceless metal. When in bright sunlight you looked into distance over its impeccable black surface, it gradually began to shimmer, then shine in the lifting heat like a revelation of water: when you looked west to the mountains you discovered yourself no longer on land, your feet had been placed on the narrow edge of the world's blue, incomprehensible sea.

III

When my parents, my sister and I moved to southern Alberta from Saskatchewan, the English language changed drastically with the drastic landscape. I knew "slough" and "muskeg" and "poplar" and "spruce," of course, and "saskatoon," but I knew nothing about "coulee," "chinook," "cottonwood," "sage," "cactus." The Native people had been inscrutable Cree, but in Alberta their names carried the blunt aggression of "Blackfoot" and "Blood." The language of lakes and momentary creeks in spring run-off and the swamps stuffed green with bullrushes for the redwing blackbirds to sway on and nest and all that stony soil that destroyed the back of any man riding his plow deep through the poplar and spruce bush of Saskatchewan became, in southern

Alberta, the language of prairie, foothills and mountains, and especially what to me seemed enormous, muddy rivers carving their way through eroded valleys ever north and east towards an ocean. In Saskatchewan I had never lived near a river, could not remember seeing one until I was taken to the hospital in North Battleford to have my awkward, mislocated appendix removed; only the school globe turning under my hand showed me where great rivers ran, and they are hard to imagine from spring creeks, almost as hard as mountains out of poplar hills.

But here a whole vocabulary of not only landscape but also of work faced you: in particular, sugar beets and irrigation. We suddenly lived beside a ditch running free all summer with thick water flickering past our house and connected somewhere to larger and larger ditches dragged in straight patterns into the flat land until they joined main ditches and finally the Overland Canal and eventually, above us somewhere in the invisible foothills, opened into a lake hidden behind a dam I could for years only imagine. But I always understood: this liquid mud settling out in our cistern, this almost clear water which we skimmed off the top by pail with great gratitude — no need for a wagon hauling barrels, always available and always free — connected us to the high distant snow sometimes visible on the southwest horizon. What I drank from our dipper was the immeasurable gift of the Rocky Mountains.

"St. Mary hits the Oldman just below the Belly."

A water geography of Lethbridge river names I was told with a schoolboy leer, whose sexual implications I then did not understand. Nor decipher why the names were so odd. St. Mary would of course be something, somewhere, Roman Catholic, but why would Paul Robeson in his unbelievable bass sing about *plantin' no cotton* on Old Man River rolling along through the valley below Lethbridge? Did it have something to do with the giant cottonwood trees that grew tangled there? And rudest of all, the Belly River — a name, I learned, first given to the entire river system flowing east to the Bow to form the South Saskatchewan because the Atsina aboriginal people once lived here and, through a mistranslation, were called Gros Ventre by the French. However, the city-founding English found the name "really unsavoury." *The Lethbridge News* reported that the 1900 English ladies of Lethbridge could but blush when in their letters home they had to name the river on which they lived and so, after numerous petitions and a careful study of water volume, the Geographic Board of Canada in 1914 banished the name to a far tributary. The present Belly River begins among the peaks of Chief Mountain in the United States and runs through no city at all, not even a village, and so can no longer be a cause for nineteenth-century genteel embarrassment.

The English petitioned to have a nice English name attached to their rambunctious river, "Lethbridge" perhaps, to double the use of their own colonial designation, or, better yet, "Alberta." Thankfully, the Geographic Board decided that the provincial use of the third name of the fourth daughter of Queen Victoria was enough obeisance to distant royalty; the board named the river "Oldman," the oldest and richest name of all.

Even after ten years in southern Alberta I would have no intimation of the mind-expanding world of story contained in that word, *Napi-ooch-a-tay-cots* in Blackfoot: "The river the Old Man played upon," in a playing field that can still be seen in the foothill wilderness beyond the Porcupine Hills. Napi, the Blackfoot creator and trickster, The Old Man known to the Cree farther north as Wi-suk-i-shak, whose stories would eventually become as evocative to me as those of Moses and Odysseus, Shakespeare and Goethe. What I did know at age twelve was that I had been moved from an isolated bush farm and a single-room log school to sidewalks and electricity and coal mines half a mile deep and sugar beets and libraries with shelves and shelves of books; the whole world had gone "so passing strange and wonderful" (Shelley 1).

IV

The wind is a sea in Lethbridge, and usually by noon the tide rises and the city begins to flood. Gradually, relentlessly, with blusters of increasing violence swirling around eddies of teasing, always merely momentary calm, every street becomes a running surf, every strong tree streaming away bent like seaweed in deep current, every building a headland to dive behind for breathing shelter. That's when the denizens of this place surrender their walking, or swimming if you will; they climb into the submarines of their cars and pickups, they power themselves inside steel through the windy seas, though often, caught by the red cross-currents of intersections, they are forced to stand still while shuddering profoundly.

Well, what did you expect? This is a city of the prairie, a word that comes into English from Old French meaning "extended meadow," and whose space is often associated with long light over water. In 1682 Sir Thomas Browne wrote about "the prairie or large sea-meadow upon the coast of Provence" (OED), and a century later another Englishman noted, "The prairies are very extensive, natural meadows covered with long grass... like the ocean, as far as the eye can see the view is terminated by the horizon" (OED).

"Pr - air - ie," *air* suspended in a high and difficult, one might say an impossible, linguistic balance between two hard bilabial and approximant consonants and two gentle frontal vowels. Or, fondled and listened to in another way, "prairie" becomes two words, "pra[ye]r" and "air[y]," their bumpy head and knotted tail strung inextricably together to create what strange amalgam creature, what improbable verbal lion, snake, goat and eagle chimera?

Strangely enough, in the Judeo-Christian and Muslim traditions many of us were born into, the movement of air we call "wind" is one evocative image for the divine; that spirit of God that breathes life into every creation and inspires (quite literally, "in-spirits" or "breathes into") all creatures with powers to help them achieve their utmost, their most exalted desires.

Prairie: a landscape of airy prayer indeed.

There can be no doubt about it: after a lengthening spring or summer or fall day of walking in the wind, I know that I have been breathed into. Whether I want to or not. And for the first time I comprehend why the city climbed up out of the deep, protective Oldman River valley and, despite its indenture to coal, built itself large on the unbounded and treeless prairie lying open to the distant mountains: it wanted the full blessing of the wind.

To live in Lethbridge is to be perpetually inspired.

v

Within the present city boundaries of Lethbridge, Alberta, lies the site of the last and one of the largest battles ever fought between Aboriginal peoples in North America. It began at dawn one day in late October 1870 near Fort Whoop-up, built illegally by

American traders from Montana only that summer, when a huge party of at least five hundred Cree warriors with their Assiniboine allies attacked a small Blood encampment on the Belly (now Oldman) River. The Cree and their allies had walked and ridden south-west more than two hundred miles from their usual lands to avenge the killing of their aged peace chief, Maskeptetoon (Broken Arm) by Blackfoot the spring before; however, unknown to the attackers, there were several larger camps of the Blackfoot Confederacy in the vicinity, and their warriors, armed with the latest Winchester and Henry repeating rifles and Colt revolvers traded from the Americans, rushed to assist the Bloods. Together they drove the Cree attackers, who had by then destroyed the small Blood camp, back into retreat over the open prairie and into the long Oldman River coulees, and eventually down into the deep valley that today lies between the city centre and the university suburb of West Lethbridge. After four or five hours of vicious fighting, they say, forty Blackfoot were dead and fifty wounded, but the Cree escaped total annihilation only by leaving some three hundred of their dead behind.

After these events the Blackfoot, for whom, like all oral peoples, geographical place names often became the historical record of their living past, began to call the Oldman River valley at that spot Assini-etomochi: "Where They Slaughtered The Cree."

"Slaughter" — a horrific word, with none of the echoing dignity and heroism Europeans attach to such killing encounters when they name them "battle." But it strikes me as an honest word here: slaughter, on a scale impossible for the prairie peoples until Europeans arrived with their guns and horses.

It is an easy walk, now, to get an overview of the field of slaughter. Stone markers and explanatory plaques have been erected at various spots; historian Alex Johnston has collected all available eyewitness accounts into an excellent booklet, *The Battle at Belly River,* first published in 1966 and reissued in 1997 as *The Last Great Indian Battle* with the added findings of an archeological dig to identify the exact western riverbank coulees, just north of today's Whoop-Up Drive, where the Cree and the Assiniboine for a time tried to make their last stand. They were in one long coulee leading down to the river, trying to cover their retreat with musket fire and arrows, but from the parallel coulees on either side of them, the Bloods and the Siksika to the north, the Peigans to the south, they were being raked by the bullets of repeating rifles. In the 1997 book the precise evidence of musket balls and shells and bullets, and a single iron projectile point over three inches long, uncovered at the various sites are exactly mapped, identified and listed. And finally, though building Whoop-Up Drive covered the battle site at that spot, two commemorative parks have been established to preserve most of the vital geographical places: Bull Trail Park in West Lethbridge, which includes the three battle coulees, and Indian Battle Park in the valley where the Cree and their horses fell from banks and cliffs into the river, staggered through the water to die in the open glades and under the massive cottonwoods.

All that a hundred-and-thirty years of facticity and forgetting can reveal about this inter-tribal violence — a typically human revenge disaster of accident and treachery, racial prejudice and hatred, courage, ambition, loyalty, overwhelming brutality and heroic as well as grotesque death — as much evidence as is still findable has been carefully gathered. Though as many as 350 men, and certainly many dozens of women and children, died in 1870 at Assini-etomochi, in the European tradition of inter-tribal violence the Battle at Belly River is, to put it very mildly, not large. To encounter a memory of a typical nineteenth-century slaughter between so-called Christian peoples, one need only fly to Brussels, Belgium, and make the short drive south to the pleasant grainfields surrounding the village of Waterloo. The day was Sunday, June 18, 1815, and on a painted, three-dimensional panorama 110 yards by 12, you can today see in one continuous, horrified stare how "heroically" more than 60,000 men and 10,000 horses were destroyed in the daylight hours of that one Christian "day of rest." Not to speak of the wounded and the maimed, the mentally shattered.

The facticity of even the largest Aboriginal battle in 1870 comes quickly to its end; there can be no archival government lists of men and supplies. For years Blackfoot men must have sung their battle exploits in the warrior lodges; around their family winter campfires, many would certainly have told stories about those coulees "where they slaughtered the Cree." Many oral accounts must have been told, but apparently only one written document by a Blackfoot was ever made, a short chapter in *My People, the Bloods* (1979) by Mike Mountain Horse (1885–1964); he gives no personal details of what his father or grandfather — both warriors in the battle — might have told him. So perhaps, for us, only informed imagination remains.

In my novel *The Temptations of Big Bear*, Big Bear, one of the historical Cree chiefs who fought at Belly River, sings a story of how his third son, Twin Wolverine, fought that violent battle in his own distinctive way. The story is, of necessity, a long lament, and as Big Bear nears the end of it he remembers the Blackoot Winchesters had so much fire-power, the Cree could no longer hold their position:

Finally we had to crawl from our coulee for the river. There was nothing to be seen but smoke and at first they didn't follow, but soon they charged so hard some of us had to retreat down against a ridge which broke off into the river below. Here our few horses left started breaking their legs, the river was deeper against the banks and sucked warriors under when they fell into it. Bear Son was screaming as the grey horse he had taken at the Blood camp snapped both its front legs trying to stick to that sheered-off cliff, "The river's all blood, blood!"

On the edge of the coulee behind us the two Sutherland brothers fighting with us screamed in a white language no one understood and when their legs were finished they lay on them and tore Bloods apart with their teeth and knives, but their yellow hair came free at last and they had to be left there, above the river for the Blood women to finish cutting what was left of them. We were down and through the river by then, some of us, and the Blood warrior Mountain Chief had stabbed Rabbit Head between the shoulders while he was crossing…and then Bear Son had him by the hair and drove his knife into his back; but Mountain Chief was still singing his power song,

"My body will be lying on the plains,
The guns, the knives they hear
Me!"

and his war bonnet had worked down on his neck and the knife stuck in that when Bear Son drove it into him. That Blood saw the handle sticking out behind himself and grabbed it and then the knife drank Cree blood, deep, and Mountain Chief pulled the knife out and stabbed again, still singing, and then held the knife up to Sun, there was nothing to see but horses' teeth foaming, coming at us up out of the river.... And I said to my sons, the two that were left, "Your brother Bear Son lies by the river." We had nothing but a few arrows left, and stones. We were throwing pieces of the black rock that burns at the horses as they kept charging us under the trees.

Little Bad Man stared at me, but my other son Twin Wolverine, suddenly, started to walk. He still held his musket and hadn't fired it once that day; he hadn't opened his mouth and his knife was stuck in his belt with not a drop on it. But now he sang, loud. The song he sang was Coyote's, which we had heard the night before at Little Bow Crossing warning us about the battle, not to go into battle but we wouldn't listen, only Twin Wolverine who walked out into the clearing toward the river where shadows already reached out black from the cliffs. He was walking into those warriors hot with our weapons and our blood and it seemed to me that I had dreamed this somewhere, before, and might dream it again someday when I was very weak. A Peigan wheeled, charged him and I saw my youngest son kneel and aim and pull the trigger and that warrior flew up arms and legs, splattered to the ground and the horse galloped on; another rode at him. He had left the musket where he knelt to shoot and as the Blood came on a beautiful sweating black horse Twin Wolverine ducked aside, the warrior was looping over and there he lay, knife through his throat. All the time my son was singing the new song Coyote had lent him, and all those warriors with Mountain Chief stopped then, not riding at him, and holding their guns in front of them as they watched him walk without a weapon in his hands to the river and lift the body of his brother Bear Son up on his shoulder and turn his back to the sun and come between them to us still singing and the wide valley there quiet at last, hearing that. (346–49)

Today you can park your car beside the cairn in West Lethbridge at the top of Bull Trail Park, and walk down the long battle coulee ridges, walk various trails in the dry cactus earth looking down either right or left to where warriors once crouched with their guns or clubs, walk down to where the cliffs drop sheer into the river. Below you, north over the bent water, where the Cree horses broke their legs and fell, you will see the eroded black heaps of earth marking Nicholas Sheran's first coal mine. You are standing between Whoop-Up Drive Bridge to the south, curving low over the river, and the CPR High Level Bridge to the north, a thin black steel line from cliff to cliff.

I have stood at that spot only once myself, and talked to no one. So I do not know whether, between the endless automobile roar of one bridge and the grinding thunder of a possible train crossing the other, anyone has ever again heard Coyote there, singing.

VI

Lethbridge is not named for its bridge, though it might well be, since the High Level Bridge of the Canadian Pacific Railway is, with the brilliant exception of the University of Lethbridge that architecturally echoes it, the most memorable man-made structure in the city. The Blackfoot, Sarcee and Cree peoples had already, in their various languages, named the river valley at that place "Black Rocks," and the first English name reflected them: the American traders named it "Coal Banks" because Nicholas Sheran dug the first drift coal mines there as early as 1874. So why "Lethbridge"?

In 1882 Sir Alexander Tilloch Galt (1817–1893), a Montreal politician and land developer who was also Canada's High Commissioner in London, organized the North Western Coal and Navigation Company which contracted to supply coal to power the transcontinental CPR then being built across the prairie. One of his London backers was the wealthy bookseller W.H. Smith — bookstores named after him still exist, even in Canada — who interested his friend the publisher William Lethbridge (1825–1901) to help him finance a distant Canadian coal scheme; shortly after, Lethbridge was named president of the development company. That long-faced English gentleman with his narrow nose, curly hair and full round beard was never near the prairie, nor did he ever make the slow sea voyage to Canada; so why was the city not named "Galt" after Sir Alexander? Or for his son Elliot Torrance Galt who travelled the prairie far and wide on horseback and first recommended that the coal on the Belly River be developed; who with his family lived in the splendid house they called Coaldale among the cottonwoods and mines on the river valley flats for some twenty years, expanding those mines and building river boats and railroads and irrigation systems and farming settlements? Indeed, if some London financier who held shares in the company (there were soon over thirty English investors) was to have the honour of his name attached to a spot on the unknown and limitless Canadian prairie, why not choose banker Edward Crabb, who in 1891 was the largest single backer with 1500 shares, two hundred more than Smith and Lethbridge combined?

Galt: since 1827 there had already been a Galt in Ontario. And if Victorian ladies blushed to say they lived on the Belly River, as they evidently did, then what could possibly be said for living in a town named Crabb?

Naming a place in what, to an European, seems to be a "new and empty" land can be a complicated affair, as North-West Mounted Police Inspector Ephrem A. Brisebois discovered, to his rage. In 1875 he and his detachment built a police post where the Bow and Elbow Rivers meet, and he simply named it after himself; but NWMP Commissioner James Macleod, who had not hesitated to name the post he built on the Oldman after himself and had allowed Inspector James Walsh the same privilege in the Cypress Hills, cancelled "Fort Brisebois" because among other things, like Brisebois' personal insubordination, he felt it was really too awkward to pronounce. As was often done with French names, it might have been translated into something easier, like "Fort Breaks Wood" or, with a bit of license, "Fort Breeze in the Timber"; we do have unique prairie names like Medicine Hat and Moose Jaw, even Tete Jaune Cache. But when a dour Scot controls naming, we're sure to be stuck with that of his ancestral estate back home; in this case, Calgary on the Isle of Mull in the Hebrides. In Gaelic that word may mean "Clear Running Water," but more likely "Pasture on the Bay."

In any case, Alex Galt knew the value of memorializing his shareholders and so gave his banker a small due by naming a street on the 1885 town plan as Crabb (the present 6th Street South), but labeled the town he forsaw with a Devon publisher's name,

"Lethbridge." The largest city in Alberta not begun as a fort: that is, as a walled or palisaded settlement of a few apprehensive Europeans trying to keep the wilderness they feared, wildness in its myriad natural and possibly savage — especially savagely human — forms, somehow at bay. No, in 1885 the wide, short-grass plain where the Alberta Coal Company Railway ended on the cliffs high above the thick black seams of coal eroded bare far below them was laid out as a wholly owned company town with a geometric grid of streets from Baroness Road (today 1st Avenue) to London Road (7th Avenue), and Galt Street (Scenic Drive) to Westminister Road (13th Street). In this staggering bare world of light, perpetual wind, horizonless land and gaunt dryness, where the most cheerful flowers were briefly blooming cactus and water at best a distant line of muddy river buried in a wide valley, the names of home helped anchor the newcomers.

The only town in Canada named after a publisher. As a writer, I like that.

And, as one might expect, the publisher's name (thank goodness it wasn't erased later, like the street names, into something Scottishly orderly like City No. 3) persists with wider, intriguing possibilities. Whatever Mr. Lethbridge's family history may be, *leth* is an obsolete Old English word meaning "hatred" or "ill-will" — modern "lethal" derives from it — and if we consider that prefix a bit more we can further find Lethe: the river of forgetfulness running through the Greek hell of Hades, or *lith*, meaning "stone." Leth-bridge, translated as "Stonebridge"? "Bridge of Hate"? "Bridge Crossing to Hell"?

Such wordplay is best left to poets, hopefully those with a sense of comedy. Beyond any "leth," the "bridge" remains fixed, and today in the centre of Lethbridge a tremendous bridge literally exists as a stunning, physical fact. Galt could not have imagined that fact when he chose the name he did for the town he needed to build if he was to make money for his shareholders – coal needs miners and miners need houses, and companies need indentured families who will re-circulate the money they earn back into other company businesses. Nevertheless, after 1909, when both namer and namee were long dead, how strangely and evocatively appropriate the name became.

The 1993 edition of Alex Johnston's book *The C.P. Rail High Level Bridge at Lethbridge* tells the story of how this improbable steel viaduct bridge was constructed. Beginning with geological formation drilling (November 22, 1906), the book presents detailed information and a startling picture album on every aspect of the work, from pouring the concrete blocks which must support the bents in that geometry of steel reaching out into the vast space of the valley – a steel spider's web slowly shaping itself in air 314 feet above the river as the erection traveller with its eleven miles of cable to lower steel girders into place crept forward over the valley on the piers already riveted in place – to a picture of the last steel girder fitting perfectly into the west abutment 5327.625 feet from the east abutment, lowered into place on June 22, 1909. This final picture even reveals two workmen jumping to the ground as the girder is lowered, and the caption notes that "this action terminated their employment with the contractor" (Johnston 28).

Strangely enough, both the river and the antediluvian layers of coal declared their fixed opposition to the bridge in unmistakable ways:

One of the wildest and heaviest Oldman River floods in recorded history ripped through the valley below Lethbridge, filling it from bank to bank, in June, 1908. The flood tore away the concrete forms and all the substructures of the bridge not already anchored deep in the earth, and knocked out the coal-burning power plant that served the city.

Barely had the river receded when contractors found that bridge Piers 21N and 22N were sinking. A shaft was dug between them, and it was discovered that the piers had been built above the long-abandoned diggings of a drift mine from which danger-ous coal gas drifted up. On July 15, 1908 a ten-year-old boy from the valley houses nearby climbed down to play on the timbers of the shaft; he was overcome by the gas and collapsed on the beams. Two workmen who tried to rescue him were also overcome; they fell off the beams to the bottom of the shaft and were dead before they could be brought out. The boy, who had not been working on the bridge but simply playing there, lived.

Of course, mere nature has never, anywhere, ultimately stopped the Canadian Pacific Railway from buckling its double-steel belt tight over the landscape of Canada. Less than a year later, in the afternoon of the day when the last girder was fitted into place between piers 65/66 and the concrete abutment on the western river cliff, one hundred Lethbridge residents standing on open flatcars rolled across the bridge.

They found themselves so high they were looking down on the backs of soaring eagles.

VII

"Lethbridge was happiness," novelist Joy Kogawa tells a confer-ence audience on "Dilemmas of Reconciliation" in 1999. "A city with restaurants, stores, Woolworths…"

She is talking about how a Canadian child of Japanese ances-try experienced World War II, particularly the memory of her family — her father was an ordained Anglican minister — being forced out of their home in Vancouver where she was born, and how at the age of six the mountain forests of Slocan, BC, surrounded her, and, a few years later, the seemingly horizonless sugar beets under a staggering Alberta sun. "To come into Lethbridge for a day," she says, "from the shack on the farm where we lived, to walk on a sidewalk again, that was happiness."

The not-really-so-innocent sidewalks of Lethbridge, which was once so strongly British that by 1916 20% of its population had enlisted for World War I military service, the highest percentage of any city in Canada. But in 1943 little Joy Nakayama (as she was then) had no idea that her fellow Canadians of Asian ancestry, the Chinese, had once been forced by city bylaw to live and allowed to have businesses only west of 4th Street in what was called The Segregated Area, a space so limited "the Celestials," as *The Lethbridge News* wrote slyly on December 23, 1910, "want to set up business in the coulees." That particularly offensive bylaw was rescinded in 1916, but the area remained predominantly Chinese, and the same part of the old town core quickly became the home for prostitution when, after 1918, the bordellos on The Point, which had originally moved up the coulees from The Bottoms of the river valley, sidled ever closer to the "nice, clean, English" business district along 5th Street. The amazing range of prostitution in Lethbridge is vividly described in a chapter of James Gray's, *Red Lights on the Prairies* (1971), though the subject seems large enough to deserve a book of its own. The Lethbridge Lodge Hotel now blocks the site of The Point, but if you walk around the building and across its parking lot and west over the bulldozed flat between widening coulees to the viewpoint overlooking Fort Whoop-Up and Indian Battle Park, you are essentially walking down the centre of the old bordello street. By the early fifties, when I first drove south along 2nd Street, the magnificent panorama of The Point and its tangled, vivid history were already buried under official forgetfulness and the rusting wrecks of an automobile graveyard.

This intersection of restricted Chinese people and officially tolerated vice, which was so beneficial for all the "proper" local businesses that it received strong and continuous support from all the "Christian" businessmen around Galt Gardens, was most active along 3rd Avenue and 3rd Street South, the block now occupied by the new Provincial Courthouse. The growth of the Segregated Area "ushered in," as Johnston and Peat write in *Lethbridge Place Names* (1987), "Lethbridge's golden age of prostitution, as the district operated in wide-open fashion until 1944." The services the area provided, not only for solitary coalminers and cowboys and laundry workers and settlers, but also, as numerous reports declared, "for the married men of the city," were regulated by City Council and enforced by City Police as discretely as they could, but for obvious economic and taxpayer reasons they would not, as at various times the local churches tried to insist, be by-lawed out of existence.

Nevertheless, in March 1942 the Lethbridge City Council could, and did, pass a racially discriminatory, paranoid bylaw about Japanese Canadians evacuated from the West Coast, a law even children had to know about. It stated "that any Japanese moved [into the district must] remain domiciled on the farms to which they are allocated, and that they will not move and reside in the City of Lethbridge." This really meant that certain Canadians could neither go to school in the city nor find employment there between the beet-working seasons.

But through the fortunate accident of our late births, when Joy Nakayama and I were growing up and attending the same school in the neighbouring town of Coaldale, this Lethbridge history of racial prejudice was, at least officially, over; by 1947 the Segregated Area was no more and the bylaw against Canadians of Japanese birth had been rescinded. For me, as for Joy, the city spreading east across the prairie from the lip of the Oldman River cliffs and coulees seemed merely wonderful. A lake park for swimming surrounded by huge trees, its cowboy name, Slaughter House Slough, long forgotten; entire blocks of great early-century houses with tall, pillared entrances and wide verandas that swept around two entire walls, their fret-work gables and round turret windows fit for Sleeping Beauties and, most amazing of all, roof shingles laid in wavy lines bending and curving around each other over rounded dormers; a steel bridge from beneath which you could see crossing, as through clouds, the steam trains of the almighty Canadian Pacific Railway, which had carried my penniless family of refugees halfway round the world from Communism to Canada on a simple Mennonite promise to "pay our debt," enormous engines shifting and bumping freight cars in the railroad yard under blasts of steam and then disappearing to sleep in their roundhouse dialed by rails turning like a clock; the corrugated-steel tipple and water tower of Number Eight Coal Mine rising above the distant cliffs of the Oldman River where the thin bridge closed into its vanishing point, and where our high school class once dropped two thousand feet, they told us, into the earth to discover blind horses walking the black tunnels there and black-faced miners with lamps in their foreheads who knelt on rock and, as it seemed in the darkness, prayed with shovels and forks all day before the gleaming, broken face of a coal

seam; and the towered, clocked Canada Post Office mirrored by
the Marquis Hotel whose magnificent lobby no child could dare
enter, and the Trianon Ballroom where a dutiful little Mennonite
kid did not even want to imagine what went on; McGuire's Mens
Wear full of clothing probably designed for English lords and Leo
Singer's Mens and Boys Wear on 5th Street where my mother
once bought me a high-necked knitted shirt (T-shirts did not
yet exist by name), and, beyond everything else, the Lethbridge
Public Library.

Surrounded by the shorn grass and splendid trees of Galt
Gardens, a huge brick building devoted totally to books.

The yellow school bus that brought shoppers from Coaldale
every Saturday parked at the corner of the Gardens, 3rd Avenue
and 7th Street. My mother and sister would go shopping and
I, after studying again — Don't Touch! — the astounding display of magazines and newspapers at the Club Cigar Store (I
did not know it had once been part of the Hotel Coaldale) while
devouring a five-cent ice-cream cone, I would cross 3rd Avenue,
pass the smiling man in the corner kiosk with all his golden pop-
corn, and walk up the granite and limestone steps into the library.
If the disorder that in 1933 caused the Carnegie Foundation to
name the Lethbridge Library the most poorly planned facility it
had ever helped sponsor — truly a "librarian's nightmare" — that
handicap, if it remained in 1948, was completely unnoticed by me.
Thousands of books on open stacks, to reach up for, to take in
your hands, to hold, to open, anywhere in their hundreds of pages.
And read. When the Senator Buchanan addition was built, I sat
in the alcove in the tall, narrow window facing east and read on.

So many, many available books; with time I began to understand that I needed one completely to myself. To keep. There

was no bookstore in Lethbridge then, but Southern Stationers offered a short shelf of The Modern Library and on December 1, 1951 (name and date recorded inside the front cover) I bought W. Somerset Maugham's 1915 novel *Of Human Bondage*. What a title for me, and how utterly typical a novel to find in Canada then: Philip Carey with his club foot and servants and a living of 500 pounds a year and having tea in an absolutely nineteenth-century English world, and his o-so-sensitive and endless search for himself; his *self!* A character I eventually found so effete the sheerest drift of wind off the Oldman River would disappear him like dust. As he jolly well deserved.

But there was the rug; that remained hooked, an existential burr caught in my memory. In chapter 106, page 654, Philip suddenly understands what his friend Cronshaw meant when he gave him a Persian rug that, he told Philip, would offer an answer to his question about the meaning of life: "The answer was obvious. Life had no meaning."

To look to a rug for the meaning of your life? Meaning came through books. No, my mother said, from only one book, The Great Book called The Bible. And when sometimes I could not completely believe her then, I nevertheless wanted to all the more.

There is another memorable line, on the final page of Maugham's novel. There Philip asks Sally to marry him, and Sally, that perfect blonde embodiment of calm English beauty, answers without a flicker of emotion,

"If you like... Oh, of course, I'd like to have a house of my own..." (760).

The ultimate human desire: a house. At barely sixteen I considered this conclusion less than ludicrous; now I cannot be so sure. The desire for house: it is perhaps too easy for those who have never truly experienced either poverty or depression (both world-wide and/or personal), or deprivation or violence or war to belittle the idea of suburb, which began in Levittown, New York, for veterans of World War II, and whose Cape Cod and ranch bungalows with their L-shaped living room-dining fenced onto cul-de-sac streets mushroomed all over North America. For centuries my forebears had lived in close clusters of homes all around the walled city of Danzig, or in the farm villages on the Vistula Delta of Poland and later on the steppes of Ukraine and Russia; only the cruelty of Canada's Homestead Act forced them here on the western prairie into the sometimes devastating isolation of single farmsteads. I worked myself through university building suburb houses, beginning with Art Batty Construction in the Lethbridge district of Glendale east of Mayor Magrath Drive in 1953. At eighteen I could walk the top plate of a 2x4 wall as easily as stroll down a sidewalk; when the milk wagon trotted by, we construction grunts bought chocolate milk and strawberry ice cream for our morning break, sawed the cold bricks in half and ate them with woodchips for spoons. Glendale, and over the years all the Lakeviews, Tudors, and so on, then University West to Varsity Heights and Indian Battle Heights — until in 1999 the builders discovered, again at long last, the beauty of the deep river valley, its marvelous shelter from the wind, and now you can follow the bent pavement south, down into the ultimate Lethbridge double-garage-facing-the-street-with-golf-course suburb of Paradise Canyon.

Paradise. Canyon. Somehow contradictory words I would not immediately associate with real estate development. To be downright bookish about it, for Dante in The Divine Comedy it is Hell which is the canyon, one of increasing horrors as it circles down into the frozen centre of the earth; his Purgatory is a dazzling mountain, but Paradise culminates in the vast white blossom of a rose on whose petals are seated the spirits of the Forever Blessed. Ultimate paradise is flower and sky.

Well, paradise. The Segregation District has been gone for over half a century; only one or two vivid, austere brick buildings, a single wooden cottage overgrown and moldering on an alley remain; paradise on earth may well be for each of us wherever we can imagine we find it; it may very well be in an unforgettable river valley. In the golden evening light of Paradise Canyon the Canada geese that raise their long necks from the golf greens to watch me walking, the motionless scatter of deer resting on the hillside above the brick and stucco houses as I drive by, seem to me to be the perfect fauna reflections of the incorruptible river that continues to slip between the black and rounded stones, past the tall, eroded clay cliffs on its unending and circular journey from the mountains to the ocean to the blue and cloud-blossoming sky.

VIII

When April snow suddenly sweeps west from the mountains, people in southern Alberta are invariably confused. This is spring? For weeks we've had temperatures of fifteen, sometimes twenty above, T-shirts and shorts have appeared on sidewalks, crocuses and small cacti on the coulee hills are budding, most of the winter sand has been vacuumed off the streets, and now this? Again? Ten below and more snow than we've seen all winter, thick heavy flakes as if we had been exiled east to the St. Lawrence Valley in February.

The meteorologists are, of course, superbly helpful after the fact. They will tell us exactly why this happened, though they themselves did not anticipate it, as if knowing the scientific reasons will make us all content and happy: "Cold air moving southwest from Nunavut [it is now an official territory and can henceforth be blamed for most of the worst weather in Canada] has collided with slightly warmer, wet Pacific air coming across the northern mountains from BC." The point is, apparently, that if the Pacific air had come via Vancouver rather than the north, we'd have had a chinook, that is, warmth and headaches and crazy behaviour and happiness all around, but, as it happens, two cold fronts bumping have made a snowstorm.

Weather Where the Black Rocks Lie in the Old Man's River is forever the result of something happening far away, something moving in on us.

And meteorologists are wrigglers who thrive in lakes of statistics. Eleven centimetres of snow has already fallen on April 15, 2000, with perhaps another four or five to come, and then, before they can be stopped, they tell us what we try not to think about every spring: that April snow actually happens quite regularly. On April 13, 1996 4.5 centimetres of snow fell, on April 5, 1993 19.4 centimetres, on April 1990, in May 1988 and also May 1884 – if you listen, they'll happily bury you in a hundred and twenty years of irrefutable snow.

On the vast, sloping steppes of southern Alberta, weather is what it is, unavoidably weather. And if you were once young in Lethbridge, it is inevitable that you will return again and again. All your life, for parents, sisters and brothers and cousins and nieces and nephews, reunions, weddings; and increasingly, as you age, for funerals. Number Two Highway carries you south on cruise control from clear, sunlit Edmonton to lowering Calgary and on south, parallel to the long sky of shining mountains.

But today the foothills and the front wall of the Rockies slowly sift away in low, grey light; around the homes of Nanton bushes are clumped with snow, by Claresholm the evergreens and the crotches of green maples are as romantically draped as Christmas cards. Beyond the white ditches cattle bend into their sprawls of hay, occasional horses stand hip-shot in the snowy stubble, and soon you find yourself driving in a layer of moving mist, as if spirits were breathing hot and low around the wheels of your car, leading you away on an endless stream like thinning memory. Vehicles approach, they float past, silent and drifting as transparent ghosts. When you ease aside at the Oldman River Crossing, down among the layered and bent cottonwoods near Fort Macleod, you see your wheel-wells are hung tight with thick icicles, your entire car has become an antediluvian animal scaled over by the flow of grey, frozen slush. In this perfect world of exquisite rime, you have crawled out of the warm belly of a prehistoric beast armoured in steel ice.

And from inside it, on CBC Radio Two a mellifluous black voice, Sarah Vaughan's, is singing. So tenderly in the sharp and delicate spring air:

I've heard of a city called heaven,
And I know I will soon be there.

2000

THE SWEET FICTION
OF OWNING LAND

Writing is the judicial method which serveth
best the invention of truth.

RICHARD HOOKER

Eight of us are walking from our log house, down the wooded hill
towards Strawberry Creek. The poplars open wide to a meadow
stripped flat for coal fifty years ago, and I gesture, whisper, "In
the evening, sometimes, the deer —" and the instant we look right
there is a great buck, bounding away. As if he's been running forever with his tail hoisted white. We can only gasp, crowd forward
together to see the blur of him before he vanishes.

But at the edge of the meadow he stops, his body in perfect
side-profile against the pale trunks of the trees. Turns his pointed
head to stare at us motionless. We can see his short antlers are
furred, sprouting fast for the fall rut. He has certainly heard us
coming, and smells us, but what does he see? A cluster of erect
creatures shuffling together, more and more heads thrust out at

him from the slope of the hill; a concentration of eyes? With an ineffable ease of muscle his body ripples, shifts, lifts itself over the barbed-wire fence and gone; only the green and gold flicker of autumn leaves.

How can I imagine I "own" this land?

We walk down the eroded bentonite scar of the strip mine and across the meadow but, moving as silently as we may along the trail through bush, we hear beaver before we see one. The hard smash of a flat tail on water, and between spruce a great blue heron lifts the spear of its long body, rises like its magnificent name from the pond and away over the cliffs. Only surface ripples intersecting each other behind the curl of the dam, and someone hisses, points at a wedge of water at our feet: a muskrat paddling, all legs frantic, for an overhanging bank. Then the water bulges, opens. The dark nostrils and ears of a beaver arrow parallel to where we stand. A vee folds over the pond away from its lodge towards the dam, turns, overlaps, forges back again, the beaver keeping an exact distance from us silently, swimming and swimming. We watch the dark head nudge higher into the gold water of the sinking sun, we strain binoculars to peer at the unblinking eye and furry ear, into the breathing, pulsing nostril.

"Grandpa! There's a coyote, there..."

Camilo is pointing across the pond to the cliff and massive driftpile of logs where the creek cuts north against the coal-seam. I look, incredulous. Coyotes often appear in open fields, even near the house, and every twilight their communal hunting howls shiver into echoes along the valley, but we have never seen one near a beaver.

"A coyote?" I can't see it.

"There," he whispers, "under those willows."

The beaver swims beyond Camilo's finger, smacks its tail on the turn and disappears in a roil of water, then emerges swimming back the length of the pond to the lodge, turns, smacks, swims towards the dam again. The shadow of a raven passes over us — whiff, whiff, whiff, whiff — and then I comprehend what I see: coyote. Under the green willows like a smudge of brownish mist, his front paws on a driftpile log and peering down, ears cocked, into the narrow channel dug by the beavers to float their logs; his body poised, intense as if none of us watching him existed.

"Oh-h-h-h," Rocio murmurs, so happy she wraps her arms around me, "we've never seen this, never."

True. It seems, after thirty years, for a moment all our eyes opened together and we could recognize what was already always here: these twilight animals whose indelible presence we have felt before, and seen singly, but who, for this moment, have materialized together around us. And the many others we do not see, mysteries that may be revealed if we live here long enough, and gently.

"A man without land is nobody."
Simcha Kravitz

Strawberry Creek bends four times through the 129 hectares more or less of land which my wife Tena and I "hold as joint tenants" near Telfordville, Alberta. On the cliff overlooking the second bend we have built a house of Douglas fir logs and cedar shakes brought from the Fraser Valley where Tena grew up, and from its decks or windows we look down on water that flows towards the North Saskatchewan River, down the tilt of the continent through Edmonton and across Saskatchewan and Manitoba, seeking Hudson Bay. Our grandchildren and friends know that the ice we skate on in winter will soon melt, and some tiny bit of that melting will eventually join the oceans that circle the globe.

We walk everywhere: through aspen and birch and white spruce forest uplands; in the creek valley of cliffs layered by sandstone, coal, clay, and thick with alder and deadfall and towering balsam, swamps floating yellow with lilies in spring and oxbows of shining brown water. We sink into moss in a muskeg dense with black spruce, where wasps burrow their nests and swarm out to nuzzle your neck and wrists with their stingers, or hike across the field which opens a square kilometre of grey-wooded soil to cloud and wind-driven sky and is cultivated by a neighbour either as crop or hay or pasture. Every season of land is the same, is different in colour, smell, cold and heat, the texture of air, the silence of footsteps or the wind in trees, in sunlight or mist or moon or stars or the shifting drift and explosions of northern lights. During the long twilight of northern summer you hear the air simmering with bees.

And the changing course of the creek; every rise and wash of it, heavy rain or spring run-off or re-channeling by beaver dams, exposes more petrified wood, more black, delicately veined Genesee leaves that were imprinted on sandstone by an immense fall of volcanic ash seventy million years ago. In the Strawberry creek bed our neighbour Bruce Morden discovered the legbone of a mastodon that lived here, University of Alberta archeologists say, one hundred thousand years before us.

We order our world with language; order it legally by words on paper. Tena and I have a large paper called "Certificate of Title" issued by the North Alberta Land Registration District; it declares we are "the owner of an estate in fee simple of land west of Meridian 5, in Range 2," etc., etc. "An estate in *fee simple*" means land in which the inheritor has power of control, of use and disposition. An estate *of* and *in* a measured and uniquely coded parcel of Canadian land: these English prepositions, so tiny and yet so crucial, echo the most absolute clause in Treaty Number Six to which twenty-one Cree and one Chipewayan chief and many councilors Xed their names at Forts Carlton and Pitt in 1876:

> The Plain and Wood Cree Tribes of Indians and all other Indians inhabiting the district…do hereby cede, release, surrender and yield up to the Government of the Dominion of Canada for Her Majesty the Queen and her successors forever… (Morris 352)

"Of" and "in," "up," "to," "for": some of the tiniest and seemingly simplest words in our language. Also the most powerful.

At least when inscribed in indelible ink on historic documents. A mere nine years later, when the Cree Chief Big Bear was on trial for his involvement in the 1885 Rebellion, Mr. Justice Hugh Richardson told him that the Cree People "had never owned the land, that it belonged to the Queen, who allowed them to use it, and that when She wanted to make other use of it She called them together through Her officers, and gave them [i.e., the Cree] the choicest portions of the country."

The land belongs to the Queen. Richardson's legal pronoun-cement, as quoted in the *Regina Leader*, October 1, 1885 was of course simplistic to the point of being dead wrong. He was speak-ing of the land in western Canada as if the Common Law of England applied to it, and that in its most ancient and medieval aspect of the absolutist legal principle of *nulle terre sans seigneur* — no land without a lord — which asserts that all land in Britain is "held" by the Crown, though not actually "owned" by the Crown. As A.W. Brian Simpson explains in *A History of the Land Law* (1986), even in medieval England the king was not seen as literally *owning* the land; rather, "the King was lord, ultimately, of all the tenants of the realm. Technically, land is not subject of absolute ownership but of tenure [Latin: 'to hold']."

Saskatchewan law professor James Sakej Henderson explains this further; the concept of land being "held" by the crown, he writes, is "a legal fiction." The word "fiction" in this context means "a conventional acceptance of something as fact that in reality is not a fact," and in their book *Aboriginal Tenure in the Constitution of Canada* (2000), Henderson and his co-authors elaborate on this astonishing legal phrase: in British law the doctrine of Crown tenure is viewed as "a legal fiction of the common law," that is, it exists as an assumption created for the purposes of justice and designed not to create any injury (67–70).

So, the concept of "crown tenure" is "a legal fiction" created for the purpose of justice to all. It may well be that this British concept of law is rooted in the Judeo-Christian principle stated in Psalm 24 —

> The earth is the Lord's and all that is in it,
> The world and all who live in it.

— and that therefore the King, who in medieval times was considered God's representative on earth, was responsible to distribute the land justly among all its possible tenants. Today, after feudal kings have vanished and the very concept of "the Lord" has faded, this fundamental principle of human right nevertheless remains our Common Law: just tenancy for all who live on the earth.

"O Canada, your home's on native land."
Elijah Harper

As Henderson points out, Aboriginal concepts of land fit together with English Common Law in the sense that they too speak not of ownership but of tenure, of holding the land as the original occupants when the European guests, as the Aboriginals called them, first arrived in North America. In the centuries since that first arrival, more than four hundred treaties signed between the Native Peoples and Whites have created what we today call Canada. These treaties, large and small, were enacted in the words of Treaty Six in 1876, the treaty that deals with the territory "our" land in Alberta lies in: "so that there may be peace and good will between them [i.e., the Aboriginal Peoples] and Her Majesty" (Morris 351).

Sadly, we all realize that Canada's largest treaties have often not dealt fairly with the Aboriginal Peoples. This unfairness must continue to be re-dressed by law, as the Supreme Court ruling in *Delgamuukw vs. British Columbia* did for the Gitksan and Wet'suwet'en people in 1997. However, I personally can feel nothing but gratitude towards those people who lived here since pre-historic time. In Canada my parents, fleeing personal and religious persecution in the Soviet Union, found a place to live as human beings with human rights, found land where they could work and hope in peace. This is true because Canada is a particular country forged by the uniqueness of the land itself and the just, united property understandings of the Aboriginal Peoples, the French civil code and English common law.

The problems of creating our country out of "the legal fiction" of crown land tenure is already there in the wisdom of the chiefs who negotiated the numbered treaties of the Canadian west. It is there in 1871 when Cree Chief Sweetgrass in Fort Edmonton dictates a letter to Governor Archibald in Winnipeg, being careful to use language a white person will understand:

> Great Father – I shake hands with you, and bid you welcome.... We heard our lands were sold, and we did not like it...we don't want to sell our lands... they are our property, and no one has a right to sell them. (Morris 170)

That wisdom is there in the rich imagery of Ojibwa Chief Mawedopenais debating Treaty Three at Fort Francis in 1873:

> we think that the Great Spirit has planted us on this ground where we are, as you were where you come from. ... Our hands are poor, but our heads are rich... The sound of the rustling of the gold is under my feet where I stand; we have a rich country; it is the Great Spirit who gave us this; where we stand upon is the Indians' property, and belongs to them. (Morris 59, 61, 62)

And in 1877 at Treaty Seven when the Blackfoot Councillor Button Chief declares it plain and straight: "The Great Spirit, and not the Great Mother, gave us this land" (Morris 270).

We can easily recognize the ideological, the legal, and the spiritual principle that underlies this statement. Paul of Tarsus, a Jewish man and the first Christian philosopher, explained exactly this to the Greek parliament of first century Athens: "The God who made the world and everything in it...he made from one every nation of men to live on all the face of the earth, having determined allotted periods and the boundaries of their habitation" (Acts 17: 24, 26).

In Button Chief's words: "The Great Spirit... gave *us* this land."

When my family arrived in Treaty Six country in 1930, no one questioned whose land it was; certainly not refugee peasants who spoke no word of English. For my Russian Mennonite parents, as for all peoples forced to flee their birthplace, land was life and with profound gratitude and utter amazement they accepted a place on the land Canada offered them.

"I remember the land being so beautiful when I was a child, as though it were newly created."
Mary Agnes Bonnetrouge

For over fifty years I have had a bluish card laminated in plastic labelled "Certificate of Birth." It reveals:

> Birth Date: Oct 4, 1934
> Name: Rudy Henry Wiebe
> Birthplace: Sec.31, Tp.52, Rge.17, W3rd, Saskatchewan

That's a place? Where a person can be born? It is, of course, the geographical numbered code for an exact western Canada location, and it is easily interpreted. Our enormous prairie was surveyed and measured into English miles in a global system of meridians, ranges, townships and sections. These coordinate numbers indicate that I was not born in any named place like a village or city, but rather — to read the code from the largest to the smallest unit — born west of the Third Meridian in Range 17, Township 52, within the square mile of Section 31. To be even more precise, I could add that I was born on the Southwest Quarter of Section 31.

Knowing the code, you can find that physical place if you want to very badly. First, drive ten miles north of Glaslyn on Saskatchewan Highway Number Four; at the Jack Pine Road sign turn west for four miles, then two miles north and another mile west to the dead end facing a spruce muskeg. Then you must walk south along the overgrown road allowance, over the hill, half a mile to where barbed-wire fences parallel plowed fields and the grass of the Fairholme Community Pasture. Climb right into the pasture, angle a bit south of west another half a mile, through a swamp, past multicoloured cows and their startled, bucking calves, to an obvious wooded knoll where, ten steps inside the bush, a cellar hole of dumped stones, several poplars and a coyote den marks the site where my father and brothers were building a log house when I arrived too soon and my mother bore me in a temporary cabin behind that house. With "Mrs. Aug. Beicht. Fairholme. Attendant at birth." I was always so impatient, my mother said, and large for the time, but as her seventh and last child I emerged easily.

Our family lived on various homesteads in the Jack Pine and Speedwell School Districts, as they were then called, until May 1947. Some two to three hundred farming people lived there with us, large immigrant families trying to clear the boreal forest into homestead grain fields, raising their children through years of Depression and war. Now on almost every quarter section of the Fairholme Community Pasture only cellar hollows and bits of logs remain — sometimes with the crushed torso of an ancient car — over eleven square miles of stony landscape and farmyards bulldozed and burned and planted into huge fields of grass. But I could tell the owners of the cattle I meet there, and the cowboys that tend them, the individual name of every child with me in school when I was learning to speak and read English; take them to the stacked jack pine walls that are all that remain of Speedwell School #4860, or to the crest of the valley where the Speedwell Mennonite Brethren Church is a sunken cellar space with a rim of its gasoline-barrel heater still visible in the hole, lead them through deadfall bush to the small cemetery — thirty graves in three rows: children, men, women — where my sister Helen was buried in 1945, the stone and hollow of her place — oh, there could be endless story telling on this rolling land of cattle and glacial erratics and white-tail deer walking the bare skylines of the east-west eskers. Stories that live in the long memories of people aging across Canada and on every continent. All we have to do is speak them.

So, how do I imagine I own this land?

Four hundred and seventy kilometres west of Speedwell, as the raven flies, I walk between poplars along Strawberry Creek: simply another part of the immense Canadian boreal forest of my childhood. The February snow is almost a metre deep. I wear snowshoes designed eons ago by boreal Ojibwa people and a parka sewn for me by Christina Felix in Tuktoyaktuk on the Arctic Ocean, which she beautifully hand-trimmed with wolverine fur along every edge and the front claws at my neck. I angle up the steep bank, past the point on the cliff where coyotes last spring destroyed a Canada goose nest, the huge eggs crushed and lapped up, come out into the clearing of fire pit and garden, cross the ravine bridge and see that the feeder beside the house is aswarm with birds. This is not the season for finch or grosbeak or thrush, but there is a downy woodpecker among the flitting chickadees, and a red-breasted nuthatch walking down a dead poplar head-first as usual, waiting to dart out at the swinging feeder. Tiny creatures, clothed in feathers, riding air at thirty below.

How do we "own" land? It is important to remember that, in entrepreneurial Alberta, private land ownership consists of only the top six inches of soil. Everything below that — and in particular all the oil and gas and coal — by law belongs to a community called "the people of Alberta." I like that, very much. The depths of the earth's resources should be shared as a public good, not benefit individuals only. And "owning" even that six inches is a "legal fiction" — *fiction,* from the Latin word *fict-us,* to fashion or form, something that is imaginatively invented — that is, the concept of ownership is created by legal words on a legal paper for the purposes of order and justice to all.

Clearly, we cannot "possess land" in the way we can, for example, possess a piece of food when we eat it and it becomes part of us; or own clothes that we alone wear until they are, as we say, worn out; or own anything we can carry. In fact, when I contemplate the land that surrounds and sustains me — as land sustains everyone; without land we have nothing to eat, no place to live on, in fact, without land it is impossible for humans to exist — I feel I no more possess land than I possess the blood heritage of which I am inexplicably born. But I *was* born and am, for the moment, alive, and therefore as a human I can speak and write about what and who *I* am, about what and who *you* are.

Consequently, in keeping with the legal fiction of justly making words, I believe the best, perhaps only, way we can begin to understand what "owning land" means is for us to contemplate, together, the magnificent question a Gitksan elder once asked Canadian government officials:

"If this is your land, where are your stories?"

The land becomes ours as we tell each other our stories.

After the animals have again moved into their evening invisibility, we eight eddy along the beaver pond. We listen to the water running at the dam. Strawberry Creek is fed by springs and muskegs, and we have never known it to stop flowing. Bright water, moving water, ho! anyone who wants, come, come down to the water.

The sun is gone beyond the trees. Evening mist rises from the pond. The willows and alders and birch and the great, grey-riven trunks of the balsam poplars begin to merge upward into white. My tall son Chris and I walk back along the path. The wall of trees before us opens to sky over the white-tail meadow. A thicker mist is drifting there, and then we see — even as we see it we know it is gone — the slender darkness of what may be a woman, may be a man, fading there, passing into brighter, golden, light. As it was and ever shall be.

2004

ON DEATH AND WRITING

"The twentieth century shall be the century of Canada!" So declaimed Sir Wilfrid Laurier, Prime Minister of Canada, in January 1904. And he would lay claim to this century again and again for over a year (House of Commons address, February 21, 1905). Eighty-three years into the century we can see more clearly; even allowing for normal political balderdash, the statement is ridiculous.

And it would have been ridiculous even if Theodore Roosevelt had said it at that time about the United States; or Vladimir Lenin, exiled in London and dreaming about the nation of workers and peasants he was convinced he would establish in his native land, a proletariat that, when he had a chance to found that nation, would prove as intractable as any nobility and he would end by hacking out a nation not ruled by a dictatorial and repressive czar, but by a party so brutally oppressive that anyone, even Lenin I think in his worst nightmares, would have prayed to avoid it; if he had had anyone to pray to, besides himself perhaps.

If the twentieth century belongs to any single nation, surely it is the nation of the dead. I mean that enormous nation of the man-made dead which during this century continues to develop with such deliberate, such dreadful, steady speed. The tiniest, most poverty-stricken of countries have often contributed most to its gross national product. Its geographical territory is everywhere, from the veldt of South Africa to the "civilized" cities of Europe and the jungles of Vietnam, or the sands of the Middle East and the bleak rock of the Falkland Islands. At times its population has grown by ten, twelve, and even fifteen million people a year; today (1984) its inhabitants number at least one hundred and eighty million, probably more for no real census has ever been, or can be, taken. Of these citizens, no more than 25% are soldiers; the rest are civilians (who always constitute the bulk of any nation), the children, the old men and women, the farm and factory workers, the mothers, the sick and the crippled, all caught within the boundaries of their proper countries by the relentless maw of this century's death machine, and ground down into violent emigration by that machine.

Scientifically, that machine has been developed to such a point of imaginative brilliance that now it provides the nation of the dead with an overwhelming capacity for growth. Indeed, it seems quite likely that the end of the twentieth century will see only one nation left on earth, and if we are ever going to have a name for it, perhaps we better hurry and suggest one now. How about *The United Republics of Total Death?*

Death is the normal end of life; I am not talking about a normality. I am talking about death deliberately planned and man-made, about human activity which has no other objective than to kill other human beings. In one sense, such activity has been with us throughout known human history; for example, the Tatars in their wars with the Russian people used to pile the severed heads of their victims in pyramids around the cities they destroyed. It is difficult, but I believe one can grasp the "humanness" of eighty-four neat stacks of human heads numbering, shall we say, between 400 and 621 each; one could even pick them up, hold them one by one in the palm of one's hand, and consider them, ponder them like Hamlet – all before they rotted completely away. But the issue becomes imaginatively ungraspable when the leader of one superpower declares that his nation would win a nuclear war with no more than 35, at most 45 million of his own citizens killed, because *the enemy would suffer more deaths than that* (USA President Ronald Reagan).

I am referring strictly to numbers. When we consider morality, the issue becomes even more difficult. For if morality concerns the human relationship between individuals, or between an individual and the larger society, then every human death caused by human violence carries with it a moral value, an aura of morality impugned. People do not die in masses; the heads in the pyramid were cut off one by one even if it could be done simultaneously; every person we kill has a name. A so-called mass killer, whether it be Eichmann or the Yorkshire Ripper, can really only be judged for each single killing because every one of his victims could claim that her or his individual death had an absolute moral value. As such, the un-morality of some killers, whether they be individuals or nations sending forth expertly trained killers in the name of a principle or their own national security, becomes morally incomprehensible to the contemplative mind. That a few people should be able to kill every human being on earth, including themselves, is of course now technologically possible but it is not, I think, morally graspable. For as the philosopher Hegel once stated, at a certain point a quantitative change, if large enough, becomes a qualitative difference. We cannot understand, we cannot express in words the immorality – do you notice how *weak* that word is? – the measureless immorality of the Founding Fathers of The United Republics of Total Death. It drives as far beyond our moral comprehension as our grappling with the imponderable curve of space: what is outside the edge of the universe, beyond that which eventually must return to coincide with itself? We cannot speak, or think, of it; we have no words or imagination.

Having begun with this most heavy of all possible introductions, what can I possibly say to justify my own recalcitrant and dogged persistence in writing fiction? There seems no more social point to making novels in the twentieth century than there would be in crocheting doilies if the Ice Age were once again advancing over our continent. And if I persist in writing novels, who will be a reader? I belong to no impoverished so-called developing nation; if I did, my work might be of romantic or revolutionary interest, condescended to perhaps but at least considered. Nor am I a citizen of the super-nations; if I were a significant writer there, it is highly likely that I would be published in all parts of the world because it is essential for every nation on earth to know what the USA or the USSR considers important. No, I belong to the unlikely northern half of North America, a nation materially rich enough to be envied by almost everyone but socially and politically largely meaningless. Canada makes the world news only when the Soviet Union destroys our hockey team, again, in an ice arena, or when a Canadian Very Public Person spends a weekend in a New York hotel with a US rock star. Is there any point in a Canadian like me writing novels?

Well, let me tell you something: I once had a brilliant chance. It happened five years before I was born; in the fall of 1929 when my parents bundled up their young family and tried to get out of the Soviet Union. Together with thousands of other Mennonites who had been living there for seven generations, they left their Mennonite villages and whatever property they had and flooded into Moscow. Officially there was no hope for them, but they wanted to make one last desperate attempt, by means of a massive gathering together, to importune, to force, to shame, whatever you want to call it, the government into letting them leave the Soviet Union. And it worked, to an extent. For no known reason, in late November 1929 about 3,800 Mennonites were given exit visas, put on trains as "landless refugees of German origin," and shipped helter-skelter to President Hindenberg's Germany. Some 14,000 others were forced back, either to their villages or, almost as often, to prison labour camps somewhere in the farthest reaches of the world's largest nation. My problem is that my mother, father, two brothers, and three sisters were among those 3,800 who were shipped out.

I began to get a clearer view of my problem in the middle sixties when the writings of Alexander Solzhenitsyn began to be known in the West; this climaxed of course with the vivid drama of his expulsion from the Soviet Union. I read everything he published, books upon books, and they were magnificent. Dear God, what a writer! And what a platform from which to address the world: secret police, torture, hunger, imprisonment, forced labour camps, exile – all rooted in the Stalin purges by terror that affect everyone on earth to this day as directly as the horrors of Hitler. I even thought of a possible short story called "Lucky Solzhenitsyn." Then, this past summer, all that Russian awareness was revived for me with a particular force.

Two of my father's brothers and their families also made that flight to Moscow in 1929; they were sent back by the police, and a few years later the brothers disappeared into the Stalin terror of 1937–38, never to be heard of again. But one of their sons, my cousin Peter, 19 years old that autumn in Moscow, did survive fifty years in the Soviet Union and in 1979 he was allowed to settle in Germany under the Soviet-West German *Umsiedler* agreement negotiated by Willy Brandt. In 1980 I lectured at the German Association of Canadian Studies in Gummersbach, and at that time my cousin was living within two miles of where I spoke; but neither of us knew the other existed. Now in July 1983, we discovered one another in a Mennonite *Umsiedler* gathering in Germany. When I saw him coming towards me through a crowd of people, it seemed I was seeing the face of my father as he was just before he died. And Peter greeted me in that marvellous Russian manner of full embrace and triple kissing, laughing, "You look just like a Wiebe, a real Wiebe!" A wonderfully cheerful, tiny man who had been to the Gulag twice, the last time in 1952 when he was arrested because a group met in his home regularly to read the Bible and pray. Though they couldn't prove that he was spreading anti-Soviet propaganda (officially there is religious freedom in the Soviet Union), he was nevertheless sentenced under Article 58 of the Criminal Code, sentenced to 25 years of hard labour. Now he tells me, "It was all right, I had only four years, only four, they let me out in the Khrushchev Amnesty after Stalin died." And he holds me, laughing and laughing, there is no limit to his happiness at meeting me.

In 1956 when Peter was released from the Kengir prison mine in Khazakhstan, I was graduating from a Canadian university and I wanted to become a writer. I had every chance to be whatever I wanted. But what could I write, really? An immigrant child born in an obscure corner of an unimportant land. I have been writing fiction for 25 years now and the question is still there; it does not go away. *What* can I write? Or should I say *whom?*

In 1921 Osip Mandelstam wrote: "Just as a person does not choose his parents, a people does not choose its poets" (2:228). I would not begin to compare myself to the greatest Russian poet of the twentieth century, but his words, for me, are profound. The poet is parent to his people; the poet makes his people known and recognizable, an acting and speaking manifestation; he begets them, he enfleshes them, yes, he gives birth to them. I was born and grew up in a rocky boreal forest bushland of northern Saskatchewan, a landscape homesteaded, cleared, and broken to the plough (wherever it was cleared; most of it remained poplar and spruce covered, thick as hair, sometimes you had to walk sideways to get between the trees), a place where the temperature could vary 150 degrees from winter to summer, born among a people who had run to the opposite side of the world to escape one of the bloodiest revolutions and civil wars and anarchies and starvations known in history: and to me it was all *invisible*. It was the world I fell into at birth, and I could not *see* it. "How do you write in a new country?" my friend Robert Kroetsch asks. How can you see yourself without a reflector? Kroetsch continues:

> People who feel invisible try to borrow visibility from those who are visible. To understand others is surely difficult. But to understand ourselves becomes impossible if we do not see images of ourselves in the mirror — be that mirror theatre or literature or historical writing. A local pride [he uses the phrase of William Carlos Williams] does not exclude the rest of the world or other experiences, rather, it makes them possible. ("Moment" 5, 6)

The true writer writes her people, her place into existence. Out of herself; and in this sense "birth" is a more natural image than "inventing." People and landscapes and historical events do not create poets: it is exactly the reverse. The American Civil War did not make William Faulkner, nor the Russian Civil War Mikhail Sholokhov. The literature I devoured as a child was most definitely not made by people who had lived on the prairie or rocky Canadian bush; they knew nothing of picking rocks and Mennonite hymn singing and Low German jokes and the swampy ooze of muskegs breathing steam from smoldering subterranean moss in the rigid winter like spirits breathing upwards through the snow. So, growing up in such a place, among such people, *what* could I write? *Whom* could I write?

Listen, let me tell you. Let me tell you the story of a Cree man named Maskepetoon, "Broken Arm," who was born somewhere around 1805 near the North Saskatchewan River, whose picture George Caitlin once painted. All the places where he lived can be seen to this day, as can the place in the Peace Hills (at Wetaskiwin, Alberta) where he met the Blackfoot/Siksika man who had killed his father. But, instead of killing him in revenge immediately, Maskepetoon told him to mount his own horse:

The Siksika looked at his friends without hope, then mounted in one swift movement and waited, his face clenched to accept whatever hit him first. Maskepetoon looked up at him.

"Both my hands are empty," he said then. "You took my father from me, so now I ask you to be my father. Wear my clothes, ride my horse, and when your people ask you how it is you are still alive, tell them it is because

The Young Chief has taken his revenge."

Slowly the old Siksika slid from the horse and faced Maskepetoon empty-handed. Then he took him in his arms and held him hard against his heart.

"My son," he said, "you have killed me."

(Wiebe, Collected Stories 11)

Listen, let me tell you another story, of an American woman who comes to Alberta from Illinois with her husband and three sons in 1906 to "make a better life for themselves" as they say, and how her first apprehensions about the prairie gradually gather into a profound fear. The story is called "After Thirty Years of Marriage," and she fears not merely loneliness; it is the space she fears, it is the solitariness of woman's work, it is her silent self. This goes beyond fear into primordial terror so deep she cannot even talk of it, but she must finally face it in her winter house, which is both her shelter and her prison; only when she puts her very head into the centre of the terror is she able to sleep without headache or dream, to sleep at last (Wiebe, Collected Stories 156–66).

There are a thousand stories for any prairie writer to tell, whether the world at large listens or not. I have told a very few of them, and once the stories have been made, of course, they will be there forever; or at least as long as there is a human ear and eye to perceive them. This came to me in a new way recently while I was reading aloud "The Angel of the Tar Sands." That very short story tells how the operator of a giant bucket dredging up bitumen sand for processing at Fort McMurray cuts into the body of an angel buried fifty feet below the earth's surface (Collected Stories 248–51). Who knows what we will encounter now that we have the technology to rip up the entire earth in an organized way.

And that thought about the Athabasca Tar (Oil?) Sands, of course, brought me back irrevocably to my United Republics of Total Death; for the sands are right there in the northern Alberta space of the Primrose Air Weapons Range where the United States government wants to test the ground-hugging Cruise missile because the terrain of northern Alberta is so much like the terrain of the Soviet Union. Developing the endless, brutal possibilities of our United Republics.

So though I would like to speak of men and of angels, I am nevertheless brought back to death — where I began. I do not believe that writing is like death. Making things with words is not at all like being killed. I once wrote that writing was like climbing a mountain, a mountain that did not and would never exist unless you climbed it. I still think that is a good way of saying it, but perhaps it is too ego-oriented. Let me try again.

Let me say that writing is like taking a long journey. You must travel every day, and every day you decide roughly where you would like to go, what you would hope to see, but you never know if you will actually get there. You do not really know where you will eat that day, or what, nor where you will be able to rest, if at all, and you may not even have a place to sleep when night begins to surround you. The only certainty is that you are travelling and that travelling with you is another person. This is a person you love. You are together in everything you encounter, whatever you eat, wherever you rest or sleep; whatever the circumstances there you two are together. And that is enough. Together you are enough for anything, anything in this world.

1984

KILLING OUR WAY TO PEACE

Ladies and gentlemen:
It is a joy to come to Vancouver in February when the cherry trees begin to blossom white along the streets. There is so much beauty and goodness in the world, and Thomas Merton, the man whom we have come together this evening to honour, wrote a great deal about both. Blessed be his memory.

Nevertheless, I have chosen a black, one could say a grotesque title/subject to talk about this evening. Because "peace" and "killing" also appear in much of Merton's contemplative writing, and today, February 13, 2003, this subject hangs over us like a black horror. For a year and a half we have had devastating war in Afghanistan; now Iraq looms before us.

War.

Aristotle, the teacher of Alexander of Greece, who is known in history as The Great because he conquered more races and peoples, more swiftly, than anyone before or after him — that is, when he died in 323 BC at the mere age of 33 years, Alexander had developed war tactics to the point where his armies killed more human beings in less time than we can now calculate — the most fundamental philosophic concept Aristotle taught Alexander was that human beings are, by nature, political animals. The word "political" comes from "polis" — city. Aristotle meant, among many other things, that we are animals who can live together in communities by means of rational policies that regulate our relations between one another, and that protect us from enemies.

More than 2,300 years later the German child Carl von Clausewitz (b. 1780), was placed in the Prussian Army by his parents at age eleven; he learned all about war fighting Napoleon. Napoleon could be called western history's "second Alexander The Great," though he had many more years to wage war over a more populated territory and with a greatly developed technology, and he certainly killed more people than the original Greek. von Clausewitz, a true disciple of the rational Aristotle, wrote an incisive book about the nature of war. Its two fundamental treatises were:

— War is an act of violence intended to compel our opponent to fulfill our will.

— War is a mere continuation of national policy by other means.

von Clausewitz's book *On War* (1832) may well be the most influential book ever written on the subject. He was a regimental commander who had experienced time and again on the battlefields of Jena, Borodino, and Waterloo, that the real work of war in his time was butchery: men standing silent, motionless in long inert lines waiting for orders while being slaughtered by artillery fire. Nevertheless, he elaborates at length on this idea of "state policy": when there are differences, problems within or between states, you may well have discussions, conferences, elections, governments passing laws, etc., to try and achieve agreement, but in the end, if these strategies do not bring the desired results for one or the other nation, you organize an overwhelming act of violence to resolve your differences.

In other words, von Clausewitz, a follower of Aristotle, is saying that man as a political animal is a war-making animal. Ultimately, we human beings settle our political differences by killing each other; the most effective killer prevails to decide how those who survive the war, however physically and psychically destroyed they may be, how they will continue to live.

Do you believe that? Do you believe that war exists, that war is forever with us because we are thinking human beings? That we are directed by our intellect, by our ability to reason, to kill one another?

Allow me to quote Thomas Merton on the relationship between reason and war; he wrote this in the middle 60s, when the Cold War (so-called) was threatening the world with nuclear disaster:

> The most obvious fact about war today is that while everyone claims to hate it, and all are agreed that it is our greatest single evil, there is little significant resistance to it except on the part of small minorities who, by the fact of their protest, are dismissed as eccentric.... [It is argued that] the best, most obvious, most incontrovertible reason for war is of course "peace." *The motive for which men are led to fight today is that war is necessary to destroy those who threaten our peace!* (*Love and Living* 114; my italics)

Does this contradiction sound at all familiar in 2003? Indeed, the political leaders of the world's only super-power now talk of "pre-emptive strikes" against anyone they *think is about to threaten* their peace!

It should be clear from this that war is, in fact, totally irrational, and it proceeds to its violent ritual with the chanting of perfect nonsense. Yet men not only accept this, they even go so far as to sacrifice their lives and their human dignity and commit the most hideous atrocities, convinced that in so doing they are being noble, honest, self-sacrificing and just.

As you know, Merton lived his, sadly all-too-brief, life (53 years) through the very heart of the bloodiest century in human history. Twenty years ago I reflected on this fact of human blood in "On Death and Writing":

> If the twentieth century belongs to any one nation, surely it is the nation of the dead. I mean that enormous nation of the man-made dead which during this century continues to develop with such deliberate, such dreadful, steady speed.... Indeed, it seems likely that the end of the 20th century will see only one nation left on earth, and if we are ever going to have a name for it, perhaps we better hurry up and suggest one now. How about *The United Republics of Total Death?*
>
> Death is the normal end of life: I am not talking about an inevitable normality. I am talking about death deliberately planned and man-made, about human activity which has no other objective than to kill other human beings. (223–25 above)

In September, 1983 I wrote these words in the shadow of President Ronald Reagan's world policy analysis of the Soviet Union as "the Evil Empire." In the summer of 1983 Mr. Reagan declared that the USA would win any nuclear war with no more than 35, at most 45 million American citizens killed, *because the enemy would suffer more deaths than that.*

The present US president George W. Bush has not dared to be so frank with us; for him and his speech writers "the Other, the Enemy" is simply Evil. At the same time, everyone on earth knows which nation has the most lethal "weapons of mass destruction," and the mightiest rockets to deliver them.

Today the Soviet Union world threat has more or less disappeared and we live in the shadow of only one world superpower; we live in the dreadful shadow of September 11, 2001 when within an hour over three thousand Americans were killed on their home soil by seventeen suicide terrorists; we live in the shadow of President Bush's declaration of "the War on Terror" and his world policy analysis of "the Axis of Evil" and his straightforward declarations, repeated almost every day, of destroying any nation he believes threatens America. We live, most particularly, under the shadow of the endless cycle of killings in Israel/ Palestine, the relentless threat of the United States to annihilate Saddam Hussein in Iraq, which will certainly require that a few Americans, perhaps, but more certainly thousands of Iraqis be killed.

What casualties can we anticipate in Iraq? The statistics of the very brief 1991 Gulf War are unclear, but reporters agree they numbered in the many tens of thousands, and, as usual, the majority were not soldiers but children, women, older people. As for Coalition casualties, mostly American, all the dead were soldiers, 213 mature human beings. And 44 of them were killed by "friendly fire."

That was war when Iraq was a military power strong enough to fight Iran and invade Kuwait. Today, after 12 years of world sanctions, what will Saddam Hussein be capable of?

Perhaps almost nothing, except brave or terrified people blown up in their homes or standing in the way of tanks, ultimately families being driven out of their shanties by American soldiers inhumanly faceless inside their robot-like military gear, soldiers who, as one TV news clip showed them recently training for door to door combat, say they have been training hard for eight years and are now "Ready, eager for the game to begin." When the TV reporter asked, "What's the game?" the young soldier cradled his huge automatic in his crossed arms and laughed, completely at ease. "You know what it is," he said. "The game with Saddam."

Yes, we know. Playing a game with one fiendish ogre; no ordinary human beings involved. Yes, we do know. The big question is: do these international policies of today's nations make intellectual sense? Is this 2003 threat of war with Iraq, to quote von Clausewitz, simply an international continuation of political discourse with the intermixing of other means (von Clausewitz 119)? Is reason, as has been argued endlessly by the two Bs, Bush and Blair, the "smoking gun" reason of "weapons of mass destruction" — leaving aside whether any can be proven to be there — is reason truly ruling the behaviour of nations? Did Colin Powell speaking at the UN give convincing reasons for war, now?

We all know: human beings are not only creatures of reason. And so I want to turn this question over. From reason to morality. Say the UN inspectors in Iraq do find twenty or more rocket shells that are not empty and uselessly dismantled, that would be capable of carrying horrible disease as far as Israel on the orders of a tyrant with the blood of tens of thousands already on his cruel hands — as Hussein and his cohorts do. To destroy that aggressive capability, infinitesimally small in relation to the powers ranged against it and miniscule in terms of the damage it can cause, how many Iraqi citizens are worth killing for those twenty rockets? How many American/allied soldiers?

And say the US does begin its war, annihilates whatever and whoever is necessary, and subsequently discovers the inspectors were right: there is nothing "mass destructive" in Iraq. "Oops"? "Sorry"?

I think reason must make one pause here; and morality even more. A moral position for this war strikes me as impossible.

One night I am wide awake, suddenly, coming out of a dream that I cannot remember. I invariably sleep on my side, and so I am staring level across the room into the darkness of our bedroom closet, the door of which I have left open. But in the closet darkness I am looking into my computer screen, and there I see how quickly, easily I have typed these words: "thousands, perhaps tens of thousands of people will be killed." And I think of us here, this group of several hundred, mostly strangers to each other, who will come together this evening, and we will sit and ponder together, and talk, on a peaceful, lovely evening in one of the world's most beautiful cities, here in Vancouver, Canada. What if this green and beautiful city were "under attack" (notice how that age-old expression for war is especially vivid in an age of F–16 and F–18 supersonic jets — under attack) and what if a "smart rocket" with a "smart bomb" (and with its penetration point hardened by plutonium) smashed through the roof of this church and exploded?

And it killed seven of you and lacerated a hundred others?

Or it landed here on stage and killed me?

Or it blew us all into the exploded debris of this church as indistinguishable shreds of bloody flesh?

We have seen the world's reaction to the deaths of seven international astronauts exploding in the atmosphere; the avalanche deaths of seven teenagers from Alberta. We have seen their individual pictures in all the media.

Awake in the middle of the night, I understood again that human beings never die as a simple mass. We may die together, in small or greater numbers, but we are always, each of us *one*, and unique; every individual human being is of an absolute moral worth. If that death happens at the hands of another human being, that is killing, and killing is a heinous crime. As Martin Buber pointed out so vividly, "The world as experience belongs to the basic word I — It. The basic word I — You establishes the world of relation" (Buber 56). As I understand this, Buber is saying that I recognize my unique *self* in those entities that are *not-me*, and most particularly I recognize my unique self in my recognition of the person *You*, who is not *I*. Therefore, when I say *I* I am also saying *You* as well, because we are a pair: my individual self-recognition of myself — I — is possible only in relation to the other — You. We all know every person on earth has a name, and when we say that name we declare this relational uniqueness — as the media does when it shows every particular body, face, and name — we declare that which distinguishes each individual human being from anything and everything and everyone else on earth.

That is what I mean when I say that each of us, in relation to another human being, has an absolute moral worth. You have the same moral worth as I. In a human moral sense there is no difference between an Iraqi child being killed by a bomb —"smart" or "dumb" certainly has no bearing on the matter — a child or the president of the US being killed by a similar bomb. There is no moral difference: a human being has been destroyed, a You, absolutely unique among billions, whether innocent and helpless or older and burdened by a life-time of power and power decisions. The understanding of a moral person must declare such a killing is irrevocably wrong.

The great teachers of Judeo-Christian thought have always taught this, by example, image and parable. Jesus said that "Our Father" cares for every single sparrow, how much more does he care for one of us? And eight hundred years before him the poet/ prophet Isaiah wrote: "Thus says the LORD: Does a woman forget the baby at her breast? Can a loving mother forget the child of her womb? Even these forget, but I will never forget you. I have engraved you in the palms of my hands" (Isaiah 49: 15 – 16).

I-You: the unbreakable connection between human beings, between us and our Creator. To quote Buber again: "The basic word I-You establishes the world of relation." So, how then can we fathom the deliberate, man-made destruction of that human unity? The ravines of Babi Yar, the napalmed villages of Vietnam, the churches and streets and ditches of Rwanda, the twin towers of New York with all those overwhelming names craved in memorial stone — as they are, in Isaiah's magnificent image, engraved in the palms of God's hands — they are in their immeasurable complexity beyond our comprehension; but one thing we know for certain: when I destroy You, the I of our basic being is destroyed as well.

Can you see that? Can you see me standing here, in front of you, and suddenly, without warning, with an overwhelming explosion of light and sound I would be disintegrated before your eyes? Or you, one of you, would be annihilated before me? Wouldn't we, each one, feel that, know that within our very body as long as our body would endure?

In that sense, the depths of immorality — do you notice how weak that word is? — the immorality of individual deaths any war, every contemporary war with all its technological extensions brings with it, is, in its massiveness, morally ungraspable even by the most grossly tuned ethical imagination. As W.G. Sebald explains in his book *On The Natural History of Destruction*, where he discusses the psychic and moral consequences of the Allied bombing, during World War II, of 131 German cities and towns, and the specific deaths in them of over 600,000 civilians, "the objective nature of...what really happened far surpassed the most outrageous dreams of annihilation" (Sebald 184).

May God have mercy on us.

For our closer consideration here, in order that we may not be totally overwhelmed, I suggest we briefly consider one, single, life and death; the unique personality and circumstances of one You who has been torn from the eternal I-You pairing of humanity. To do that, I want to tell you a story based on an historical event, the story of a life, a death, and how the living dealt with it, an edited excerpt from my novel *Sweeter Than All The World*. The speaker is David Loewen and the listener Adam Wiebe; the conversation takes place in Fernheim, a Mennonite village in Paraguay during the 1980s.

Adam Wiebe from Canada is, as I tell him, my sort of lop-sided double-cousin: my third cousin on my father's Loewen side, my second cousin on my mother's, the Wiebe side. We laugh at that, and Adam tells me again he's a good listener, he didn't fly to Paraguay almost at the bottom of the world to hear himself talk. I tell him I've heard the world is round, and he's so far north in Canada that maybe it's he who's at the bottom, and we laugh again. He speaks Lowgerman, that makes it very easy for us together, and so I start:

"I was named David for my grandpa when I was born on November, 1925, a Sunday my mother said, in the Mennonite villages north of the Russian city of Orenburg.... I was the last of eleven children she bore, though only six of us lived, including me.

"Orenburg Colony had once been well to do, and growing, but then came the Russian Revolution and the Civil War and by the winter of 1925–26 no one had much of anything, my mother said, except empty bellies and dying children....

"I have no memory of seeing my father. None, though I have stared at the one picture we have of him, trying. I was barely four when they took him and he was gone. But when my mother was dying ten years ago she talked to me then about that, and our first year in Paraguay. She talked so much in the hospital, like she never had before. She wanted to tell me more and more day after day, about my father, *Mien Jahonn* as she always called him, 'My John', and also about my oldest brother Vanya here in Paraguay, both taken from us so fast, so horribly. 'Vanya! Vanya!' my mother still wailed for her oldest child on her last bed, though he had been deep in the Chaco sand for thirty years and there was no tear to her eye.

Long ago she had cried enough forever in Russia and in Paraguay too, that was more than a knife through the heart, she said."

[After a lengthy account of enduring the Stalin regime's growing violence in the 1920s, David explains:]

"By October, 1929 we were in Moscow, and by a miracle got out of there on December 12, praise God."

"And your brother Vanya, how old did he get?"

"… December 24, 1930, twenty-two years, eleven months, one day."

"But then you were already here. Except for your father, you were all already safe in Paraguay."

"Safe from the Communists, yes, but there is still everything else on earth."

"What was it, here?"

"First typhus. In our first year in the Chaco desert less than three hundred and fifty families buried ninety-four people, forty-four of them children."

"Ninety-four, in one year?

"My sister Maria's two children too. Heat and dysentery, and forty-three of typhus, one whole family died out, parents and three small children, and all the orphans… they said the Chaco was too dry for typhus, but we brought it here, we brought it along with us."

"Ah-h-h," Adam says. He is looking at the empty orange skin between his long fingers, fingers so pale and soft it could be he has never in his whole life so much as touched a shovel. Suffer? He looks up, and smiles sadly, so I tell him,

"We had no doctor in the Chaco. After a month of dying a Paraguayan one came from Asuncion, and he said people on the river boats coming from Argentina sometimes had typhus."

Adam nods, "Epidemic typhus, carried by lice, aided by dirt and bad water."

"Our ministers could do nothing but pray and read the Bible, my mother said. Our 'Great Dying' as we call it to this day. It all comes from the hand of God, they preached, health or sickness, want or plenty, but during the 94 funerals in 1930 our ministers often broke down crying when they said it. My mother remembered the one verse they always read,

'And King David built an altar to the Lord on the threshing floor, and sacrificed burnt offerings and peace offerings. Then the Lord answered the prayer for the land, and the plague was stopped.'

Mennonites certainly aren't kings, my mother said, but after our long, hard journeys to reach the Gran Chaco, we did sacrifice, all of us, until the plagues finally stopped, they truly did."

Adam says slowly, "I guess it doesn't matter how far you travel, you always carry...things along with you. But sacrifice children...such suffering? The ministers said it was from God?"

"All life comes from God, they said, and suffering too, because of sin."

"But that verse about David, I think he sacrificed animals on an altar for something he had done wrong, some exact sin, I think he made God angry by lying with a woman or counting people, I don't know exactly — what big sin did you people here do?"

"I don't know. Maybe because we escaped the Communists, maybe we were supposed to help pay here for what our relatives were still paying in Russia."

"Pay? My parents escaped too. Pay what?"

"For evil, pay for sin in the world. The sin of Adam."

My cousin Adam from Canada stares at me, almost as if I had meant him! I say, "In the Garden of Eden, the snake and Eve."

"I know," he says. "But some people seem to 'pay' a lot more than others."

"My mother always said, who can argue with God."

"If we were Jews we would."

"Jews don't believe in the New Testament."

Adam makes a hard sound in his throat. "Well, we're supposed to, and the New Testament says Jesus paid for all sin, for everybody, on the cross, so why do we still have to pay more?"

I don't know what more to say. My mother certainly thought longer about this than I and, if she knew, she never told me. I can only ask Adam,

"You in Canada, what do you pay for sin?"

"Humm! Not very much. Hard work, my family started in a log house no bigger than a shed, they worked like slaves — but no hunger or Communists, certainly not typhus or…" then he laughs, and I hear his thoughts change in his laughter. "Maybe my debt is piling up interest, who knows how big it'll be when I have to pay!"

We laugh a little, together, as people do when there is nothing to say about something that is not funny.

"But your brother Vanya," Adam says, "that wasn't typhus."

No. Not typhus. In the ten days he visits me I tell him our worst and best story, the one that started our life in Paraguay in 1930 when we already had no father because of Stalin. Tell him, as I can. My mother told me Vanya's will was unbreakable. He was the head of the family, he must work. Not the heat and bittergrass campos and thorn-brush sand flats and mosquitoes nor the endless labour of building a village out of nothing in a strange and often frightening land could stop him, by God's grace we had escaped the Land of Terror and he would build our home again as our father surely would have if only he had lived.

But my own small first Chaco memory is not of Vanya working. In my memory I see the big bandaged head of my brother lying on a mat in the terrible heat of our house tent, the strips of my mother's cleanest, whitest sheets soaking blotches of blood around his neck and head crushed by a wagon yoke for oxen, a yoke of red quebracho so hard they called it 'axe-breaker', so heavy it sank in water like steel, and that was what smashed Vanya, beat him to the ground behind the small corral where we kept our cow, a Paraguayan beast so wild she had to be roped and tied up, both head and foot, her back legs spread wide against two posts to strip a small bottle of bluish milk out of her. My brother Vanya did that twice a day, my mother said, the milk was for me and our little Frieda, but that day just before Christmas 1930 in the worst of the summer heat when she heard him, she knew no cow would make him scream like that, she heard the thud! thud! thud! of red quebracho as she ran crying his name from our tent and around the corral.

"What?" Adam asks me, "what happened, what?"

For fifty years I have not said a word to anyone, nor asked, nor has anyone in Fernheim spoken to me of it. Mennonites know, they understand silence. Now this "lopsided double-cousin" from Canada, a doctor with soft hands so rich he can fly around the earth and probably talk to all those big men, too, who control the way the world is and have never heard of us or the miserable Paraguayan Chaco and how you labour to simply endure here, decade after decade how you wait for a drop of rain. Adam Wiebe comes out of the sky and listens to me, but in seven days he'll be gone. He laughs about his debt to sin growing; children being sacrificed to pay it. They're just words to him, words, would he laugh if it was his daughter, his son he had to watch die? I hope for them is that they will never have to suffer like our parents – but I don't think even Canada is the heavenly Canaan, not yet.

My mother said on her deathbed: only God and forgiveness can end pain. And each one forgives for himself; no one can forgive for others, you must do it for yourself, for yourself alone.

"David, what happened?"

Adam is peering at me so hard and Wiebe grey, as if he intends to find Vanya in my eyes. I could tell him I don't look like my brother at all, that I have the long nose and heavy eyebrows of my Wiebe mother, he should be looking at my ears. In the one picture of our family taken fifty-two years ago in Russia I know that both Vanya and I had our father's ears, even as a baby on my mother's lap you can see it, our ears sticking straight out and so broad, if we were heads only we could fly away.

I tell him, "My brother's neck and shoulder, the left side of his head was smashed. We had no doctor then in the Fernheim, only Heinrich Unruh who had been a hospital orderly in the First World War. He knew how to bandage a wound. Such horrible pain in the heat boiling our tent, I remember his face wrapped up and soaking bloody. He died after three days."

"God. With a wagon – oxen – yoke?"

Quebracho wood. There were only two wagons and four oxen then, my mother said, in our village – there was no school yet, but they had started the adobe houses – and Vanya had finally gotten two oxen yoked under that unbreakable yoke and pulling together, he could quietly talk any animal into doing its proper work except that beast our first cow, my mother said, the yoke was still warm when that man lifted it up.

"Who? Who did it?"

One of our village, one of us. Actually three of them came to argue and yell at Vanya, my mother told me, they were his age but only one stayed longer, he was so strong to lift that red quebracho high enough. And enraged, violent enough to do it. What was the matter between them? Why were they so angry at Vanya? I asked my mother as she lay on her last bed, tell me, you have never said anything, the man may be dead now or one day I could meet him on the street, who did it? And why? Why did he crush my brother's head?

She would not open her eyes, she would not tell me. Perhaps she could not, God had given her the mercy of washing her blackest memories clean long ago in forgiveness. Who can deny their mother on her deathbed, who would force her, draw out what she has already given away? She told me only what I myself already knew because I saw it, five years old and I can never forget — or want to. My brother's body lying inside the bulge of a bottle-tree log our neighbors had cut and dragged out of the thorn bushes which is all the forests in the Gran Chaco are, and had sawn the tree open down the middle, dug out with shovels and hoes the pulp in the great bulge of the stem where the tree stores its water, dried it out until the smell of it was almost gone in the sun and then the women laid Vanya wrapped in a sheet down inside it and the men covered him over with the sawn half so there was only the thorn-studded grey barrel of the dead tree left, it seemed to her, my mother said, as if they were sinking a piece of the thorn-bristling Chaco, laying it back deep into the Paraguay sand, trying to bury this terrible land into itself, but they never would be able get all the Mennonites quiet and buried and in no more pain, not even if they prayed and shoveled forever, and the poor young Mennonite who had done it kneeling by the hole, weeping as they broke the edges of the hole in and the sand flowed down over the bulging tree laid flat, as they filled the hole until it was heaping high on the far edge of the school lot, here, next to our farmyard. She told me how the Paraguayan Army captain who had met Vanya on his freight trips to the railroad came to the funeral with his soldiers and said to her he would deal properly with the killer, as Paraguayans do, but my mother forbade the captain his vengeance, no, she would hear nothing of it. She told him she must forgive the weeping man as Jesus had taught, and she invited the man to our tent and, crying, she finally could do that with her whole heart.

And she told me again how that suffering young man came to work for us then, walking every day from his parents yard at the south end of our village and how he helped her build our sleeping and cooking houses, cut the bittergrass for the roof and plowed our land with that yoke of oxen, trained so well, and learned to plant kaffir and Paraguayan beans and sweet potatoes and cotton, he helped us do our share of village work on fences and road and school, for three years, always bringing his own food for the day though he always ate it with us, but it was our little family — I was five and getting bigger and I shovelled too — our family with my sister the oldest child left now barely sixteen, and we tore away our first corral and built a larger one farther back on our lot for the Beast our Paraguay cow and planted the garden and later, when we learned how, also planted our Chaco orchard, apricot trees and berry bushes and, after years, lemon and orange trees where our tent and our corral had first stood, where it happened. He worked for us every day for three years and then that was the end of it.

Adam says, slowly, "Three years — you would have been eight by then... surely, you remember who he was?"

"I don't," I blurt out, and I realize everyone older in the colony must think I know, I have never said a word about this to anyone, not to my sisters, not to my closest friends. But I can say it to this cousin, this stranger: "He worked with us, but I don't remember, not his name or his face... what I remember is nothing but him walking down the street, towards his family's house, the back of a big man, walking away. And one day he never came again."

Adam is staring into the orange trees.

I say at last, "I think he left the colony, Brazil, maybe Argentina... but I don't know."

And I think to myself, as I have so often: I see him kneeling beside the grave, head down and weeping; I see him working in the distance, I see his back walking away. I cannot see his face; nor think of his name.

And on her dying bed my mother told me nothing more. For her, and for me — who can understand this? — that man remained a shape we once knew existed, but he was gone. Like the outline of a person against the stark sun, after a moment there is too much light and it disappears. Heinrich Unruh was alive and only a little over eighty years old, he would certainly have remembered something to tell me — and all the older people in our colony — but why ask them? It was my mother who had to tell me and my mother said, No, no, leave that what it is with you, and be thankful. On earth, if God is good, you can sometimes forgive a few things long enough so you don't have to drag them after you all the way into heaven before the Throne of Grace. And anyway, she said, God already knows, He understands it all, why should we turn over and over in our hearts the little we know and the more that we don't? Let it rest in the sand, and in God's heart, that's enough for all of us, here.

Adam asks me, "Have you forgiven that man?"

And then, very quickly, "I'm sorry. Please, forgive me."

After a while he says, "That's really the second story in the Bible. The two sons of Adam and Eve."

"I know," I tell him, and his eyes are so quiet now and grey, I know somewhere he knows about pain, or will soon. "I've read it so often, I still can't understand why Cain killed Abel."

"In the Bible it's because of God, and something about fruit and sheep."

"Well," I say, "we don't have sheep, I like oranges better than cow meat!"

We laugh a little again; nothing to be said.

"How about God?" he says.

"I don't think people have to kill each other because of God, anymore. I think He can take care of Himself."

We are under the bright green orange trees. I tell Adam we are standing where our first corral stood, I can't tell exactly, but our feet may be on the exact spot.

He looks down at his polished shoes, dusty from Gran Chaco sand that grows every seed you plant into a miracle of goodness if only you can find enough water for it. I live in a garden of Eden really, a Garden of Eden of God's forgiveness and forgetting; if only the garden had four rivers flowing through it.

We walk through orchard and garden, we walk past the white adobe school which is also our church, walk out into the staggering brilliance of December Paraguay sun. East over the communal pastures the vultures float high as they always do, riding air on their giant wings. That's good, if they weren't up there we would know one of our cattle was dead. Beside us in the field beyond the fence five horses rest in the morning heat; a dapple grey mare suckles her foal. At the corner of the fence; between pasture and street and school, is the gravestone of my brother Vanya. (310–332)

The barest shadow of this story of violence — a story of strangely inexplicable forgiveness and forgetting — was told me personally by the ancient father of the young man who was beaten to death in 1930. It was during my first visit to Paraguay, 1966, and the old man gave me a copy of the life-memoir he had written of their emigration. One of the agreements of Mennonite settlement in Paraguay was that, as long as their activities did not infringe on native Paraguayan rights, the colony could administer its own legal affairs. So, in the very first year the Russian Mennonites came to the Chaco and tried to build a settlement in the desert, a year filled with hunger, heat and drought, labour and sickness and epidemic dying, the year they were most unprepared and suffering, they also had to deal with a murder in their very midst. As that ancient father told me, "That was when we lived through what it meant to be peace loving; what our Lord taught in his prayer, 'Forgive us our trespasses as we forgive those who trespass against us.'"

Those precise words are not included in the story as I wrote it; nor the actual gravestone he showed me, which simply had on it the name of his son and his dates, and below that the engraved statement: *Gott ist die Liebe* (God is (the) Love). It is a story told in the Chaco to this day. In the Fernheim Mennonite Colony, State of Boqueron, Paraguay. And the gravestone is there in Village # 5, called Friedensfeld: Field of Peace.

If in Canada one of our children was violently killed by someone, we parents, the ones most brutally affected, would not have to make any decisions of procedure or conscience; we would not be asked for our opinions, our names would not even be legally mentioned; the perpetrator of the crime would be arrested by police and tried by law in an impersonal trial formulated as

"The Queen vs. so-and-so." "The Law," which in a statue before the Supreme Court of Canada in Ottawa is represented as a blindfolded woman holding high the balancing scales of justice, "blind Law" would decide everything for us in the nameless name of "The Queen." But my relatives in Paraguay lived in the very same village as the killer; he was their neighbour, a member of their church. He might well be deeply sorry for what he had done, but his sorrow would never return their son to life; and, even more difficult, the family had to decide how he should be punished for the evil he had done. Overwhelming though it was, they followed Paul's admonition in Romans 12: "Never repay evil with evil. Do all you can to live at peace with everyone."

Perhaps you feel I have moved rather far from my original subject, which I began with the von Clausewitz hypothesis that the violence of war between nations was fundamentally a "continuation of national policy with the intermixing of other means." Please understand me: I am discussing the principle we all hold most dear, humanity's ability, and basic right, to make self-aware decisions about how to act within society. In western cultures we call this the free will of human beings: as individuals, we make hundreds, perhaps thousands, of independent decisions every day about exactly how we will act. We more or less take that for granted.

Well. There's a Lowgerman rhyme I remember from my childhood: *Waeah de Wohl haft, haft de Kwohl.* Whoever has the choice, has the torture. As we all know, choice always means both gain and loss. To walk one path means we cannot walk another, and yet, often enough, especially in our day, we do long to walk both. Too often we think we can simply have everything, especially if we are powerful; and that applies both to individuals and to nations.

We desire the pleasures of relaxed happiness, *but* also the adrenalin rush of physical action.

We desire the quiet of home and peace and love, of self-actualization and beauty, *but* also the meaningful activity of "making a difference," of "being involved," even to the point of dying for what we hold as greater than our own personal and single identity:

— an astronaut putting his/her body on the line for the cause of science

— a soldier training to, if necessary, kill and/or die for his/her country

— a suicide bomber blowing up him/herself and others for a "greater cause"

— a "human shield," of which there are a number now in Iraq, non-Iraqi civilians who are there to stand beside/with Iraqi people when a war begins.

We human beings are capable of making such decisions; like the family who will forgive a murderer, the decision is not necessarily rational because we are not only rational creatures; far more, we are (thanks be to God!) believing, feeling, sensitive, remembering creatures and we most often make our choices on that basis.

And so do nations. Nations after all are communities of peoples and they act on their beliefs, on their historical teachings, on their feelings as well. When Saddam Hussein says to his people, "We will fight to the last bullet!", when George W. Bush says to his people, "We will fight this war against The Axis of Evil, and we will prevail," we know they are not speaking rationally. Thinking people know Hussein's military power may inflict some hurt on opposing armies in a war, but it will be overrun by overwhelming power, and that long before "the last bullet." As for the USA, the past fifty years tell us that, despite its population, wealth and almost inconceivable military weapons truly capable of "mass destruction," in major, drawn-out wars America has not prevailed. In 1953 Korea was a partition stand-off whose problems even as we speak loom larger and larger with every nuclear device the North Koreans test. Further, Vietnam was a humiliating disaster with tens of thousands of American dead, a forced withdrawal and negotiated surrender in 1975 that no president since ever dares mention.

Strange. It must be noted: since the dropping of the atomic bombs in 1945, the huge ideological wars the USA initiated in Korea and Vietnam have provided either disasters, or ongoing, festering international problems; the small wars they fought with limited objectives: Granada, Panama, expelling Iraq from Kuwait, have been, we might say, "more successful." But this new war on Iraq, where will it go? How can it end? The buildup has been more than strange; it's a horrifying mystery; the endless repetition of "weapons of mass destruction" has worn itself out into meaninglessness, and all the more because we know at least a dozen belligerent nations have nuclear bombs and at least two, India and Pakistan, regularly threaten each other with them. Nor can it be the fact that Hussein is a brutal dictator: dozens of nations are controlled by military dictatorships and we tolerate, as in Zimbabwe and Congo, or actively cooperate with them, as in Pakistan and Saudi Arabia.

And the pious repetition of "freeing the people of Iraq" and bringing them "democracy" contains very little rationality either: if the Iraqi people are allowed a democratic "one person one vote" election, the majority Shiite Muslims will control the country, and that would mean it would be drawn so much closer to Iran, whose population is 95% Shiite. But Iran is also one of Mr. Bush's "Axis of Evil" nations, and such a strengthening of ultra-conservative Islamic forces is frightening indeed: the next fixation of the USA might very well have to be Iran, a nation with a population and an area almost four times larger than Iraq; within the past week we heard that it is developing uranium mines within its borders. Is that a fact? Where will this so-called program of "saving the world from weapons of mass destruction" and "freeing peoples from evil dictators" end?

Can threatening people, killing people, bring our world peace and happiness?

Iraq and Iran are not problems like North Korea, which is a relatively small, relatively poor, weak nation on a distant Asian peninsula isolated and contained by its surrounding giants of China, Russia and South Korea. Iraq and Iran are at the very centre of our capitalist world; the lands where western cultures and religions began; they are the world's second and fourth largest oil producers; they will not be a Vietnam which, when it turns into a debacle, can simply be withdrawn from and subjected to national amnesia.

Why would any thinking person imagine that if western nations, some of whose leaders apparently have Bible studies and prayers meetings in their offices every morning, if these so-called Christian nations attack and kill thousands of Islamic believers in the lands where they have lived since before written history, how can these nations rationally hold that they will bring peace to the world? The taped message sent to the world on February 11, two days ago, whether spoken by Osama bin Laden or not, gives us an ice-cold warning: an attack on Iraq will be considered an attack on all Muslims, everywhere in the world. I believe Nelson Mandela is correct when he declared that, in attacking Iraq, the president of the United States is a man of absolutely no foresight.

The Preamble to the UN Charter would agree. Less than three months after Hiroshima and Nagasaki ended World War II, the UN Charter Preamble declared: "We the peoples of the United Nations [are] determined to save succeeding generations from the scourge of war, which twice in our lifetime has brought untold sorrow to mankind." In 1963 the Second Vatican Council called for an entirely new evaluation of war, stating: "The arms race is an utterly treacherous trap … [it] will spawn lethal ruin … Divine Providence urgently demands of us that we free ourselves from the age-old slavery of war … all war can be completely outlawed by international consent" (Merton 116).

Both these statements are humane and rational statements of our world's political situation, and yet the one super-power on earth, whose leaders tell us again and again that it is not only the most powerful but the most democratic, free, humane and avowedly *Christian* nation as well, these leaders are fixated on perpetrating a massive, organized campaign of violent killing. Could we say irrationally fixated? The world lived with the Cold War of Soviet Communism for 44 years while restraining itself from the disaster of a killing war — and in the Cuban Crisis, which most of us remember living through, we were within a word of nuclear holocaust — and eventually the Cold War collapsed from within; the USA supported Saddam Hussein for 12 years, and has been in conflict with him for another 12; why, now, in order to get rid of him, are the Iraqi people to be sacrificed to supersonic bombs? And the precarious stability of an historical,

vital area of our earth, already riven by confrontation and killing, massively destroyed? Why?

We can all, only, conjecture:

– it has something to do, as Colin Powell pointedly mentioned to the UN, with the attack of September 11 – (to be
cynical) revenge?

– it has something to do with oil – money?

– it has something to do with Israel – political lobby power?

– it has something to do with the long, on-going American
travail of power and pride and intrigue in the larger Middle
East, something perhaps no US government will ever explain to
the world because it is too damaging, too humiliating, perhaps
something so shameful, so horrible as – may God protect us –
Saddam really does have nuclear missiles and warheads because
years ago – when Iraq and the US were allies against Iran, when
the Iran Crisis of 1979–80 toppled the most foresightful, most
peace-loving president the US has had in the last fifty years,
Jimmy Carter – perhaps the reason for this war, now, will prove
to be that during the Reagan regime (to use their favorite word)
the USA gave Iraq nuclear bombs.

We will know then that this fixation on "war war war" is not
just a kind of willful, overbearing, bullying, irrational, the-world-
be-damned stupid use of power, as it appears to be now. It has to
be more than some overweening drive to force the world, through
an ultimate brutality, to recognise: "We've got the technology
and the machines to bomb anyone we want back to the Stone
Age, and we'll do, it because no other nation has the weapons to
stop us." If, for example, 20,000 Iraqis die in this "war," 15,000
of them will be civilians; and if 200 Allied soldiers die, including 22% from "friendly fire" as in Kuwait, it's not *war* between

armies. It's much more like chaining people in cages and then machine-gunning them. "Winning" such a "war" should overwhelm us with shame.

Thomas Merton did not live to see the full horrors of the Vietman War, napalm and jungle booby-traps, but he had seen it developing all too dreadfully. In *Love and Living* he wrote, prophetically as always:

> The awful fact is that though mankind fears war and seeks to avoid it, the fear is irrational and inefficacious. It [i.e., the fear] can do nothing against a profound *unconscious proclivity* to violence which seems, in fact, to be one of the most mysterious characteristics of man, not only in his individuality but in his collective and social life.... The only possible conclusion is that man is so addicted to war that he cannot possibly deal with his addiction. And yet, if he does not learn to cope with it, the addiction will ruin him altogether. (114 – 15)

Mankind's "profound unconscious proclivity to violence." I would suggest it is not totally unconscious; most addicts are only too aware of their addictions. They live with them every second, as we are all, now, subjected as we are to endless talk of war, war, war. I think Walter Wink in *Sojourers Magazine* a year after the first "victory" against Saddam Hussein in Kuwait, takes this matter of "addiction" one step farther when he explicates at length our western "Myth of Redemptive Violence." He writes: "Violence is the ethos of our times.... What is generally overlooked is that violence is accorded the status of a religion, demanding from its devotees an absolute obedience-unto-death" (Apr. 18, 1992).

I cannot quote this full length, but he concludes:

> We see a mounting impatience with the laborious pro-
> cesses of civilized life and a restless eagerness to embrace
> violent solutions.... [In our nation] the myth of redemp-
> tive violence has become the cornerstone of foreign policy,
> enshrined in the doctrine of the national security state.
> Might is right. Everything depends on victory, success,
> the thrill of belonging to a nation capable of imposing
> its will...among the nations.

If this was evident in 1992, how much more so in 2003?

I must conclude. You understand why, despite the peacefulness and
freedom we enjoy in Canada, the beauty of the cities in which we
personally live, the cheerfulness and unexpected goodness we so
often experience even from complete strangers, on February 13,
2003 I have no cheery, sparkly word of bright assurance to leave
with you. Rather, let me say that the latest DNA research seems to
indicate that we, the only surviving human species, called homo
sapiens, came from a single ancestor living perhaps 60,000 years
ago on the coast of East Africa. The present visible differences
between all living humans, as contemporary scientists tell us,
are quite literally skin deep and evolved during the past 30,000
years. In terms of DNA, of blood, we're all one extended family.

Now we already know that homo sapiens is, by an incredible measure, the most complex organism ever to live on earth.
Scientists also tell us that, of the millions of living organisms
that have ever existed on this planet, 97% are now extinct. Dead
and gone.

In my most pessimistic moments I sometimes think: perhaps that is what will happen to us, we brilliant, sensitive homo sapiens. Perhaps from a meteor crashing into our planet, perhaps from volcanoes and earthquakes crumpling up the earth's protective crust, or perhaps (more likely?) we will do it to ourselves. We are so incomparably, brilliantly intelligent, we are such super-powers that we could by violence destroy ourselves, totally. Life could again belong only to such living creatures as can hide themselves from the cataclysm deep inside the earth, in the darkness of the sea, under the sheltering layers of such antipodal ice as may yet remain. Perhaps that is what the vision of Saint John means, the one recorded in his Book of Revelations concerning Armageddon, when the earth is visited by a greater violence than "anyone has ever seen since there have been men on earth... Every island vanished and the mountains disappeared, and hailstones weighing a hundredweight fell from the sky on the people" (ch. 16).

When or if that happens, it may well be by mankind's own choice, our violent doing.

As for us, here and now, we still live in the time of much human goodness, and, if you will, divine mercy; or perhaps it should be called divine forbearance. It is still possible for each of us, I-You, all named and known people, even as those afflicted Jesus followers in Paraguay seventy years ago did, we can continue to pray as St. Francis taught us:

"O divine Creator, make me an instrument of your peace."

2003

THE BODY KNOWS AS MUCH AS THE SOUL

On the Human Reality of Being a Writer

Up from the bed of the river
God scooped the clay;
And by the bank of the river
He kneeled Him down;
And there the great God Almighty
Who lit the sun and fixed it in the sky,
Who flung the stars to the most far corner of the night,
Who rounded the earth in the middle of His hand;
This Great God,
Like a mammy bending over her baby,
Kneeled down in the dust
Toiling over a lump of clay
Till He shaped it in his own image;

Then into it He blew the breath of life,
And man became a living soul.
Amen. Amen.

The conclusion of "The Creation," the great poem written by James Weldon Johnson (261). He was born seven years after the Civil War ended, and throughout his life he carried the heritage of his slavery in his very name (for 14 years he was the secretary of the National Association for the Advancement of Colored People), so American college students know his poetry well. But let me tell you, over forty years ago, when I was a student in a small Mennonite high school in Alberta, his magnificent re-telling of the Hebrew creation story rolled, rang through my body like a sounding bell. Precise, indelible words: BED SCOOP FLING HAND MAMMY BABY BLOW LUMP CLAY

The human artist/sculptor who works with lumps of clay may, in that sense, be the most "god-like" in the Judeo-Christian tradition of "making." As the French poet Paul Claudel describes it, "Sculpture expresses the need to touch" (xvii). The sense of touch is, of course, the most *physical* of all our senses: touch alone requires that we place us body against body and, as we know, the more "touchly alert" the parts of bodies we place together, the more physical, the more *bodily*, our response becomes; must be.

And speaking of sculpture, Claudel continues: "Even before he can see, the child waves its tiny swarming hands about. The almost maternal joy of possessing the plastic earth between... hands... of modeling, of possessing — henceforth enduringly between his ten fingers — these full forms [you see about you]...it is for these that desire first appears in [the artist]" (xvii).

Paul Claudel is of course writing about the sculptures of his sister Camille Claudel, whose genius he notes is that "The sculptural object, for her, is what has become capable of being detached [from the surrounding clay, that is, become a discrete, separate body], what can be gathered up and possessed between intelligent hands" (xviii).

I have entered the Camille Claudel Room in the Rodin Museum, Hotel Biron, Paris; I have felt the irresistible force of desiring to touch, to somehow comprehend with all my physical body those indescribable forms she shaped. I cannot here detail the incredible flowering of her art, nor the disaster of her life. (For 30 years, before she died in 1943, she was forced to endure the slow, living death of a lunatic asylum.) But what I can say here is this: if sculpture expresses the need to touch, I am convinced that writing expresses the need to, first *listen*, and then *see*.

I am not talking primarily of how we mutually *experience* an art shaped by words — that is, any writing — I am talking much more about the making of that writing. The writer first encounters the embodiment of language — that most incredible, most uniquely human ability — by hearing it: FLING LUMP CLAY — and if you cannot hear that embodiment, and in that very instant also see it, you are not a writer. I differentiate senses here for simple clarity, but which is primary, or which is most evocative, or most enduring is really a function impossible, and probably unnecessary, to explicate. Story spoken aloud, poetry seen and silently read from a page or recited aloud from a podium, drama acted out and/or spoken by actors on a stage or on a television or movie screen — these are creative acts imbibed by our very bodies, felt and experienced there, the more fully experienced the more *fully embodied there* until, at their most experiential, we are as it seems taken out of our own, particular, bodies altogether and become part of those other bodies that are there written before us. *For,* I would say, *the power of words, of writing, is in their body.*

To illuminate what I mean, let me tell you a story. My novel, *A Discovery of Strangers*, concerns itself with how the Yellowknife Dene of Arctic Canada first meet white men. This particular first encounter of physical bodies takes place in 1820, when five English naval personnel with their sixteen voyageur paddlers attempt to reach the Arctic Ocean overland from Hudson Bay, and are forced to spend the winter with the Yellowknives north of Great Slave Lake. The winter begins in early September and lasts for ten months, and during that time the Dene elder, Keskarrah, hears of the biblical creation story. He recounts the story to his wife and two daughters as they work around the centre fire in their lodge:

> [Lying on his back, Keskarrah] speaks upwards, into the smoke praying upwards.... "I've heard it said that These English began from mud. Richard Sun [the scientist on the expedition, John Richardson] told that story, white mud I suppose though he didn't say it exactly that way.... [He said] "You must know this, we men were made first from mud and the spit of The Great Soul Everywhere." ... I've never heard a story like that, about such spit, but it would be wonderful to see happening. Or feel, such spit, even if you never saw it. It would be like good rain, I suppose, which in summer makes very small things grow out of the ground in every place, so that story could be told, I can't doubt that. I told Richard Sun that if I'd been spitting and playing with such mud and finding a man in it, I would have used much more and made him bigger and stronger, a lot stronger like a bear; myself." ...
>
> "Richard Sun [also] says the woman Whitemud was supposed to be the companion and helper of the man.

She happens out of his rib while he's sleeping, but when he wakes up and there she is, his rib a woman out of his sleep, she doesn't help him at all, hey! she eats this one berry which is so large it grows alone on one big tree and then she gives it to him to eat and that makes everything in the world go completely crazy. Even the woman and the man."

[His wife Birdseye and daughter Greenstockings] are looking at him, puzzled, and he explains fast, "That's the part I can't understand, though I have been thinking about it. If People don't eat, they die — and Whites eat far more than People. How can one tree berry have so much power that eating it matters to everything else? Forever? Aren't there plenty of smaller berries for the man to eat? Our first man ate berries alone for a whole summer and nothing happened to him. But Richard Sun says no, that's probably because there was no woman yet. Once there is one, Whitemud man always has to eat at least as much as the woman, he can't eat less, and that one big berry she eats easily enough off the tree is too much for him. After that they both do everything all wrong."

"It's very strange," he adds thoughtfully, "hard for us to understand. Maybe it's eating *together* that's so bad for them — I've never seen a White woman so I can't tell — maybe that's why White men never travel with one?"

Greenstockings has not heard his contemplative speculations that are tangling him further; she is thinking about the rib.

"A rib from a tree?" she asks him, smiling and ready to laugh. That's a good story. A tall tree surely has as many ribs as branches. As it is, there are never enough women in the world so men never leave them alone, but if women were as numerous as branches, the fewer men would be kept so busy running after them that at least some women would be left in peace some of the time, maybe as long as the female caribou who with their growing calves live completely free from males for an entire year. She laughs aloud for happiness: what a happy story! And in her laughter senses the essence of her father's contemplations. [She says to him,]

"So — just never eat with [women]!"

"No no," Keskarrah, always a man, spoils it. "The rib is from the man, one rib only, that is where Whitemud Woman comes from."

Greenstockings asks, "These English do have their own women, somewhere? And their first woman has a man for her mother?"

Her laughter catches in her throat, then bursts out even louder at this truly incredible story; Birdseye and little Greywing answer her and suddenly the lodge is shaking with laughter....

"There's trouble," Keskarrah's tone quiets them immediately. He is lying with his eyes closed, as if he has already wandered much farther than he wanted to. Indeed, as if he has betrayed himself.

"The Whitemud story," he says, "is not happy.... Stories are like ropes, they pull you to incomprehensible places. This rib story could drag us tighter together with Whitemuds than the endless killing of animals.... Hey! a story can tangle you up, so badly you start to think different."...

He lies motionless, contemplating the luminous darkness under his own eyelids. Searching.

"Everything," he says softly, "is becoming dangerous....
These strangers are here now," he says with staggering
sadness. "It must be their fault. Never before has anything been all wrong with the world." (*Discovery* 123 – 25)

We understand Keskarrah's sadness, his sorrow at this Genesis
story better once we know the Yellowknife story of creation. That
story was first recorded in English by naturalist Richard King in
1835, told to him by an elder named, appropriately, Old Soul on
the Back River. Old Soul did not pretend he knew how a human
male first came into the world, but he felt it must have been in
summer, when there are plenty of berries for food. In the novel
Keskarrah tells the story this way:

"Man was alone, and lonely; he had only berries and roots
and leaves to eat and [he didn't know how to cook anything, like a woman does, and so] when winter came he
grew desperately hungry. He sank deep in the snow as
he watched rabbits and caribou and ptarmigan travel so
lightly on it that finally he dreamed his feet, they were
much bigger and he was running over snow everywhere
as easily as the animals, as swiftly as wind smoothing it,
whispering among birch. So at last he turned to the trees,
he peeled the white, thin birch and bent them into large
hoops. He stepped inside them, and he knew his feet
were in the right place — but he didn't know what to do
with the centre; there was no woman to see the strings
of babiche possible in animal leather and so weave the

webbing to bind his feet inside the wooden frames he had made.

"The bent birch lay there, empty, and every day he travelled, hunting. But in deep snow every animal ran easily from him; every day he returned with nothing, and always hungrier. Then one day he heard a noise in his shelter, so he ran as fast as he could and a ptarmigan flew out of the opening at the top before he could get there. The next day he hunted until dark, and then from a distance he saw smoke rising from his shelter. He rushed there and the beautiful ptarmigan flew out again, but inside he saw a fire burning and his snowshoe frames drying beside it, their sad emptiness half woven over with babiche.

"'The ptarmigan has done this,' he said, amazed as the fire warmed him.

"So next morning before leaving he covered the roof opening and did not go far; he returned early, breathing as quietly as he could sinking deep in the snow. And there he surprised the ptarmigan starting the fire again in his lonely shelter, the snowshoes lying almost complete with babiche webbing. The bird darted around, tried to fly out but could find no way to escape, and when he caught it, between his hands it turned into what he had often dreamed: someone like himself but O so different!

"Woman, yes, who made everything beautiful happen, fire to cook meat and tanned hides for clothing and lying together hot as bears and children forever because she alone could fill the frames he had dreamed and bent.

She changed when he held her, but her holding changed him as well. Frame and woven centre, when she fastened the snowshoes to his feet he became a bird, flying over the soft, deep snow everywhere in the beautiful world, and she prepared the animals he captured, they ate together and lived, long ago my mother told me this story of beginning," sang old Keskarrah, "O my mother, long ago my mother," he sang. (*Discovery* 90 – 91)

When I first encountered the basics of this story in Richard King, and then a variation of it in chapter one of *The Book of Dene*, it struck me like a revelation. From a nomadic caribou hunting people in an arctic wilderness comes this astonishing story of the creation of man and woman, a story without temptation, without heavy "disobedience," without eternal guilt written into the very body of all humanity by that elemental, necessary declaration of the body *eating*. No; the exact reverse is true. The story underlines that human act of eating (the act by which we of necessity sustain our physical bodies) is not the action by which evil enters the world, but that eating is made possible by the very relatedness, the sameness of all our animal bodies — after all, when a person eats an animal, or an animal eats a person, and both are nourished to health and strength thereby, such eating is simply a profound, inherent declaration of our physical, animal sameness: "Your body is mine, therefore, my body is yours." Which is, of course, also the Eden story of the rib, of the "one flesh" declaration by the Lord God in Genesis.

But in the Dene creation story the flesh stands without guilt; it emphasizes only female and male companionship, the endless possibilities for a transforming complementarity.

We know this power of touch, of complementarity, is there in all our bodies; we know it in every cell of our flesh, of our bones, of our tumultuous blood. I am certain we do — even if we are Mennonites and trained in certain denials! Who, in our most conservative (could one say "apprehensive"?) manifestations, have sometimes tried almost to mirror some Muslim peoples in the hiding of our bodies under all-effacing clothes. We have reserved these strictures especially for women — and I am happy to see that the women of Goshen College refuse to suffer such effacement. And why should anyone suffer it? We were breathed by God, yes, but before that could happen we were shaped by His hands: if we take that story seriously — and I do, I am deadly serious about that story — then surely we should recognize that the body is primary. It is there, first. It has to be *there*, so it can be breathed into.

The hundreds of continuing stories in the Bible underscore that primacy, and for Christian believers, the Bible's great, all-subsuming story turns upon it. Jesus is born first as a tiny, ordinary, physical baby; that baby's normal human development slowly reveals that Jesus is God's Son, and his mature man's body dies the way any human body would when physically abused and tortured and finally hammered onto and heaved up on a Roman executioner's cross.

Have you ever heard a minister or theologian discuss the implications of Jesus' physical body, I mean seriously, the way we live in our own bodies every day? Well, I have always thought that novels may go where ministers fear to tread: in my novel called *My Lovely Enemy*, the protagonist James Dyck — born a Russian Mennonite — meets Jesus and asks him about his body, specifically what he did with his penis when it insisted on having an erection since, as every man knows, a penis can exhibit a some-times embarrassing will of its own. When my church conference magazine the *M.B. Herald* reviewed the novel (mostly giving me advice on how I should have been written it differently), it was flooded with outraged letters. Church boards passed motions of censure on the editors; one board of elders wrote that the book, "offends the morals, pollutes the mind, and degrades the person of Jesus."

Nevertheless, not only do the Bible writers insist that Jesus had a complete human body but, far more drastically, they also declare that he returns from the dead in a complete, physical, *embodied*, return. They tell us that Mary Magdalene knows Jesus when she hears him speak her name, that Thomas knows Jesus when his open wounds offer themselves to the touch of Thomas's terrified fingers. And when Paul presents the Jesus story to the most searching intellectuals of his day, to the Athenians debat-ing ideas on Mars Hill, the bit of his speech Luke records for us is where Paul lays the general physical body of all humanity, and the particular physical body of Jesus together, right on the line:

> God who made the world and all the things that are in
> it…from one blood created every race of men to live over
> the face of the whole earth. He has fixed the times of
> their existence, and the limits of their territory, so that
> they should search for God and, it might be, feel after
> him and find him. And indeed he is not far from any of
> us, for in him we live and move and have our being. As
> some of your poets also have said, "We are his offspring."
> (Acts 17, 24–28)

How much more *physically* could Paul speak of Jesus and creation? Notice: "one blood"; "fixed the time"; "fixed the territory," i.e., the *place* where you live; "search for God"; "*feel* after him"; "in him we live and move"; "we are his offspring." But his listeners are Greek philosophers; no doubt they have been raised on Plato's theory of ideas, a concept of ideals perceptible to our senses only as they manifest themselves in the shifty physicality of their shadows. No wonder that when Paul declares, "God has given proof of this [that is, of Jesus's bodily, in body and at the same time divine, perfect appointment] to all men by raising Jesus from the dead," they mostly sneer and leave. Though a few listen, and believe; as a few always do. Their bodies declare it, within themselves.

In our contemporary world, it seems to me that Mennonite preachers or theologians have not been strong witnesses to this "*raising* of the *body* from the dead." Despite what the Bible insists, we seem to be fundamentally dominated by Augustine's Plato-influenced love of the ethereal spirit, of the literally untouchable soul; they are so much nicer, somehow — cleaner and perfectible. In most of our thinking, sin clings like a leech to the body, sucking itself tight onto it, never letting go, the very blood and flesh of its attachment must be torn away, the body disfigured if sin is ever to be, even momentarily, overcome. On the other hand, if a concept is mystically indescribable enough, something soulfully and unspeakably "spiritual," we will hear sermons about that forever. Every Sunday morning the word "love" is so endlessly thrown about in all Christian churches that one is reminded of nothing so much as the television repetition of Pepsi or Coca Cola. An ineffable word, so bathetically overused, has been battered to mean nothing actually graspable: meaning everything, it can only mean nothing at all. Mennonite preaching all too often abjures the body; the peasant, farm physicality of most of our origins (at least of my generation) has been mortified into abstracted, church-community general decencies and rules, something we feel we could suitably utter to children, in a vaguely soulish tone, of course.

Some of you will remember Scott Holland's story, which he told here at Goshen College last October. Scott Holland, an intellectual, postmodernist thinker, and also a minister-at-large for the Ohio Conference of the Mennonite Church. He tells how he and Menno Coblentz, an aged farmer, were walking together in the country one Saturday morning and Menno asked him, "Hey preacher, why can't the strange feelings of the barn and field ever enter the meeting house? It seems there is church talk and then there is everything else."

More Mennonite preachers, like Scott Holland, should work at trying to answer that question.

I believe that Mennonite writers are working harder at it than any theologians. Particularly the poets, and most particular of all the women poets like Di Brandt, Jean Janzen, Sarah Klassen or Audrey Poetker. It is most fitting therefore that I read a poem by Julia Kasdorf, who studied here at Goshen for several years, a woman who, to quote Gerald Stern, "has learned the secret to poetry, to snarl the music with the thought, and always to keep them together, as Chaucer taught." This poem from her superb first collection, *Sleeping Preacher*:

The Body Remembers
for David

Before they were married, Opa slept
on the floor beside Oma's bed.
The wedding feast was just
cabbage soup, not a bone
to cook in the village.
Even in Canada, Oma stewed borscht
without beef. In California, among orchards,
your mother cooks *geschmuade Bonen*
without ham. The body remembers
famine, but I make *Kartoffelsuppe*
thick with cream and stroke
your white ribs with my lips.
I kiss your stomach, innocent as a fish,
and crush my small, olive breasts
on your chest. The blades
of our pelvises collide
in defiance of grief
as we pull and thrust
against all the suffering
sown in our cells, all those stories
of bodies enduring torture and hunger
for God. We knock together
like two muddy shoes, knocking
history loose from our limbs,
knocking through Zurich and Danzig,
knocking off kulak and milksop
(all the names they once called us),
knocking until we are nothing special,
just a woman and a man on a floor
in Brooklyn, where Arab melodies
and Burmese cooking waft
through our windows like ghosts.
(Kasdorf 38)

I will let you conjecture why, from the story in Genesis, women might be able to live with their original, naked bodies and all their bodies' wondrous attributes and abilities better than men. It seems to me axiomatic that they do so; to this day. Before those flaming angelic swords close Eden away forever, the Lord God promises Eve the multiplication of sorrow in her childbearing; Adam in turn is promised the sorrow of eating the fruits of the now-cursed ground. I won't venture on a close reading of that text here, but simply point out that the era we call the Middle or Dark Ages was also the time of the great abbesses, from Bridget of Leinster in Ireland to Hildegard of Bingen in Germany. The word "abbess" is, of course, the feminine form of the word "abbot" who rules over an "abbey," the original word coming from Aramaic, "abba," meaning "father." To be an abbess, therefore, literally means to be a "fatheress," in the same way that any male, even an abbot, could develop into a "motherer." (Many languages have even more genius for these kinds of relational endings than English, but English is not bad if we push it.) It was in those ages we call "Dark," when the most imaginative and spiritual women in the church deliberately avoided bearing children, that they created the retreats and schools and hospitals of their magnificent abbeys, places where both children and women and men were physically, intellectually and spiritually nurtured; and it was there that the equality, the indivisible union of body and soul was most clearly taught and celebrated. On the other hand, the leading men of the church, from Origen in the third century — who castrated himself in an attempt to remove temptation, and found that he was, nevertheless, more enslaved than ever to his body — to Augustine in the sixth century — who brilliantly taught the fundamental corruption of humanity because of The Fall (it was always in capitals for him) and chained all Christians ever after to the inescapable doctrine of original sin within their fallen bodies — to Pope Innocent III (what a name for the most powerful, and most power-hungry pope who ever lived!), Innocent III who persuaded thousands to commit their bodies to the holy wars of the Crusades and who banned abbesses, forever, from hearing the confessions of their nuns and returned them again to the absolutions of male priests. It would seem, that for powerful Christian men, the female body was largely an object of overwhelming temptation; for some reason, in that body they could instantly recognize the, for them, devastating beauty of lust, but rarely, if ever, the sublime beauty of the temple of the Holy Spirit.

(And even as I wrote this, I was struck by the strange consanguinity of English sound between the words "temple" and "tempt." Both come from Latin, one meaning "the dwelling place of a deity," the other "to put to the test, often by touching, to test by feeling." In a place where the deity dwells, you test things by feeling them? Strange, strange.)

The Dark Ages gave way to the so-called "enlightened" Reformation, and ironically the most enlightened male reformers of the sixteenth century helped women not at all; neither Zwingli nor Luther nor Calvin, and not Menno Simons either. By 1563 the Council of Trent, the Roman church's "Counter Reformation," forbade abbesses every temporal power they had for centuries exercised outside their cloisters, which had included sitting as nobles in political councils even to the level of the German Diet; henceforth every abbess was strictly subordinated to her local bishop. The Protestant reformers of course took women out of the abbesses altogether, out of the hospitals and schools, the artistic movements they had fostered for over a millennium, and harnessed them all once more, all the more firmly, into childbearing and childrearing only. Both Martin Luther and Menno Simons married former nuns and had large families. "Your bodies will be saved in childbearing," Luther pronounced, even though one of the most fundamental scriptures for him was Psalm 51: 5: "Behold I was shapen in iniquity, and in sin did my mother conceive me." Thomas Aquinas, the Divine Doctor, had once argued that Original Sin was *not* transferred by propagation but, with Luther, Augustine's teaching once again ruled Christians: in sin *were we* conceived.

And so, consistent with the way they interpreted the Lord God's declaration in Eden, the Reformers returned women all the more firmly to the multiplication of their eternal sorrow. Five centuries later, many Christians (and that includes women) still refuse to conceive of a woman as other than either a temptation or a "mammy bending over her baby." I pray for us all that we will never again merely say "Amen" to that; we must, by now, understand what it implies.

For as a writer, I am faced with the obvious physicality of the places, the people I can tell stories about. Like the clay the sculptor works between her fingers, moulds with her "intelligent hands" until, as in Camille Claudel, the "body [is] a cavity in the huge space modeled" (xvii), a palpable, passionately developed obsession in physical form in body, so the writer must face the revelation em-body-ment will open out of words. As Di Brandt's poem expresses it so perceptively:

mother why didn't you tell me this
how everything in the middle of life
becomes its opposite & all the signs
turn unreadable every direction a
dead end why didn't you tell me about
the belly's trembling just when you
need strength how the brain turns to
mush when it most needs to be clear
when you promised us passion & warned
us about boys why didn't you tell
about the body's great emptiness its
wanting the void the tight ache of
heart's muscle in the middle of the night
the shaking of knees
(Brandt 55)

The body remembers, it always remembers. Because the body
knows.

1995

FLOWERS FOR APPROACHING
THE FIRE

Last summer (July 1997) I was asked to introduce an exhibit called *The Mirror of the Martyrs* then opening at the Provincial Museum here in Edmonton. This exhibit of physical items, audios, pictures and books, which had travelled to over 40 different places in North America, recalled the political and religious conflict during the Reformation in Europe some four centuries ago. The program declared it to be "the drama of people, obedient to state and church, torturing and killing people who claimed a higher obedience."

Anyone who saw this exhibit was faced with inevitable questions:

— Why would supposedly good people imprison, torture, and kill their fellow citizens?

— Why would good and decent people resist state authorities to the point of enduring deaths reserved for the worst of criminals?

These are hard and complex questions, and I would like to briefly lead your thinking about them in a series of seven notes. These "notes" are not exhaustive; they are simply points of meditation, among many possible others, to ponder.

Note One: The exhibit at the Provincial Museum is gone, but the questions it raised certainly are not. In fact, they are the kinds of questions Edmontonians working with the Mennonite Center for Newcomers continuously face. They are the kind of questions that many of you have experienced not only in your mind and imagination — as I have, thinking over the years about these matters — but some of you have experienced them in your very flesh and bones. Because you know your relatives and friends, persons you love, have experienced pain and suffering; perhaps they are enduring them at this very moment. One of the most important purposes of the MCN, this Edmonton organization we celebrate tonight, is to provide assistance and understanding to people who have been forced to live through such horrors in our twentieth century world. Perhaps that is why the organizers of this benefit asked me to repeat some of the remarks I made last summer about the Martyrs exhibit: because we all know very well that violence and martyrdom continue. In fact, statistics underscore what the media newscasts of the world tell us: this our century now drawing to a close, so "civilized," so alert to individual and even animal and environment "rights," the twentieth century has had more martyrs, Christian, Jewish, Muslim, Buddhist, political, racial — you could all add groups to that list — more martyrs than any other century in history.

I will try to differentiate between suffering and martyrdom in a later note, but before I do that I must warn you that what

I have to say tonight is no pleasant entertainment. These stories are brutal, they cannot help but be, and any touch of beauty in them only underscores their violent ugliness. But we all know what life can be like, how side-by-side contradictions so often exist, and this leads to:

Note Two: The fact that, the large and highly popular exhibit which immediately preceded *The Mirror of the Martyrs* at our provincial museum last summer was a bitterly ironic comment on our human situation: how we long for beauty and gentleness and peace for ourselves, but how we are so powerfully, so perversely attracted to the violence of past human history. The museum's preceding exhibit was *Genghis Khan, Treasures of Inner Mongolia*, and I cannot think of two subjects that could, shown one after the other, demonstrate more vividly the farthest bounds of human experience and values.

Genghis Khan was the kind of man history gives us only too often: the ultimate incarnation of the terrifying, unstoppable warrior leader. Genghis Khan, a nomadic Mongolian herdsman driven, as it seems, by pitiless vengeance to try to conquer, by force, the entire world known in the thirteenth century. And he very nearly did so; when he died in 1227, his empire stretched from the Pacific Ocean to the Black Sea and his army was at the gates of Vienna. He was capable of doing this, as historian John Keegan puts it because "he was untroubled by any of the monotheism of Buddhist or Christian concerns for mercy to strangers, or with personal perfection" (Keegan 206). Then, in contrast to the horrors of Genghis Khan and his army, and the literally millions of human beings they destroyed, *The Mirror of the Martyrs* exhibit followed; it told us the stories of "the defenseless Christians" of the sixteenth century.

The merciless warrior who by mass killing becomes a world despot, the defenceless or non-resistant believer: both are human beings, yes, homo sapiens are quite capable of both. They are opposite human extremes — and when you think about it, you might consider which it might be easier to be — but these very extremes, Keegan notes, have shaped our civilization. They do so to this day. Think of the human extremes of this century, as seen in men like

Joseph Stalin or Martin Luther King

Adolf Hitler or Mahatma Gandhi

Idi Amin or Nelson Mandela

You can make your own list. And as you do so, please notice what women come to your mind. Are there many? For example, with whom would you contrast Mother Teresa? Are the horrible extremes to be found only among *men*? If so, why is that?

Note Three: The stories I want to talk to you about are in this immense book I hold: 1157 large, double-column pages. I have here both the most recent 15th English edition, published in 1987, and this rare, leather-bound copy of the first complete English translation, published by the Mennonite Publishing Company in Elkhart, Indiana, in 1886. The book was first published in Dutch, in Holland in 1660 by Thieleman Jansz van Braght, and he compiled and wrote it from innumerable published and oral accounts. It contains the life stories and death accounts of over 4000 individuals, beginning with Jesus himself and is, without a question, the greatest historical work and the most enduring monument of Mennonite writing. Listen carefully to the full title, as Joseph Sohm translated it in 1886:

BLOODY THEATRE,

or

MARTYRS MIRROR

of the

DEFENSELESS CHRISTIANS

who Baptized Only Upon Confession of Faith, and Who Suffered and Died for the Testimony of Jesus, Their Savior, from the Time of Christ to the Year A.D. 1660

A long and complicated title. We need to take a few items in it apart to consider what this huge book really is.

First of all, it is called *The Bloody Theatre*. Why?

Well, "bloody" is obvious enough. When a human limb or head is chopped off, as often happened, there is an enormous spout of blood. How many litres of blood does a human body contain? An unimaginably horrifying sight, a visual assault we sheltered Canadians really cannot conceive of. And many people saw that, because one major element of sixteenth-century religious executions was that the public *must* see them. The events described in this book were not done in secret: these were not night arrests, disappearances that loved ones could search after for years and find no trace of; these were not the hidden killings that twentieth-century tyrants love so much. This was bloody, public theatre.

The title in the original Dutch "Tooneel" means "a stage, a place for display, for acting." In German it's "Schauplatz": a place where you see things that are exhibited; it also means the physical building where you stage plays. So this first section of the title makes it absolutely clear that, in the sixteenth century, martyrdom was an open, public act: a drama, complete with opening arrest, with imprisonments and often tortures to try and force people to confess more and/or change their minds, with long trials and debates and counter-arguments — all happening before an observant public — with eventual conviction and then, the climax of the drama, the execution. The point is: people were supposed to see every detail of the drama and, in particular, be present at the execution.

The time and place of execution was announced by public crier walking throughout the town. The city square, where it often took place, would be packed with hundreds of spectators. The condemned persons were brought in carts guarded by soldiers to prevent any outbreak of support on their behalf — sometimes they were led in chains, that is, if they could still walk after their torture — and if they still had a tongue, they would preach or quote Scripture or, more usually, sing hymns of faith that often they had composed themselves. Thus they exhorted the public to stand fast, or to convert to the faith. More often they were gagged or tongue-screwed to prevent them from testifying, but they could still turn, smile, nod their beaten heads to the crowd, lift their chained hands to heaven.

And the spectators to this "bloody theatre" might well include the family of the condemned, there to encourage them in their final witness of faith. The crowd could respond as it pleased: in silence, or weeping, or shouting curses, or blessings and prayers, but the latter could be dangerous: you might be arrested on the spot, and you'd be next on trial. If you revealed too much, you could be dragged out of the audience and yourself become the leading actor in the next performance of this horrific drama.

Truly a bloody theatre: the ultimate drama of life and death. This was no acting: it was literal life-on-the-line theatre. The fire really burned; the persons chained to stakes (often on high platforms so all could see exactly how they reacted to the flames) were literally reduced to ashes. This takes a long time: a living human body is largely liquid, it does not burn easily; and it takes even longer if you lay the fire farther away from the post, which was sometimes done, as part of the sentence, to increase the pain of dying. The condemned roasts, slowly.

This was all done in public; a show. I suppose that if it were done today — as we hear some countries occasionally do — our equivalent of exhibiting might well be prime-time television. I have no doubt that such a show would now have a world audience of billions. But in the sixteenth century, as Michel Foucault has pointed out, the theory of learning was that knowledge is constructed largely by analogy: you learn to know by recognizing the resemblances between things. You learn by watching, by doing. As Foucault writes, "The function of the public torture and execution was to reveal the truth... A successful public execution justified justice, in that it published the truth of the crime in the very body of the man to be executed" (Foucault 44).

For van Braght, the compiler and writer of this book in 1660, true language was exactly a mirror of nature, of what had actually taken place. He writes that the book "is a representation or exhibition of the blood, suffering and death of those who for the testimony of Jesus Christ, and for their conscience sake, shed their blood" (van Braght 16), and insists that his language literally reflects the innocent life and wrongful death experiences of the martyrs: the text in this book mirrors an exact reflection of what was said and done. Hence this title: *The Bloody Theatre, or the Martyrs Mirror of the Defenseless Christians*: a long title for what is, for me, one of the world's most enduring and significant books.

Note Four: The word "martyr" needs some discussion. "Martyr" and "martyrdom" are often used too vaguely to reveal the true power of what they mean.

Martyr comes from the same Greek word as the one meaning "witness"; its Aryan root simply means "to remember." As such, it is a word parallel to the Latin "confess," and in the early Christian tradition "martyr" is the word for those who "witness" or "confess" to their Christian faith to the point of death. Building from that, today the word carries the wider meaning of anyone who endures great suffering, even to the point of death, through steadfast devotion to a belief, a religious faith, an ideal or a cause. The *martyr* is one who will not renounce a personal conviction, who endures and witnesses to his or her belief to the limits of life, into death itself.

To keep this meaning clear, those who die in wars, in terrorist attacks, in racial purges, in genocide, in "ethnic cleansing" — that grotesque phrase invented to make us think, momentarily, that a bloody massacre is no more than a simple washing away — those who suffer this "cleansing" due to their ethnicity — these people are not necessarily martyrs. I am in no way trying to deny the significance or pain of their suffering; I am merely trying to be accurate about the use of the word *martyr,* which I take to be that *martyrdom* means it must be possible to *renounce* something in order to avoid the pain, the punishment your non-renunciation brings.

For example: two of my father's brothers, Peter and Heinrich Wiebe, were arrested, tortured and eventually murdered in Orenburg, Soviet Union, during the Stalin so-called "purges" of 1937–38. I would not call my uncles martyrs. Their deaths were prolonged and horrible, but they were not killed primarily because they testified to a Christian faith. Thousands of others who were not Christians died in the same way at that time in the Soviet Union: none of them could renounce anything to avoid their fate. In the same way, most of the millions who died in the Holocaust were not martyrs either. They could not deny, renounce their Jewish or their Gypsy blood: they suffered *geno-cide* – another horror the twentieth century had to invent a word for – but theirs was not martyrdom in the sense we mean here.

Of course, these words can overlap: Martin Luther King was assassinated, but was he a martyr? He could not renounce his black ancestry, but perhaps he could have renounced his vision, so which was the reason for the lethal bullet? Probably both. Meanings do overlap, but let's try to be clear in our thinking when they do.

The over 4000 people whose life and death stories are recorded in *The Martyrs Mirror* died not because of their race or their political convictions, but because they steadfastly refused to change their religious beliefs. The Reformation in Europe transformed Christianity forever, yes, and eventually for the better, but for more than a century it was a time of grotesque killing in the name of "true" Christianity. There were particularly many "executions" of believers in Holland because Holland was under the political control of Spain and the Spanish kings, both Charles V and Philip II, believed they ruled by divine right. They considered themselves to be God's representatives on earth and, since they were Roman Catholics, only such believers could live in their domains. They used their secular armies to enforce that religious concept: if you were suspected of "wrong belief," the army arrested you and then you were examined in a trial by the church authorities, i.e., the Inquisition, to make you declare your "heresy."

Two key test questions were always asked of you:

1) Did you baptize your infant when it was born?

2) Do you believe that in holy communion the bread and wine turn into the literal flesh and blood of Jesus Christ?

If you could not immediately and unequivocally answer "Yes" to both, you had proven yourself to be not of the true Roman Catholic faith; therefore, you either recanted or you died.

Holy Roman Emperor Philip II's policy towards Holland during his long reign (1556 – 1598) exemplified Ferdinand II's Inquisition maxim: "Rather a desert than a land full of heretics." His instruments for this policy were the Cardinal Granvelle of the Inquisition and the Duke of Alva with his army. Together they formed what was called "A Council of Blood" and they killed over 18,000 people for their faith. They raged especially hard in Flanders (now partly in Belgium), from Antwerp to Amsterdam and The Hague. I cannot review here the horrors of what was done: much is recorded, with stomach-turning vividness, in this large book. A good deal of it is given in dramatic form, the actual records of trials, the questions asked by the most learned theologians available and the responses given by ordinary working people, many of whom could not read or write but who had memorized entire chapters and books of the Bible. For example, in 1549 a man named Eelken was arrested in Leeuwarden; he "boldly confessed his faith" before the lords.

Eelken was then asked again, "What do you hold concerning the sacrament?"

Answer: "I know nothing of your baked God."

Question: "Friend, take care what you say. Such words

cost necks.... What do you hold concerning our holy Roman church?"

Answer: "I know nothing of your holy church. I do not know it; I never in all my life was in a holy church."
(van Braght 484)

And so it goes on. The dialogue at the trials is usually not so cutting and ironic; but it is always deadly for the believer. Eelken is executed with the sword, a relatively merciful death, quick and without prolonged suffering, if you got a good swordsman.

Most of the stories are not so defiantly up-beat; the deaths are not so quick, and the believers are ordinary people, not heroes; they suffer the extremes of hope and despair. As many women as men suffered: for example, Ursel van Essen who, together with her husband Arent and two other women, was arrested by the troops of the Duke of Alva in Maastrich in 1570. They all refused to renounce their faith, and Ursel was particularly tortured. She was placed twice on the wheel of the rack (842) and stretched, her body caught and held in that position by a ratchet, notch by notch. However, despite unimaginable pain she steadfastly refused to speak the names of any other believers, and it is recorded that a Jesuit advised that she be scourged: "The executioner tied her hands together and drew her up [on a hanging post] and, as she was hanging there he cut open her chemise with a knife baring her back, and severely scourged her with rods; this was done twice in one day" (842). (Jan Luyken made an engraving of this for the 1685 edition of The Martyrs Mirror.) Finally, enduring all pain, on January 9, 1570, she was led out separately, so that she and her husband could not comfort each other, to the place of execution.

She asked the lords:

"And may I not sing a little, and say something now and then?" But this they would not permit her... the executioner had a piece of wood which he put in Ursel's mouth, and tied up her mouth with a cloth.... Thus Ursel went to the place where she was to be offered up, the people complaining greatly, because her mouth had been gagged so that she could not speak one word.

When Ursel arrived at the scaffold which had been erected, she ascended it quietly as a lamb, and went directly into the [straw] hut, and the executioner immediately set fire to the same; and thus she was burned to ashes, and became a burnt offering unto the Lord. (844)

Note Five: Torture. We must, for a few moments, consider this frightening word. Let us be formal about it. A French encyclopedia definition quoted by Foucault: *torture* is "Corporal punishment painful to a more or less horrible degree...an inexplicable phenomenon that the extension of man's imagination creates out of the barbarous and cruel" (Foucault 33).

In the hands of the state, "death-torture is the art of maintaining life in pain, by," as it were, "subdividing" life into a "'thousand'," endless deaths each more painful than the last. Foucault theorizes that there is a kind of "legal code of pain" (34), and the fact that the person groans, cries out in suffering is part of the ceremonial ritual that is required in "proper, legal" torture. The legal point was that the kings and the bishops of the sixteenth century (and perhaps some rulers, including imams, to this day) held it was their moral obligation to assert their power in the world over what people did and thought because they were acting on God's behalf by enforcing His Divine Law on earth. In that sense, the death of the person at the end of the formal judicial ritual takes on even greater intensity because the death "hastened by pain…occurs exactly at the juncture between the judgement of men and the judgement of God" (46). The judgement of men, the final burnings, these are the earthly representations (for all to see and learn) of the eternal judgement of hell to which these heretics are now going. "The eternal game has already begun: the torture of the execution anticipates [begins and leads into] the punishments of the beyond" (46), which will last for all eternity.

And herein lies the ultimate power of the martyrs singing songs, testifying, waving with joy to the throngs as they were taken to execution. They did not curse the emperor, or the church, who had such overwhelming power to hurt their bodies. They accepted the torch quietly, even gladly, not because they were fanatics, or out of their minds — no — but because they thereby gave the ultimate witness to their faith: they believed this judicial torture, this excruciating fire, represented nothing but the final act of what "carnal" men could inflict upon them. By their calm, by their very joy they declared that this fire of wood and straw was earthly, momentary, and though its leaping flames would certainly torture and eventually kill them, this was not for them the gateway into everlasting, burning hell. No. These flames were their bright entrance into the Eternal City of God.

Note Six: Spain's enslavement of the Dutch could not last, and to try forcing a form of religion upon so many, brutalizing and killing them publicly, expropriating their property, causing many of the most industrious citizens to flee the country taking their skills and what property they could with them — military rebellion erupted. By 1581 the Dutch Prince William of Orange united North Holland against Spain, but war raged on in many vicious forms — in all, over 80 years of conflict until the Dutch gained their ultimate freedom from Spain in 1648. By the late 1650s then, when van Braght began working on *The Martyrs Mirror*, there was very little inquisition or burning of heretics in Holland. So, why did he write it?

He believed times that are "quieter and more comfortable" can be very dangerous for those who would live "the true separated Christian life which is the outgrowth of faith" (8), and he wanted to strengthen the believers' faith with these stories. They must be remembered, "the many beautiful examples of men, women, youths and maidens who faithfully followed their Savior Christ Jesus in the true faith...well knowing that they [who would] live godly lives must suffer persecution."

And then, when van Braght has told the hundreds of stories that constitute the sixteenth-century persecution, he writes one of the finest declarations of freedom of conscience ever composed. I excerpt:

> Who would execute judgement of conscience upon a human being? Who can fathom a man's heart save He who sees all things... and penetrates the hearts and knows the thoughts of all men?
>
> God alone can judge us — the human examiners of faith can easily be blinded, deceived by lies and a hypocritical life....
>
> It behooves a king to tolerate all sorts of doctrines, persuasion and heretics in his country [for if] in any

country several princes, differing in religions should come to rule one after another [as was often the case in Europe, with England the best known to us] and each seeking to enforce his faith, they would pollute the land with the blood of its inhabitants, such a country would be nothing else than a hell... a lamentable misery, as ships on the turbulent ocean are rocked by storm and wind till they at last suddenly perish. But how can they so greatly hate and cast out any one for their faith, even though he should err? This is not the nature of the children of God, who do not suppress even the unrighteous, even as it is not the nature of sheep to devour wolves, but to flee from them, and suffer devouring. (van Braght 1099)

Perhaps that is too strong for us, in our century: that we should, for our faith, willingly "suffer devouring." To put it another way: that the righteous subsume, within their very own bodies, the pain and suffering of others. Can we, who perhaps believe ourselves to be righteous believers, can we accept such a burden?

I do not know; I cannot speak for anyone. As van Braght illustrates so often in this formidable book, each person chooses for himself or herself; each must give personal account, even, he insists, the very king himself. What I do know is that the people whose stories he has gathered for us to read four centuries later, they took up this burden of suffering with fear and joy. For it is exactly at that moment of accepting pain, in joy, that the powerlessness of the martyr becomes the greatest possible strength. At that moment of heaviest burden, overwhelming suffering, no power on earth can touch you.

Note Seven: My title for this talk, "Flowers for Approaching the Fire," comes of course from another story in this book.

My friend Mary Wright told me that she had a copy of the 1886 edition of *The Martyrs Mirror*. Her family came to Didsbury, Alberta, from Ontario early in this century, and the book had been passed on to her as a family heirloom. Then Mary's daughter, Megen Collins, told me another story about it. She remembered the book always being around, it was very large and she'd never read it, but sometimes, when she opened it and looked at the pictures, sometimes there were prairie flowers drying between its leaves.

Now, I love books. I don't really believe in using them as a flower press but, in this case, the more I thought about it, the lovelier the story became. Believe me, this is a book very difficult to read. Even in short bits, 16 centuries of cruelty done in the name of Christianity is hard to take. Yet, between these horrible acts of human beings, the wild, uncontrollable beauty of flowers is laid.

And of course, when we think of flowers, Christians remember the inspiring words of Jesus: "Consider the lilies of the field, how they grow; they toil not, neither do they spin, yet I tell you, not even Solomon in all his splendor was dressed like one of these" (Matthew 6:28). Those poor, tortured men and women, facing all the assembled, rich, splendidly dressed lords of the state and of the church: in the eyes of Jesus, who was truly "dressed" the most beautifully? Pressing wild flowers between the leaves of this book is right, and lovely.

And in this immense library of lives gloriously lived and ended, there is also a flower story to discover. It is the 1527 story of a zealous Lutheran minister — van Braght was completely ecumenical in his accounts of martyrs — named Leonard Keyser:

In the second year of his ministry Leonard Keyser was apprehended in Scharding, Bavaria [a Roman Catholic jurisdiction], and condemned by the Bishop of Passau and others...to be burned on Friday before St. Lawrence day in August.... Having bound him on a cart, they took him to the fire, the priests going alongside, and speaking Latin to him, but he, on account of the people, answered them in German.... When he came out into the field, as they were approaching the fire, he, bound as he was, leaned down at the side of the cart and plucked a flower with his hand, saying to the judge, who rode on horseback alongside the cart: "Lord judge, here I pluck a flower; if you can burn this flower and me, you have justly condemned me; but, on the other hand, if you cannot burn me and this flower in my hand, consider what you have done and repent." Therefore the judge and the three executioners threw an extraordinary quantity of wood into the fire, in order to burn him immediately to ashes by the great fire. But when the wood was entirely burned up, his body was taken from the fire uninjured. Then the three executioners and their assistants built another great fire of wood which, when it was consumed, his body still remained uninjured, only his hair and nails were somewhat burnt brown, and, the ashes having been removed from his body, the latter was found smooth and clear, and the flower in his hand, not withered, or burnt in the least, the executioners then cut his body into pieces, which they threw into a new fire. When the wood was burned up, the pieces lay unconsumed in the fire. Finally they took the pieces and threw them into the river Inn.

This judge was so terrified by this occurrence that he resigned his office, and moved to another place. His chief servant, who was with the judge, and saw and heard all this, came to us in Moravia, became our brother and lived and died piously. That it might not be forgotten our teachers have recorded this as it came from his own lips, and now cause it to be promulgated and made known. (421)

"That it might not be forgotten." What is it we should not forget?

We should not forget those who know have suffered, and especially those who died as martyrs for their faith and convictions. We must remember them, remember their witness. And tell their stories to each other again and again.

And, I would say, there is one other thing we should not forget:

When you are approaching the fire, remember this:

flowers are your best, your only protection.

1998

LOOK TO THE ROCK

My fellow pilgrims:

We gather here today, in Tokmak, Ukraine, from around the circle of the earth, to remember, and to give thanks. I greet you with the words of the poet and prophet Isaiah:

Listen to me, all you who follow what is right and seek the Lord;

Look to the rock from which you were cut,

To the quarry from which you were dug....

For I am the Lord your God...

And I have put my words in your mouth,

And hid you in the shadow of my hand...

And I say to Zion, "You are my people."

(Ch. 51:1, 16)

The quarry from which we are dug is the bedrock of Jesus Christ himself, the rock from which we are cut is the faith of our ancestors. Here, today, we want to look to that rock dug from that quarry, and remember.

Four hundred and eighty years ago our spiritual forbears in Switzerland studied the Scriptures and, with great joy, they discovered a new understanding of how to be a disciple of Jesus. It meant committing themselves to following him both in his teachings *and* in his life. When in January, 1525, Georg Blaurock knelt before Conrad Grebel and said, "I beg you, for God's sake, give me the true Christian baptism!" he was not a helpless baby having a rite administered upon him; he was a responsible adult confessing his faith in Jesus Christ; he is a deliberate adult declaring his decision to follow Jesus.

From this rock of decision, of joy, of free-will commitment, are we cut.

And we remember the consequences. Even as the fire of this new Gospel spread north with adult baptisms through Europe, just as quickly did persecution by state church and state government follow.

— January, 1527, Feliz Manz in Switzerland, drowned;

— May, 1527, Michael Sattler in Germany, burned at the stake; two days later his wife Margaretha Sattler drowned;

— November, 1527, Weynken Claes, a widow in Holland, burned at the stake.

Four of many; and always there were more, and more. The sixteenth century became a hell of blood and burning. You can read the stories in the thick martyr books published in every language of Europe. As the writer of the Book of Hebrews declares: "What more shall I say? For time would fail me to tell of [all the faithful who suffered]. They were too good for a world like this one" (11:32, 38).

What can you do when you are hounded to death for your faith by those who have power over you? You can:

— renounce your faith — and some did;

— you can try to fight the powers with their own violence of fire and water and rope and sword — and some did;

— you can try to be a secret believer — but how can a faithful Christian life be kept a secret, hidden in a corrupt world?

— you can suffer and die — and thousands did;

— or you can flee. Not the flight of cowards, nor the escape of those who seek a promised land which will be forever theirs, no, rather the journeying of those who renounce human violence and who flee to find a refuge, somewhere, anywhere on earth where they can live their faith in peace.

Many, perhaps most of us, in this room today are the descendants of those who in the past five centuries have fled. Our Swiss and German ancestors found refuge in North America with the English Quaker settlements of Pennsylvania; our Dutch ancestors fled east to where the good Roman Catholic citizens of Danzig and the King of Poland offered them refuge in return for their hard work in reclaiming the Vistula Delta. For over two hundred years they lived there, following their motto of "Work and Hope." God blessed them as a community of believers, as artisans in the city, as farmers building beautiful villages and farmsteads protected by the dikes and windmills they built on the Vistula marshlands. But the continual wars of Europe over-ran them, and when Frederick the Great of Prussia came to control their destiny, it was time for many Mennonites to flee again. Beginning in 1789 our forbears left the lowlands of Prussia for refuge here, on the strange, high steppes of Ukraine, its long hills and winding rivers. And here too, with hard labour, they found civil peace and God blessed them with freedom and many children and a burgeoning prosperity. And so much independence that the community often disagreed, even quarreled within itself — Flemish and Frisians, landless and land owners, conservatives and progressives, Mennonite and Mennonite Brethren — but the Czar's land was vast enough to contain them all, and especially here in Ukraine their communities blossomed into what we now call "The Mennonite Commonwealth." Churches, schools, hospitals, factories, estates, art and music, railroads grew and flourished, and above all so did personal freedoms; the "quality of life" of individuals improved like an endless blessing from God.

Yes, the Mennonite world here flourished in faith and prosperity, until World War I and the Bolshevik Revolution destroyed all Russian worlds together; within a few years no person alive in what had once been the Czar's immense Empire was spared possible destruction.

Those of us who have come from North and South America are here today because our parents and grandparents fled from this land of Ukraine in the 1870s, in the 1920s, in the 1940s. On those far continents we have found, so far, peace, much prosperity, and above all freedom to practise our faith. Today the worldwide Mennonite family has grown to over a million baptized believers. But many of our personal families who remained in the Soviet Union until its collapse experienced violence, cruelty, fear, destruction that may well exceed the suffering of our ancestors in the sixteenth century. You, sisters and brothers from Germany, and you the enduring believers of Ukraine, understand this more clearly than anything I could attempt to describe.

But today, October 10, 2004 we can meet, peacefully in Ukraine. We can come together and tell each other our stories, however sad or happy or amazingly miraculous they may be. That is the most beautiful thing we human beings can do together: not yell at each other, or quarrel about land, or kill one another because of an idea or, worse, kill because of God. No! We are human beings, created from the mud of the earth and the breath of our Creator, and we talk! We tell each other stories, as, by his brilliant example, Jesus himself taught us. Our past gives us the stories by which we can live our present story.

Let me, for a few moments, tell you a story of mine.

There once was a Mennonite colony — it exists no longer — of twenty-five villages north of the city Orenburg near the Ural Mountains in eastern European Russia. Both my father's and my mother's parents moved from the colonies here in Ukraine to be pioneer settlers on the steppes there; in 1929 my parents with their five children were the only members of either large family to get out of Russia in the dramatic escape now known to Mennonites as "The Flight Over Moscow." Almost seventy years later my wife Tena and I were in Orenburg for the first time. My cousin Johann showed us "The Grey House" at #24 Kirov Street where, deep in the basement where their cries could not be heard, the KGB questioned those they arrested, often questioned them to death. High over the houses Johann pointed out the walls and roofs of enormous Orenburg Prison on the banks above the Ural River, and then we crossed the bridge into the valley where the river turns against the rock cliffs below the city. For decades this valley was a park, a playground for families, walks for lovers to wander hand in hand, until one spring the river washed away the bank and exposed bones, thousands upon thousands of human bones. The river revealed that the lovely park below Orenburg was in reality a massive grave, covered trenches filled with the bodies of men murdered during the Stalin terror of 1937–38.

Today the river valley is a park no longer; it is a memorial. We stand in silence, look down the rows upon rows of memorial birch trees now planted there, each one bearing a plaque with a name and a date of birth, though it is of course impossible to plant enough trees to name all those who were destroyed. We remember in particular my father's two brothers, the elder Peter Jacob Wiebe and the youngest Heinrich Jacob Wiebe, whose bones are here, somewhere, slowly moldering back to their elements, and as we kneel there to weep, to pray, to touch the long-suffering earth which nourishes this green May grass and these shining birches, we remember the son of that Uncle Peter Wiebe, also a Peter — the name means "rock" — my cousin Peter Petrovitsch Wiebe who was twice torn from his home during the night, also tortured in The Grey House, also starved in Orenburg Prison, but somehow, by the strange mercy of God, survived all that to work for years in a Kazakhstan prison labour camp and who in his old age was free in Germany, who lived surrounded by children and grandchildren and great-grandchildren to whom he could tell, again and again, the inexplicable mysteries of his life: how God had been good to him and had kept them all, through all pain and suffering and labour and death, kept them faithfully in His loving care.

My cousin Peter's rock of faith overcame the Gulag. And now he rests in the bosom of Abraham. And when I remember us in Germany during the 1980's telling each other stories in the language our mothers spoke with us, it is as if I were seeing the long, long pilgrimage of our Mennonite people reaching back through the centuries, our ancestors working in hope and with great courage, leaving their homes again and again in order to remain true followers, faithful disciples of Jesus. For in the stories that Peter told me, I could hear even more clearly the voice of God speaking through Isaiah:

Listen to me,
All you who follow what is right and search for God;
Look to the rock from which you were cut,
To the quarry from which you were dug....
[Listen to me,]
For I am the Lord your God...
And I have put my words in your mouth,
And [I have] hid you in the shadow of my hand...
And I say to you, "You are my people."

Thanks be to God (*Dank sei Dir, Herr*).

2004

WORKS CITED

Aquinas, St. Thomas. *Summa Theologiae*. Second Part, Part 1 (1265 – 1274).

Aristotle. *Politics*. Trans. H. Rackham. London: William Heinemann, 1932.

Atwood, Margaret. *Strange Things: The Malevolent North in Canadian Literature*. Oxford: Clarendon Press, 1995.

Blondin, George. *Yamoria The Lawmaker: Stories of the Dene*. Edmonton: NeWest Press, 1997.

———. *When the World was New: Stories of the Sahtu Dene*. Yellowknife: Outcrop, 1990.

The Book of Dene. Dept. of Education, Government of the Northwest Territories. Yellowknife: 1976.

Brandt, Di. "questions i asked my mother." *Questions i asked my mother*. Winnipeg: Turnstone Press, 1987. 55.

Brody, Hugh. *The Other Side of Eden: Hunters, Farmers and the Shaping of the World*. Vancouver: Douglas & McIntyre, 2000.

Buber, Martin. *I and Thou*. Trans. Walter Kaufmann. New York: Charles Scribner's Sons, 1970.

Cameron, William B. *The War Trail of Big Bear*. Boston: Small, Maynard & Co., 1927.

Cardinal, Gil, and Rudy Wiebe. *Big Bear*. Dir. Gil Cardinal. Canadian Broadcasting Corporation, 1998/9.

Carson, Anne. "Foam (Essay with Rhapsody): On the Sublime in Longinus and Antonioni." *Brick*, 68 (Fall 2001): 143 – 49.

Claudel, Paul. Quoted in Reine-Marie Paris, *Camille – The Life of Camille Claudel*. New York: Henry Holt, 1988.

Collinson, Richard, ed. *The Three Voyages of Martin Frobisher, in Search of a Passage to Cathaie and India by the North-West, 1576 – 78*. London: Hakluyt Society, 1867.

Cowper, William. "Hope." *Poems: 1782*. London: The Scolar Press Limited, 1973. 140 – 79.

Dempsey, Hugh A. *Big Bear: The End of Freedom*. Vancouver: Douglas & McIntyre, 1984.

———, ed. "The Starvation Year: Edgar Dewdney's Diary for 1879." *Alberta History*, 31, (1), 1983.

Dickinson, Emily. "I heard a Fly buzz (465)." *The Complete Poems of Emily Dickinson.* Ed. Thomas H. Johnson. Boston: Little, Brown, 1960. 223–24.

Dillard, Anne. *The Writing Life.* New York: Harper & Row, 1989.

Dyck, Arnold. *Koop enn Bua op Reise.* Steinbach, Man.: Derksen Printers, 1942.

Dyck, Peter P. *Orenburg am Ural.* Clearbrook, B.C.: Christian Book Store, 1951.

Foucault, Michel. *Discipline and Punish: The Birth of the Prison.* New York: Vintage Books, 1979.

Fraser, William B. "Big Bear, Indian Patriot." *Alberta Historical Review* 14.2 (Spring 1966): 1–13.

Friesen, Gordon. *Flamethrowers.* Caldwell, Idaho: Caxton Printers, Ltd., 1936.

Fuentes, Carlos. "The Two Shores." *The Orange Tree.* London: Picador, 1994.

Gray, James H. *Red Lights on the Prairies.* Toronto: MacMillan, 1971.

Green, L.C., and Olive P. Dickason. *The Law of Nations and the New World.* Edmonton: U of Alberta Press, 1989.

Henderson, James (Sakej) Youngblood, Marjorie L. Benson, and Isobel M. Findlay. *Aboriginal Tenure in the Constitution of Canada.* Scarborough: Carswell, 2000.

Highway, Tomson. "Hearts and Flowers." *Our Story: Aboriginal Voices on Canada's Past.* Np: Anchor Canada, 2004. 177–99.

Hobbes, Thomas. *Leviathan.* Oxford: Clarendon Press, 2012.

Hood, Robert. *To the Arctic by Canoe, 1819–1821: The Journal and Paintings of Robert Hood, Midshipman with Franklin.* Ed. C. Stuart Houston. Montreal: Arctic Institute of North America, 1974.

James, Henry. "The Art of Fiction." 1888. *The Art of Fiction and Other Essays.* New York: Oxford UP, 1948. 3–23.

Johnson, James Weldon. "The Creation." *Poems Worth Knowing.* Ed. Claude Lewis. Toronto: Copp Clark Co., 1941. 259–61.

Johnston, Alex. *The C.P. Rail High Level Bridge at Lethbridge.* Lethbridge: Lethbridge Historical Society, 1993.

Johnston, Alex, and Barry R. Peat. *Lethbridge Place Names and Points of Interest.* Lethbridge: Historical Society of Alberta, 1987.

Kasdorf, Julia. "The Body Remembers." *Sleeping Preacher.* Pittsburgh: U of Pittsburgh P, 1992. 38.

Keegan, John. *A History of Warfare.* Toronto: Vintage Books, 1994.

King, Richard. *Narrative of a Journey to the Shores of the Arctic Ocean* in 1833.... London: R. Bentley, 1836.

King, Thomas. *The Truth about Stories*. Toronto: Anansi, 2003.

Klein, A.M. "Portrait of the Poet as Landscape." *The Collected Poems of A.M. Klein*. Toronto: McGraw-Hill Ryerson, 1974.

Kogawa, Joy. *Obasan*. Toronto: Lester & Orpen Dennys, 1981.

Kroetsch, Robert. "A Conversation with Margaret Laurence." *Creation* by Robert Kroetsch, James Bacque and Pierre Gravel. Ed. Robert Kroetsch. Toronto: New Press, 1970. 53–63.

———. *A Likely Story*. Red Deer: Red Deer College Press, 1995.

———. "The Moment of the Discovery of America Continues." *The Lovely Treachery of Words: Essays Selected and New*. Toronto: Oxford UP, 1989. 1–19.

Langer, Suzanne K. "Language and Thought." *Language Awareness: Readings for College Writers*. Eds. Paul Eschholz, et al. Boston: Bedford/ St. Martin's, 2000. 96–101.

Laurier, Sir Wilfred. *House of Commons Address*. 21 February 1905.

Leacock, Stephen. "I'll Stay in Canada." *Canadian Anthology*, ed. C.F. Klinck & R.E. Watters. Toronto: Gage, 1958. 209–213.

Mandelstam, Osip. "Thrust." *Sobranie Sochinenii*. 3 Vols. Ed. Gleb Struve and Boris Filipoff. Washington, D.C.: 1971.

Maugham, W. Somerset. *Of Human Bondage*. New York, The Modern Library ed., copyright George Doran Co., 1915.

Merton, Thomas. *Love and Living*. Eds. Naomi Burton Stone and Patrick Hart. Toronto: Bantam Books, 1979.

Milloy, John S. *The Plains Cree: Trade, Diplomacy and War, 1790–1870*. Winnipeg, U of Manitoba Press, 1988.

Morris, Alexander. *The Treaties of Canada with the Indians of Manitoba and the North-West Territories, Including the Negotiations on Which They Were Based, and Other Information Relating Thereto*. 1880. Toronto: Coles, 1971.

Naipaul, V.S. "Jasmine." 1964. *The Overcrowded Barracoon and Other Articles*. London: Andre Deutsch, 1972. 9–16.

O'Connor, Flannery. "The Nature and Aim of Fiction." *Mystery and Manners: Occasional Prose*. New York: Farrar, Straus & Giroux, 1969.

The Oxford Annotated Bible with the Apocrypha, RSV. Ed. Herbert May and Bruce Metzget. New York: Oxford UP, 1965.

Persky, Stan. *Delgamuukw: The Supreme Court of Canada Decision on Aboriginal Title*. Vancouver: Greystone Books, 1998.

Pinker, Steven. *The Language Instinct: The New Science of Language and Mind*. London: Allen Lane, 1994.

Ponting, J. Rick, ed. *Arduous Journey: Canadian Indians and Decolonization*. Toronto: McClelland and Stewart, 1986.

Redekop, Magdalene Falk. "Translated into the Past: Language in *The Blue Mountains of China*." *A Voice in the Land: Essays By and About Rudy Wiebe*. Ed. W.J. Keith. Edmonton: NeWest Press, 1981. 97–123.

Russell, Peter H. "High Courts and the Rights of Aboriginal Peoples: The Limits of Judicial Independence" *Saskatchewan Law Review* 61 (1998). 247–76.

Sebald, W.G. *On The Natural History of Destruction*. Trans. Anthea Bell. Toronto: Knopf Canada, 2003.

Shakespeare, William. *The Complete Plays and Poems of William Shakespeare*. Ed. William A. Neilson and Charles J. Hill. Cambridge: Riverside Press, 1942.

Shelley, Percy Bysshe. "The Daemon of the World: A Fragment." *The Complete Poetical Works of Percy Bysshe Shelley*. Ed. Thomas Hutchinson. London: Oxford UP, 1940. 1–14.

Simpson, A.W. Brian. *A History of the Land Law*. Oxford: Clarendon Press, 1986.

Stanley, George F.G. *The Birth of Western Canada: A History of the Riel Rebellions*. London: Longmans, Green, 1936.

United Nations Charter. United Nations. Victoria, BC: Colonist Presses, 1945.

van Braght, Thieleman J. *The Bloody Theater or Martyrs Mirror of the Defenseless Christians Who Baptized Only Upon Confession of Faith, and Who Suffered and Died for the Testimony of Jesus, Their Savior, From the Time of Christ to the Year A.D. 1660*. Trans. Joseph Sohm. Scottdale, PA: Herald Press, 1886; 15th ed. 1987.

van Herk, Aritha. *Places Far From Ellesmere*. Red Deer: Red Deer College Press, 1990.

Venne, Sharon Helen. *Our Elders Understand Our Rights: Evolving International Law Regarding Indigenous Peoples*. Penticton: Theytus Books, 1998.

von Clausewitz, Carl. *On War*. Trans. J.J. Graham. Ed. Anatol Rapoport. Harmondsworth: Penguin Books, 1968.

Wiebe, Rudy. "After Thirty Years of Marriage." *Rudy Wiebe: Collected Stories, 1955–2010*. Edmonton: U of Alberta Press, 2010. 156–66.

———. "All on their Knees." *Collected Stories.* 178–90.

———. "The Angel of the Tar Sands." *Collected Stories.* 248–51.

———. "The Blindman River Contradictions: An Interview with Rudy Wiebe." *Collected Stories.* 346–56.

———. "Broken Arm." *Collected Stories.* 3–21.

———. "Life Story." *Collected Stories.* 310–11

———. *Big Bear, Extraordinary Canadians.* Toronto: Penguin Canada, 2008.

———. *Of This Earth: A Mennonite Boyhood in the Boreal Forest.* Toronto: Knopf Canada, 2006.

———. "Where the Black Rocks Lie in the Old Man's River." *Place: Lethbridge, A City on the Prairie,* Rudy Wiebe (author) and Geoffrey James (photographer). Vancouver: Douglas & McIntyre, 2002. 90–126.

———. *Sweeter Than All the World.* Toronto: Knopf Canada, 2001.

———. "Bear Spirit in a Strange Land." *River of Stone: Fictions and Memories.* Toronto: Vintage Books, 1995.

———. *A Discovery of Strangers.* Toronto: Knopf Canada, 1994.

———. "On Death and Writing." *Canadian Literature* 100 (Spring 1984): 354–60.

———. *My Lovely Enemy.* Toronto: McClelland and Stewart, 1983.

———. *A Voice in the Land.* Ed. W.J. Keith. Edmonton: NeWest Press, 1981.

———. *The Scorched-Wood People.* Toronto: McClelland and Stewart, 1977.

———. *The Temptations of Big Bear.* Toronto: McClelland and Stewart Limited, 1973.

———. "Western Canada Fiction; Past and Future." *Western American Literature,* Vol. VI, # 1, Spring, 1971.

———. *The Blue Mountains of China.* Toronto: McClelland and Stewart Limited, 1970.

———. *Peace Shall Destroy Many.* Toronto: McClelland and Stewart Limited, 1962.

———. "Fall Sunday in Hyde Park." *Stet: The Gateway,* University of Alberta, Edmonton, March, 1959.

———. "The Power." *New Voices: Canadian University Writing of 1956.* Eds. Earle Birney, et al. Toronto: J.M. Dent & Sons, 1956.

Wiebe, Rudy, and Theatre Passe Muraille. *Far as the Eye Can See: A Play.* Edmonton: NeWest Press, 1977.

Wink, Walter. "Myth of Redemptive Violence." *Sojourners Magazine,* April 18, 1992.

Rudy Wiebe was born in 1934 near Fairholme, Saskatchewan. Wiebe has a BA in English and MA in Creative Writing, both from the University of Alberta. He studied under a Rotary International Fellowship at the University of Tübingen in West Germany, and in 1961 he received a Bachelor of Theology degree from the Mennonite Brethren Bible College. In 1962–1963 he was editor of the *Mennonite Brethren Herald*, a position that he resigned because of the controversy over his first novel, *Peace Shall Destroy Many*. From 1967 to 1992 he was Professor of Creative Writing and English at the University of Alberta. Wiebe has published twenty-five books, including ten novels and the non-fiction best-seller *Stolen Life: The Journey of a Cree Woman*, co-authored with Yvonne Johnson. He was awarded the Governor General's Award for fiction for *The Temptations of Big Bear* in 1973, and again in 1994 for *A Discovery of Strangers*. He is also the winner of the Lorne Pierce Gold Metal of the Royal Society of Canada for his contribution to Canadian literature (1987). Wiebe has served as chairman of both the Writer's Guild of Alberta and the Writers' Union of Canada. His book of essays, *Playing Dead,* was the first book in NeWest's Landmark Editions series. Wiebe lives in Edmonton, Alberta.